M000013555

From #Selfie to Selfless

LIVING THE LIFE
YOU WERE CREATED FOR

Kristen Perino

Deep River
B O O K S

From #Selfie to Selfless: Living the Life You Were Created For
© 2017 by Kristen Perino

Published by Deep River Books
Sisters, Oregon
www.deepriverbooks.com

All rights reserved. No part of this book may be reproduced or transmitted in any form or by any means, electronic or mechanical, including photocopying and recording, or by any information storage and retrieval system, without permission in writing from the publisher.

Unless otherwise marked, all Scripture passages are taken from the Good News Bible (GNB), published by The Bible Societies/ Collins © American Bible Society.

Quotations marked (NIV) are from THE HOLY BIBLE, NEW INTERNATIONAL VERSION® , NIV® Copyright © 1973, 1978, 1984, 2011 by Biblica, Inc.® Used by permission. All rights reserved worldwide.

ISBN – 13: 9781632694546
Library of Congress: 2017946503

Printed in the USA

Cover Design by Connie Gabbert

Table of Contents

This book is dedicated to some of the most
selfless humans I know
(who weren't aware that I've been admiring their
selflessness for years in different capacities):

Mom & Dad
For selflessly loving me since my first breath.

Lori Sase-Bechok
For selflessly giving feedback on these chapters,
even between your agonizing doctors' visits.

Jeannie Mai
For selflessly fighting the war against human
trafficking like a boss.

*My Monday night Community Group through
Vintage Church LA*
For selflessly listening to me ramble on and on
week after week; you were where this all began!

Dear selfless, gorgeous, intelligent, clever reader,

I have been praying for *you* since the first night I started writing, and continuously throughout this entire process. I have been praying that you hear God's voice. I've prayed that you laugh. I've prayed that you feel understood. I've prayed that you feel God's love and acceptance for the path you've traveled thus far, and exactly where you are right now. I've prayed that you find deep meaning and purpose in living from "selfie" to selfless. And I pray that you continue to enjoy your journey, even after you finish the last chapter.

I've worked very hard (along with God) to make sure that I offer you a book that is worth every penny of your hard-earned money. This was written with YOU in mind, so as my guest of honor, I truly hope that you enjoy!

CHAPTER 0

A Good Christian Author

(Yes, it IS called Chapter 0. Let's start from zero, the origin, the very beginning, the starting line of how all of this came about.)

#Confession: I honestly debated making up (and when I say "making up," that really just means lie) a more profound way of telling you how this book came about, but the cold, hard truth is that I never prayed to write a book. I know, we are literally one sentence in, and I already sound like the worst Christian ever. *#StopJudging* I do mean it wholeheartedly when I say that I'm the number one fan of God's love, but writing a book was never something I had prayed for. Writing a book was never even on my radar, not even in my wildest dreams. If I am 1,000% honest, asking God to send me my husband took the prime-time spot in my prayer life. Pleading with God, I requested that he would send me my handsome partner-in-crime for life, someone to be my forever plus one, the sharer of my rent, the skip in my step, the beat to my heart, the annoying pain in my neck, and the chef to my breakfasts in bed.

Call me whatever judgment you'd like, but I never prayed for a book. Are you CRAZY? Why would I ever pray to write a book? There had been many other challenges in my life that I accepted and conquered, talents and gifts that I possess, but writing a book was never a challenge I saw coming, nor a talent that I would ever publicly claim. It was more responsible to leave writing professionally for the more qualified authors who had intriguing thoughts, and degrees to back up those thoughts (and could actually eat without spilling on their clothes). My thoughts consisted of how to get through an entire day without rolling my eyes at someone, how to handle my fashion PR career with an ounce of grace, how to fight Los Angeles traffic without cursing at anyone, how many people liked my last Instagram post, and how to love my family well. I was an avid observer of Christian authors. I cheered them on, and I loved my cozy seat on the bench, but then God suddenly called me into the middle of the game, and I responded with, "WAIT! You want who to do what?" (One of my greatest talents is being extremely illiterate when I'm confused, hence that charming response.)

Who, ME?!

One random Monday night in spring of 2016, after leaving my small group in the Brentwood neighborhood of Los Angeles, I felt God tell me, *"You know, Kristen, I've taught you a lot of lessons during our adventurous walk together. I think you need to start writing them down. I need your voice."* I thought to myself, *God needs MY voice? No way, Jose. Does God know who he is talking to? He could NOT be talking to me.*

Bless, I continued in my head, *God is just so busy, and there are so many people in the world—simple mistake. He must be thinking of another "Kristen" (there are a ton of us). God definitely wanted someone who was more pulled-together than me, someone with less attitude, someone who didn't have a glittered past like mine, or someone who was more loving.* What on this good earth would I have to offer besides what shoes to wear with an outfit, or how to respond appropriately to a bad-date-text? I work in fashion PR; I did not go to seminary school, I am not a public speaker, and I'm likely to offend someone with my absurdity (if I haven't already).

There is something about God, though, when he wants to get your attention. You can run, but you can't hide (not even in my tiny apartment, and I did give it my best shot). God allowed my soul to be roused, so even as annoyed as I was, I followed this teeny, tiny breadcrumb trail that he planted in my heart and decided to see where it led. When I got home that night, I humored God for the sole purpose of proving my point that I had nothing to offer (have I mentioned how stubborn I can be?): I sat down on my bed with a pen and fresh page in my notebook and started to write. (Yes, no computer involved. I am "old school.") As I sat in silence, waiting for a lightning bolt from heaven to strike down, I quietly reflected on all the noble, intelligent authors whose books I had admired over the years. I thought about the way they wrote, their genius conclusions that made my heart stir, and I longed to have that same impact on someone else, like they had on me.

After not much time (because patience is not my finest quality), I came up with the title "Surrendered Warrior." True to my usual behavior, I did not consult God on this title decision, and I personally deemed it an "honorable and very Christian title." (Please don't even ask me what "very Christian" means, because I couldn't tell you). I felt like I was a warrior for God (which I genuinely try to be), but I also felt surrendered (which I also attempt to be every day). But after scribbling my way about halfway down the page, I got complete writer's block. *See, God? I told you that I have nothing to offer!* But God wasn't standing in my way; I was blocking my own way with selfishness. I was writing entirely for my own fulfillment and ego: MY insight on how to live life to the fullest, MY truth to fight off negativity, MY experience with being attacked and how to be a soldier through those difficult times. As this writer's block built a heavy wall in my head and heart, I felt God say to me, *"Kristen, WHAT ARE YOU DOING? WHAT IS a surrendered warrior?! I never told you to write that! This is all YOU! I want to LEAD YOU to write about something you know."*

This left me dumbfounded and actually feeling really embarrassed; God caught me, right then and there. I was trying to be something other than myself to see how it looked on me—to see if I could "pull it off." I was *trying* to be a Christian writer. I was trying to be a surrendered warrior. I had this notion of what a Christian writer looked like (I was already planning out my book tour outfit purchases), how these respected authors wrote, and what they titled their work. I was trying to fit into shoes that weren't my size, or wear some makeup that did not match my skin tone, and ended up looking ridiculous. God wasn't calling me to be a "Christian writer"; he was calling me to be me; to share his love through my story, flaws and all, with my voice, with my heart, and to candidly share the joy, the pain, and the lessons that he has so graciously taught me in hopes that you might relate and feel God's love touch your heart through experiences in this book.

When I finally submitted, I thought about it: *OK God, WHAT could I possibly write about?* Dating? Girl, please; not unless God wanted me to write a "what not-to-do" guide. OK, how about marriage? That was as probable as giraffes going to space—nowhere in the near future. Finances? I refer to my closet as my greatest investment: I keep my money right where I can see it. Listening to me about finances is like consulting a four-year-old for driving directions: useless. I genuinely felt like I had nothing to offer. *But God does not care about our past or personal disasters; he cares about our possibilities.* God's not looking at my resume; he is looking at my willingness. God doesn't care if I am qualified, because he knows that I am capable. Even though I couldn't quite recognize my potential, God already saw the finish line, and he was about to rock my world with the heart of this book, while giving me a heart for something I never saw coming.

The Great Whisper

So here I sat, on my bed, late at night. God called me out and now I was trying to understand what he was doing—where was I supposed to go from here? Back to my drawing board of topics I went. As I tried to calm my heart once more to hear what God wanted me to do, I interrupted my own thoughts again by doubting: *But who wants to hear some sob stories or a personal vent sesh? I mean, isn't that what your best friends are for? I would never subject a stranger to listen to me rant about life from my perspective. That even sounds awful to me!* But suddenly, as I was staring at my freshly turned, blank journal page, I felt God whisper, *"Repeat after me, Kristen: It's NOT ABOUT ME!"* I instantly underlined those three words like I had never seen them before. That simple phrase popped off the page and smacked me across the face, giving my soul the wakeup call it was craving. Then in a flash, hours flew by as the words, pages of writing, and ideas from God came flooding. My hand could hardly keep up. I felt God say, *"See! You do have something to write about. You have been very good at being selfish in all areas of your life. You've come a long way, and I am going to use your stories to share with others, but you still have far to go, and I have a lot to teach you through this."*

I literally laughed out loud. God has the *best* sense of humor. He is very, very clever. God, my loving Father, knows how to get me right when I need him. He totally calls me out when I am not being real, and he encourages me in a very honest way. God never wants us to be self-deprecating, but he longs for us to see truth and humility in our lives. Imagine your very best friend; they know you to your core, they can tell when you are lying, and they have enough love for you to call you out when you are acting *#TotesCray* (English translation = totally crazy). God doesn't condemn me, and he doesn't condemn you. He lovingly corrects me when I need it most, and he would graciously do the same for you if you allowed him. When I start going off path like little windup toy, he simply picks me up and sets me back on track with his loving ways.

As this "Selfish" epiphany settled into my soul, two thoughts instantly came to mind on opposite ends of the spectrum: 1) He STILL has lessons to teach me? I felt like a child in the car moaning, "But aren't we there yet?" I was exhausted and husbandless (even boyfriendless!); I was tired of learning, and ready for a vacation from it (*#WheresMyPassport*). And 2) While I was sitting in my bed deciding how to be politically correct, plotting out my Christian memoir of being a "surrendered warrior" (again, whatever that means), and privately planning my outfits for my book tour, God shook my heart and said *"RIGHT THERE! THAT'S WHERE IT IS! IT IS NOT ABOUT YOU, KRISTEN, AND YOUR PLANS. I have something so much greater for you if you would just let me use you! If you write this book your own way, you will continue to have writer's block and will get nowhere. If you would simply just calm down and let me lead, then I have some pretty awesome things to unveil to you, which you can share with many other sisters and brothers that you have yet to meet."* Proverbs 19:21 says, "People may plan all kinds of things, but the Lord's will is going to be done" (GNB).

So, here we are. I have a God-given PhD in being selfish, and God has entrusted me as an expert to help rid society of this terrible epidemic. I have learned to be selfish with my money (spend it how I want to), selfish with my time (what do I want to do this month?), selfish with my relationships (how are they benefiting me?), selfish with my work (is that the title I deserve?), and the list rattles on. I am quick to hold up both hands and claim what I have been and what I am, a *selfish human being*. Again, this is not to be self-deprecating, but my selfishness is as simple and true as the sky is blue. I have a million other loving qualities and caring traits, many incredible talents and skills, and some ugly habits (beyond perfecting selfishness), but the key to shifting my life and my purpose was this conclusion: *living selfishly is not satisfying.* I am not encouraging you to sell all your belongings and live on the streets with a megaphone condemning all to hell to prove your point. (PLEASE definitely don't do that.) I know God wants you and loves you just where you are at, just like he has loved me exactly where I am at. No radical adjustments necessary. My only hope is that you would experience this incredible peace and encouragement that you are not alone.

~~Self-Help~~ ~~Kristen-Help~~ ~~Earthly-Help~~ God-Help

This is not a self-help book. If you're anything like me, you've probably already tried helping yourself in every way, shape, and form possible, and it didn't work. Or maybe "self-help" books slapped a Band-Aid on your heart long enough to fix the boo-boo, until the rain came and loosened up the Band-Aid just enough for it to lose its grip, exposing your wound once more, still unhealed. I love Oprah more than champagne, but her Super Soul Sundays couldn't fix the void inside of me. I love yoga, and the healing it brought to my body, but I was still left searching (and sweaty and sore). If you're looking for a real transformation of the heart and head, something that will give you peace beyond any understanding, you need God's help. You didn't create you, so how could you know what needs to be fixed? God created you, and he's literally the only mechanic that can help sort out the issues. That's why I prefer to reference this book as a "God-help" book. I believe we all need God's help. And asking for help isn't a bad thing. It's a great thing! If you are lost while driving, you turn to your GPS or maps to lead you along the right path. You rely on GPS to guide you to your final destination, so if you trust GPS, then I'm hoping you can trust God with the direction of your life. I'm just here to do the writing and have been praying that God will do the healing.

CAUTION: this book is not to beat you over the head to make you feel bad about your life, but it's not filled with helpful advice to make you *feel better*. Honestly, sometimes, you might not feel better at all, and I'm sorry. It's like going to the gym: it's not always fun, but it's so necessary. Shifting our hearts from *#selfie* to selfless may not always be enjoyable because it will cause personal sacrifice: sacrifices like time, ego, comfort. I know I am usually called to be selfless with my time on the exact days when time is the last thing I have to offer. But when I allow God to take hold of my clock and calendar, he somehow makes more out of my twenty-four hours than I ever thought possible. Sacrificing my ego is not always fun, because I enjoy being right! But when I sacrifice that part of me at the foot of the throne, an extra layer of selfishness sheds from my heart. I think that if you join me in shedding selfishness, you will be so rejuvenated afterwards, and hopefully inspired by the knowledge that you are not on this journey alone.

The blunt truth: sometimes living a life that's not all about you is *not fun* at the beginning. If I'm honest, I really wish it *were* all about me. That sounds way more fun! But *fun* and *a life full of purpose* can be two different things. "Fun" hasn't gotten me very far. It would give me a great high in that moment, but would leave me feeling very dissatisfied once the sensation floated away. After vacations, romantic relationships, and retail therapy couldn't fix my itch for fun, I started the search for something greater, something deeper. Sure, I still have fun and love to enjoy life. But going from *#selfie* to selfless has brought me something so much better than "fun." This realization has given me joy—pure, soul-deep, no-one-can-take-away joy. Once I claimed this joy inside of me, it led me to be aware. Aware of my surroundings, my community, realizing that I was created to make an incredible impact, and that ordinary people like you and me can be used for extraordinary purposes. Once I laid myself down at the cross, I realized the bigger picture, the more exciting picture: It's not all about me. It's about God! And what an exhilarating, stimulating, sensational life that is to live. WOOHOO!

But *why* is it an exhilarating, stimulating, and sensational life to live? Because God is so loving, so kind, so passionate about *you* that he didn't create you to just roam the earth for some decades, collect social media followers, go on trips, go to college, get a job, raise a family, go to the spa, and then die. Clarification: *none* of those things are bad. (I *love* going to the spa. I am a more kind and compassionate person at the spa. I tried to convince God that I hear him better at the spa, so if he could continue to fund that habit, that would be wonderful. He didn't believe me.) But we were created for SO MUCH MORE than these earthly habits! You, my beautiful friend, were created to break chains and not live in the earthly confines of "what makes a life." These things are fine, but don't lose sight of your vision, your goal, and your purpose: to shed the selfishness of everyday life and start living to leave a legacy. Not a legacy to be written on a plaque or observed by strangers in generations to come, but a legacy that would leave hearts changed when they witness the love, passion, and selflessness of Jesus Christ that resides in you. YOU have breath in your lungs for a reason, and when you figure out just how valuable you are, the enemy (AKA Satan) will groan, "Crap. She figured it out." Take the enemy's wool off your eyes, and realize your possibilities!

One of the reasons I love social media is that it allows us to share amazing quotes, thoughts, and scribbles with one another. I saw an anonymous quote that read, *The devil whispered in my ear, "You're not strong enough to withstand the storm." Today I whispered in the devil's ear, "I am the storm."*

Girlfriend, you are a force to be reckoned with, but that force doesn't come from being self-centered; it comes from being selfless. This book is to encourage you to live your life as the glorious storm you were created to be. You are meant to shake things up while drenching dry places with hope and raining love over all those so thirsty for it. God created us to experience his love to the greatest extent—with massive adventures, thrilling challenges, and exciting hurtles. But it doesn't end with us. We are then to give hope to others by sharing it. God has an incredible, unbelievable plan for us, for YOU, for me, for your dog-walker, your babysitter, your boss, your mailman, your teacher. So many people sadly miss this incredible hope, joy, and peace because it is only unlocked when we understand the humbling fact that God might actually have it under control. We are to simply get out of our own way, trust him, and repeat to ourselves, "This is NOT all about me." There is an "I" in "selfie," but there is no "I" in "selfless."

A Real Girl, Living in a Real World

Now don't get it twisted. I am not some fairy hippie who thinks that some magical god will make all my problems go away, or make me into a flawless person, if I simply say a few prayers. I would hope that I treat life as responsibly as I can—like I've mentioned, I work in fashion PR. I have a 401(k). Life still throws its curveballs, and many times I still strike out.

The same will be true for you. I don't expect wars to stop, poverty to end, or every child to have a home by the time you finish this book. I do expect, and desirously pray, that your world be profoundly changed, your heart would be renewed, and your outlook would be altered by the fact that life is not about you but about God's love for you, Jesus Christ's sacrifice for you, and the life you were specifically created for. So many incredible blessings have YOUR name on them; if only you would get out of your own way and let the Creator of the universe care for you in the way that he so desires. This is not about a religion; it's about a relationship. And it's not about you, but about your relationship with a living, loving God.

I have never once regretted moving from selfish to self-less, and I have an incredible amount of faith that you won't regret it either.

CHAPTER 1

There's No Place Like Home

The bedrooms we sleep in, the zip codes we claim, or the places we raise our family: these are our temporary homes (Hebrews 13:14). This was a really difficult concept for me to understand. Whenever I move, I am the ultimate "nester." I love to paint walls, sort out the décor, get all my things out of their boxes, figure out what chairs will be placed where, and so on. I want the new, unfamiliar space to feel like my own as quickly possible. I "pin" dozens of ideas on Pinterest, I screenshot inspiration from Instagram accounts, I scope multiple stores for the best deals, and I save photos from décor magazines. I always crave that cozy, lived-in "home" feeling, where friends can feel welcomed and I am able to host celebrations for my nearest and dearest. I long for a place of my own to call home. This isn't a shameful feeling to have, as I know this is how I am wired, but the issue isn't the instinct to nest; the issue creeps in when I start to idolize where I live, put my self-worth in what fills my closet, or start to envy someone else's property. I have seen myself get way too attached to specific apartments, neighborhoods, a walk-in closet (I am still grieving that loss), and physical "treasures" like purses, shoes, jewelry, photo frames, or even blankets. All of these things I seek out for the pursuit of comfort, but God did not place me on earth just to be comfortable. What a boring existence that would be. Could you imagine what people would say about me at my funeral if I lived that way? "Kristen Perino was a lovely person, good contributor to society, and *lived a very comfortable life*. She really didn't make an impact, but she was nice." That is *not* the legacy I want to leave behind, but as I go through my day-to-day life, that is the story that I've been writing. I constantly lose sight of the big picture and actively choose to focus on my daily comfort. I start to focus too much on my wants and needs, and before I know it, I've forgotten about God's opinion quicker than Instagram updates its feed. If the Bible verse, "For your heart will always be where your riches are" (Matthew 6:21), is true, then where does my heart lie? Is it kept in the depths of my physical treasures and earthly comforts? Or is my heart safely kept in heaven, where my eternal home is?

Easily Distrac . . . There Goes a Butterfly!

Many days, it just feels like I cannot concentrate on God, his love for me, his purpose for creating me, or how I should live. There I am praising God in church, just ready to "give it all away," then by the time I walk to my car after service, I'm already thinking about what else I can accumulate to make this life happier. I was literally praising Jesus seven minutes prior; how does that happen? I have been professionally diagnosed with Attention Deficit Disorder, so some might jump to that explanation, but if I've learned to channel my attention in everyday life, why can't I channel my focus on God? Oh, right, it's because I'm focused on myself. No matter how many times you attend Sunday services, *worldly attachments will detach you from God.* Even if you decide to follow God with your life, it's those daily decisions (or for me, hourly decisions) to not get sidetracked that make the relationship so much more meaningful. Many times our lack of focus or concentration on God causes confusion—and confusion causes chaos. To avoid chaos, we need to make the effort regularly to *choose* to not get deflected.

If you are as easily distracted as me, then you will have to make the repetitive effort to choose to focus on God. I have found that I need reminders of God's purpose for my life to keep me distracted from the accumulation of this world. Distractions like verses on Post-its, a screensaver on my computer or phone with a reminder of truth, or a cross hanging from my car's rearview mirror to remind me in those hours of Los Angeles traffic that yes, I am loved and will make it! Your relationship with God will not survive on one vow of surrendering your life to him. Rather, it will be built through action if you choose to daily remind yourself that the world around you is not your home; you have a heavenly residence that's already been paid for, and a lease that will never expire. *#Hallelujah!*

Grandma Sunny

My Grandma Sunny had the most incredible house. She lived there for nearly fifty years, and every time I would go over there, it just felt like home. It was a good-sized corner lot in Newport Beach, California, but the home itself was nothing extravagant or fancy. She had a decent backyard, where I remember riding my Little Mermaid tricycle in circles. She had a large driveway, where she would stand and wave to me until my car was out of sight every time I departed. She even let me host a surprise birthday for one of my best friends in the backyard. When I got my license, I would go visit her for lunch every other week. I spent a lot of quality time in that house, and I cherish loads of remarkable conversations with her in nearly every inch of that square footage. We made jokes like two teenagers inside the large pantry in the kitchen. She gave me life advice while sitting in the dining room. We soaked up the sunshine, and each other's company, in the backyard. We sat shoulder to shoulder on the stairs, giggling, when she didn't have even strength to make it to the second floor. I discovered vintage treasures in her closet, and she would give me a story on each piece I revealed. She even attempted to teach me to cook in the kitchen. (I am *still* workin' on that one! *#PrayForMe*)

When the inevitable came around, and Grandma Sunny went to meet Jesus, not only did I lose one of my best friends, but I knew my family had to sell the house, too. I had to say good-bye to my exceptional Grandma, but I also had to part with the home that held most of our memories together. Selfishly, I was so disappointed that we couldn't keep the house in the family, but I fully understood that it just was not a logical move to do so.

During that time of grief and letting go of my dear Grandma Sunny, I felt God encourage me by whispering, "*If you think this home is great, just wait for what I have for you in heaven! Keep following me and don't forget that this is not your final home. This is not where your heart should be. Keep your heart focused on heaven; your final home for eternity.*" God understood that I was grieving, but he also didn't want me to lose sight of the larger picture. This is not about me, my comfort, or my memories on earth. These things are a gift, but our eternal, everlasting gifts await us in heaven. This is your temporary home as well. Don't get too attached, because it is fleeting and there is something so much better coming!

Let's Play "House"

My girlfriends and I love to go for weekly "Walk-n-Talks" around the neighborhood, where we walk to get our bodies moving, but chitchat to also keep our friendships moving. As we stroll around, we scope out our favorite homes (in the least creepy way possible) and note what we would do to make them our dream homes. My votes are for a walk-in closet, Jacuzzi, big yard, and open family space (*#AGirlCanDream #HelpMeJesus*). Every now and again, my girlfriends and I get swept away in the idea that when we finally settle down to own our own homes with families, THEN we will be comfortable and satisfied, so we start to yearn for that comfort. Every homeowner can tell you that owning a home is not comfortable some days. Updates cost money, repairs often come at the worst times, things break, and upkeep takes constant maintenance. The financial market fluctuates with dips and highs, so at any moment you could lose a chunk of hard-earned money within a snap. All of this occurs because *these are our temporary homes!* Despite their sturdy appearance, they were not meant to last forever, nor are we supposed to rely on them for our comfort or identity all our lives. We are meant to enjoy our homes on earth and fill them with memories, laughter, family, friends, and so much love, but we are not meant to invest our worth or happiness in where our address is.

Confession: I am an "Equal Opportunity Accumulator." I want to accumulate all things and everything. Nothing is off limits. I don't necessarily hoard. I am just as keen on throwing things away as I am on accumulating them, which actually means that I might even be more wasteful (we will leave that verdict up to heaven). I want to accumulate things I can touch, feel, and see, because they seem like tangible ways to fill my discontent. My desires have a vast range from a new purse to a handsome husband. Literally, I crave any sense of comfort that I believe will calm my anxious soul; I am all over the map. When I start to believe that this life is all about me, I constantly request things of God for my own comfort.

I know that God is excited to bless me with the desires of my heart—an incredible husband one day, a solid home to raise a family, and even that new purse that I'm craving—but only after I come to the sobering realization that it's not about me. *We were not created to accumulate, but we were created to emulate the love of Jesus Christ.* God wants to give me gifts on earth because he loves me so much, and he wants to pour blessings on your life because he loves *you* so much. "Seek your happiness in the LORD, and He will give you the desires of your heart" (Psalm 37:4). He longs for us to be happy during this life and excited about all he has to offer, but he will not allow earthly things to provide our hearts' sole fulfillment. God wants us to seek after him. Chasing the "affluent things in life" to gain us satisfaction cheapens love, and God's love is not cheap; it is quite possibly the richest love we could ever encounter.

Society and the world would LOVE for you to continue thinking that it's all about the here and now—whatever makes you happy and satisfied is what you should act on. How many times have you heard, "Do it if it makes you happy"? Buying a Chanel bag would make me cry tears of happiness, but that doesn't mean I should do it. (I would not be able to pay rent, and I would literally be a homeless woman with a Chanel bag. #Priorities) We are called for so much more!

God absolutely wants you to be happy and fulfilled, but fulfilled with things that people and time can't take away from you. Purses get lost, homes get broken into, moths bite into clothing, cars lose their value, and gifts get stolen, but your faith is something that will never lose its worth. Having faith in God while on earth is probably one of the best investments you could ever take a chance on. Many people invest everything they have in the stock market; we all know how that fluctuates (hello crash of 2008). Many people invest all that they have into a mansion on a hill; yet I have witnessed way too many landslides when an ounce of rain comes. When we take charge of our own emotional investments, and forget that we should be investing in heaven, we lose the right to turn around and blame God when things go awry. It's quite hypocritical to thank ourselves when we have a beautiful home, or an investment works out to our favor, and then only blame God when terrible things happen to us. How is that fair? When it becomes all about us, then we are quick to take credit for good, but blame God for any bad. Everything on earth is entrusted to you as a gift; it is temporary. You cannot take anything with you when you die. Physical things in this world will all one day be forgotten. It is not about us and our contentment on earth! It is about getting our eyes off ourselves, and praising God through the best and the worst situations that God brings us (even in a landslide down the hill).

At the Eye of the Self-Centered Storm

In the world of fashion PR, life moves faster than even conceivable. Fashion seasons transform rapidly week after week, trends are constantly updating, and it's far too easy for self-worth to be decided by what bag you're carrying or what shoes you have on. Opinions of what's hot and what's not are decided for you by magazine editors, bloggers, celebrities, and YouTubers. I have met some amazing people in the industry. I really do love my job, and I am so blessed to work with the kind people that I have. But during your time on earth, I encourage you to keep what you see in perspective. Not everything is always as it seems, especially with what the world offers us. When we look around horizontally at everything happening around us, judgment gets cloudy, and it's tough to see the truth. But the second that we glance up, shift our focus vertically, and remind ourselves this is just our temporary home, the craziness quiets and the millions of distractions fade to the background. Colossians 3:1–2 says, "You have been raised to life with Christ, so set your hearts on the things that are in heaven, where Christ sits on his throne at the right-hand side of God. Keep your mind fixed on things there, not on things here on earth." All we need to see is one person, one God, who loves us so much and is encouraging us to not get too comfortable where we are at, because we won't be here for long.

We all entered this world selfish. Just take babies for example. They don't naturally want to share their toys. They don't wake up from their naps thinking about anyone else. Their world is all about them. They don't care if mom and dad are tired, because they are hungry! Even though we enter the world as self-centered people, I don't want to leave that way. My hope is that we would grow, learn, challenge ourselves, be uncomfortable, and leave this earth changed as giving, selfless people. God encourages us in Matthew 6:31–34:

> So do not start worrying; "Where will my food come from, or my drink, or my clothing?" Your Father in heaven knows that you need all of these things. Instead, be concerned above everything else with the Kingdom of God and with what He requires of you, and He will provide you with all of these other things. So do not worry about tomorrow; it will have enough worries of its own. There is no need to add to the troubles each day brings.

The most awesome part about living a Christ-centered life is realizing that I don't have to figure everything out during my time here on earth. God is longing to take care of me, if I would just surrender myself.

Home Is Not Always Where the Heart Is

The idea of "home" is not a positive thing for many people. The sad truth is that millions of people grew up in broken homes filled with neglect, abuse of many kinds, abandonment, and layers of pain. If any of these are relatable to you, first of all, please let me just say, I am so sorry. You are so loved, and worth so much more than the pain you've had to endure (Psalms 34:18). Unfortunately there is no lobotomy procedure or time machine to wipe those memories clear of your past (and if there was, I wish I could offer it to you!), but there is a father in heaven who has an incredible future for you, filled with everlasting love in eternity. The past cannot be taken away, but hallelujah, we can look forward to our future! The Bible promises, "I consider that what we suffer at this present time cannot be compared at all with the glory that is going to be revealed to us" (Romans 8:18). In your final home in heaven, you will be valued forever, cherished endlessly, hugged and cared for constantly, joyous always, and free of any horror you had to endure at your earthly home. The closeness and promises that we feel from him now are just a tiny sliver of the incredible love we will soak up for the rest of time. "No eye has seen, no ear has heard, and no mind has imagined what God has prepared for those who love Him" (1 Corinthians 2:9 NLT).

OK, even though it's going to be so awesome that we can't imagine, let's just try for a second. Could you picture block parties with your heavenly neighbors? You can leave your most precious toys out on the lawn and no one will steal them. Children will be able to play in the streets freely without the fear of harm. No neighbors will gossip about you. You won't need to struggle to pay rent or compete to "keep up." You won't even need to lock your doors, because no one will creep in at night to cause you any harm! And I will be able to *finally* run around in my socks on the pavement. *#Hallelujah!* (My mom was not a fan when I would go play dodge ball after school in my socks, only to return with ghastly holes). If you have no sense of excitement toward your home in heaven because you compare it to your home here on earth, well then my dear friend, you are sadly mistaken. GET EXCITED. Comparing your home on earth to your home in heaven is like comparing a tricycle to a Mercedes Benz, like comparing a Zack Morris-sized eighties cell phone to an ultra-sleek iPhone, like comparing a dirty shack to a mansion on the beach. Do not let the enemy feed you lies about your final home in heaven. It will be INCREDIBLE.

Whatever home you come from here on earth (wealthy, poor, broken, stable, crazy, boring, loud, empty, or anything in between), do not forget that this life is not all there is. Your address in heaven is waiting for you to enjoy for all of eternity. You are just moving through this life like a little hitchhiker with a godly purpose. This life is like a tent, and your heavenly address is a mansion. If you were ever told by loved ones that you are not welcome at home, well then the joke is on whoever told you that, because you ARE SO WELCOME in your forever home in heaven. One fine day, when I reach my final destination in heaven, I cannot wait to see Jesus waiting for me at those pearly gates, arms wide open, saying, "Well done good and faithful servant; welcome home."

Questions:

1. In what areas of your life do you make yourself too "at home" here on earth?
2. What is your idea of "home"? What was your home life growing up? Talk to God and write down.
3. Bonus Question: As you continue to be the incredible steward of God's gifts here on earth and build your treasure up in heaven, what will your heavenly home look like?

#TruthToRemember ➜ Don't get too comfortable with what the world has to offer; this is our temporary home.

CHAPTER 2

Life from Center Stage

In today's world, we all have an audience. Most of us don't perform world tours with sold-out shows or grace the big screen
in the latest blockbuster, but we all have someone watching
us. Some audiences are larger than others, but regardless,
a person is a person, and they are still observing your every
movement. Instagram follow counts flourish into the millions,
and Facebook likes accumulate quicker than I can spell Sha-
kira. Literally any person with a computer and video camera
can make their own YouTube videos for millions to follow.
Even if you have never downloaded an app, you still have colleagues at work who are watching you, children at home who
absorb everything you do, friends who pay attention to your
actions, and so on. Whether your audience numbers fifteen
or five million, what is the content you are showing your audience? What type of life are you living? Is it one for yourself,
glorifying you, or are you glorifying God? The content that we
post on our personal social media accounts is obviously from
our perspective, but we need to make the real decision of
what guides our perspective.

Faith in Jesus had lingered in my life for a long time, but
I never highlighted it, or even hinted at it, on my social media
accounts. Let's just say that my relationship with God was
"private," as I wasn't ready to change the security setting to
"public." God guided my heart and daily decisions, but he did
not guide my choices on social media. I did not want to be

"seen" with God in front of my audience; the fear of becoming a "weird Christian" was very real for me. He was my friend that I waved to from afar, but would never sit with at lunch. I was afraid to associate my name with God's, lest be thought guilty by association. I have two eyes and a brain; I have observed how people view God. Many people see God as unjust, condemnatory, judgmental, or completely fake, or they simply don't like him. I wanted people to like me. Additionally, I was fearful that when I mess up, the mask would come off, I would once more be revealed as a flawed human, and my relationship with Jesus would look like a fraud. If I was going to talk the talk, then I needed to walk the walk, but I felt an unending pressure that my "walk" needed to be immaculate, and if I fell or tripped, then my "talk" was hypocritical. I didn't want the pressure to appear perfect to my audience, because I knew how unrealistic that was for my life. I thought that if I took that leap of faith and demonstrated to my audience that "hey, yes I do love Jesus," then I might be ridiculed if I had a glass of wine or dated from an app. I was longing for clarity on how to stand for what I believe in without alienating those around me.

Frustration festered inside of me because I knew that God calls us to a life of authenticity with him and to not blend in with society (Romans 12:2), but I wasn't the average church-goer. I felt like I didn't quite fit in with the world, but I didn't quite fit in with the church either. I was somewhere awkwardly in between. I have dabbled with drugs, I am not a virgin, I have walked without God, and I've carelessly stumbled down paths I had no business going down. What the heck was I supposed to show my online audience, suddenly and perfectly filtered photos of joy, peace, and love? My worst fear was coming off as hypocritical. My friends from years past, who knew "Crazy-Party-Kristen," would likely roll their eyes at my efforts for purity. On the flip side, if I posted a photo at a bar with friends, my church group might gossip over their "concern." Hopelessly unsure, I was tormented with how to present myself to my small audience. I didn't want it to seem like my faith was phony, or appear as though my newfound revival in Christ was a fad. I longed to be honest, to be genuine, and just be a normal flawed woman in Los Angeles who was trying her best to follow Jesus. #TheStruggleWasReal

But God is SO GOOD. He saw me right where I was, and he refused to leave me there. He bent down and whispered a simple reminder: *"It's not about you, Kristen! Stop getting so wrapped up in what others might think. I created you; I know your heart, so just be yourself and remember that you are a daughter of the Most High. The rest will fall into place."* Well, Hallelujah. Can I get an Amen?! I had been dazed with confusion about the woman I was, or who I belonged to, or what I needed to represent. When I was looking only at myself and those around me to tell me who I was, I became increasingly unsure of myself. The moment that I looked up to heaven and heard God lovingly whisper a caring reminder, this clarity washed away all doubts in my mind.

We are placed on this earth to love and bless others. Jesus never once told his disciples to be super religious, distracting with their rituals, and unrelatable to their neighbors. To put it bluntly: we are called to live an honest life of humility and love, and not freak people out with over-the-top religious antics. Let's be a generation that breeds openness, encouragement, and good-ol'-fashioned kindness on our social media accounts.

Comfortable in Your Own ~~Skin~~ Social Media

The debate over what to post on social media may seem trivial and petty, but it reflects so much more than just a photo or a quote. So many quotes, captions, comments, and photos have sparked national outrage, stripped people of their dignity with harsh words, and allowed people to fight with complete strangers thousands of miles away. My mother used to say, "What comes out of your mouth is a reflection of what is in your heart." Well, in this day and age, the equivalent would be "What you post on your social media accounts is a reflection of what is in your heart." If your heart is seeking attention, then you will do whatever you need to do to get that, even if it means posting some skin-baring photos. If your heart is seeking validation, then you may purchase a bag that is way beyond your bank account, just to post it and watch the envious "likes" and comments accumulate. If your heart is seeking superiority, then your fingers will type so quickly they'll nearly produce smoke as you shame someone with hurtful words. Many people will do whatever it takes to accumulate more "likes" on social media, but how far are you willing to go?

With God's loving grace and many lessons learned, I became much more settled in the person I am and who God created me to be. I love incredible fashion, but now feel aware of when I start to idolize it too much. I love humor and comical quotes, but feel convicted when they are taken too far at someone else's expense. I love wine (I *AM* Italian), but I feel God tap my shoulder when enough is enough. I am a very chatty person, but I try to keep my tongue in check with language and how I interact with people. I finally got to a place with God where I am myself—the crazy, loud, curious, rambunctious person he created me to be—but I am constantly trying to tailor it to represent my Father above, and not just me. I needed to show my audience a little more of God's love and a little less Kristen. Once I was at a quality place with my spiritual relationship, I knew the person I was called to be in front of my tiny audience: a very real girl just trying to make the most of the love God has given me and the desires he placed on my heart. I don't have all the answers, but when my audience sees me, I would hope that I don't shine, but God would shine through me. This isn't my show, and I had to relinquish control. Even when I speak about fashion, God is there. When I speak about a new restaurant, God is there. When I walk my dog, God is there. When I go on a date, God is there. When I mess up for the 387, 479th time, God is there. *My goal became to always keep it real, but keep it focused on a very real relationship with God.*

The Power Struggle

Social media can be used for incredible purposes: sharing love and encouragement, distributing news (global and local), growing businesses, raising awareness, keeping in touch with traveling friends and family, etc. Many people have done an amazing job using their social media platforms for good, but I know that we are a very capable, creative generation that can expand this positivity exponentially. Like many things in this world, social media is not bad; it only becomes bad when it becomes all about us! As humans, we are really good at taking something positive and polluting it. Of course, your social media accounts are your own, so you are going to share and post from your perspective, *but what guides your perspective*? I would pray that God directs my outlook on life, so that would direct what I share, what I don't, and how I share it.

In an age when self-recorded YouTube videos garner millions of views and selfie Snapchats rule the memory on our phones, it's no wonder why we value our own voices so highly. Anyone and everyone can be their own star, so why stop to observe what God might be doing in our lives? We don't care for God's approval when we have hundreds of followers already filling that void. Nothing about sharing fun or informative videos is bad. (I learn all my hairstyles and cooking lessons on YouTube.) Let me repeat; *nothing* about sharing your own fun videos is bad. I don't want to get a zillion comments thinking that I am anti-selfie or anti-Snapchat, or that I think Instagram is from the devil and anything social media is a sin. Trust me, if I am having a great hair day, I need to selfie that evidence so I can keep a reminder that my hair is still capable of having a miracle. I am Instagram's number-one fan; I think it's the greatest thing since sliced bread. I chronically over-post. Selfies with friends or family are some of my most cherished photos. Listen, my loved one, God created an incredibly gorgeous person when he created you, so selfie until your heart is content. It only becomes bad when we become so obsessed with our own voice, our own content, our own reflection, and our own opinions that we blindly forget what God has to say. We are meant to share the voice God gave us, but our voice is not meant to speak over him. There is a very fine line, and it's not black and white. Not all selfies were created equally. It is so personal, and only you will know when you've gone too far. I just encourage you to check your own heart and motives; be aware of the ratio of how many times you speak to how many times you hear God speak. I use a couple "heart filters" to check my motives before posting: 1) If a person saw this photo or caption, would they be shocked to know that I have a personal relationship with God? 2) Am I posting this with the intent of bragging? Keep in check with how often you selfie, and how often you offer yourself to God.

I saw an encouraging quote online the other day that read, "You are so enough. It is crazy how enough you are." I instantly felt two things: 1) These are the times that I *love* social media—the times we use it to give friendly, encouraging, awesome visual reminders to one another to reiterate our true worth, and 2) I knew God was speaking that quote directly to me. And he is speaking that to your heart as well. (He's just using the words on this page to get your attention.) But then God rocked my world and took it one step further and made me think; what if we said that back to him? "Heavenly Father, you are so enough. It is crazy how enough you are." You are sitting here reading this book right now because ALL of this is about a relationship, not a religion. Relationships are a two-way street. We can soak up God's outpouring of love throughout our eighty years on earth, but if we never reciprocate that love, does that really qualify as a solid relationship? God doesn't need our love, but he wants it, and he longs for it because he longs for you, the incredible person he created. As the group of spicy world-changers I know we are, wouldn't it be awesome if we threw our hands up in the air, dropped our insecurities, shook up society norms, and said, "Hey God, this is not my show. I am tired of this comparison game. You can take every piece of my heart, including my social media, because YOU are enough. It is so crazy how enough you are, Lord."

But! Before we move on; because I love and care about you; I am going to get real with you. With every declaration of how "enough" our identities are in the Lord, there is a very real enemy lurking nearby to tear you down (even on social media!) and make you feel miserable about yourself. This deceitful predator will show up in any way possible to make you feel insecure—like you are not "enough," or like your heavenly Father is not "enough." When you hear whispers that you are not pretty enough, reply with, "Not Today Satan!" When you feel self-conscious that you don't have enough "likes" on your posts, reply with, "Not Today Satan!" When you hear lies like "you aren't skinny enough" or "you're too flat chested," reply with "Not Today Satan!" When you hear teases that "your clothes are not cool enough to post on social media," it's time to *yell*, "Not Today Satan!" (The enemy better not whisper lies about my wardrobe; that is just crossing the line! #BoyBye)

Follow Carefully

The other night I was lying in bed, simply wanting to check my Instagram and update a post I was inspired by. I had every intention of going to bed within the next five to ten minutes. Well, I had clicked on my friend's page, then saw another mutual friend in her photo, so I was curious what this long-lost friend was up to, so I clicked on his page, and probably repeated this same cycle about nine times, until finally I ended up on Reese Witherspoon's page, and I was suddenly like a lost child in Target: *How did I get here? Where am I? What time is it? I want to go home. I need to get out!* I'd just wasted a lot of time, and my heart felt empty. Somehow a feeling of insecurity, self-doubt, and anxiety crept in. How did this happen? I went on my Instagram to repost something inspirational, and I ended up feeling ugly forty-five minutes later. I was comparing every "unfiltered" part of my life to everyone else's perfectly posed, perfectly timed, perfectly dressed photos. As I investigated further into my sudden self-loathing to figure out where it came from, I had to take a hard look at two major components to my sadness. Whose pages was I looking at? 1) Strangers, and 2) Non-believers. Let's look at the problems more deeply:

1. **Admiring the life of a stranger.** I am really, really good at making up fantasy scenarios of the lives everyone else is living around me, but I am very realistic about my own. I have no idea about these people's lives. I have no idea about their struggles, their pasts, their worries, their health, their friendships; I don't know anything other than I really, really, really like their outfits, so somehow they magically have a life that I want. How did I get so shallow? Yes, I love their outfits, and they took awesome photos, which should be applauded! Good for

them! But there is a big difference between applauding and idolizing. When my imagination kicks in, I want their lives, because I start to believe that their lives are better than mine. THAT is when social media turns to the dark side. Admiring is fine, but lusting over someone's life is not.

2. **Following Non-believers**. Following people, friends, family, etc., who do not believe in Jesus is absolutely fine (as we are still humans in this world, and we should not be hiding under a rock from anything outside the church), but I do encourage you to take a hard look at the content they post and how it seeps into your head and heart. At twenty-nine years old, I would like to think that I am not so impressionable anymore; I have my own career and am confident in the woman I am. But I have found that even the most confident of women can still feel less-than by simply looking at photos of other women, the clothes they are wearing, the men they might be seducing, the "perfect lives" they are living. A lot of social media has become modern-day marketing, so it is usual for these posts to come across as natural behavior, but it might as well be an advertisement on a billboard, or a specially planned-out commercial on the television. Why am I allowing myself to follow people who are not adding to my life or lifting me up, but rather tearing me down? And why call things that tear me down "inspiration" or #goals? I really do look to social media sites for inspiration, but we all have that fine line in our hearts where it turns from light to dark very quickly. I encourage you to figure out where that line is. Or better yet, scroll through your Instagram feed (or Facebook, or Twitter, or Snapchat, etc.), and see whether the people you are following

feed your soul or take a tiny piece of it. Once I became aware of what was happening, I started following really inspiring leaders—actors who didn't post provocatively or who used their social media to bring awareness to causes (i.e. actress Amanda Seyfried, who posts consistently about animal rights, or actress Emma Watson, who is a UN Women Global Goodwill Ambassador and constantly posts about different causes).

Post the Post, Walk the Walk

There is an old saying that goes, "You talk the talk, but can you walk the walk?" This acknowledges that one might be good at talking but fail to follow up their words with actions. I've always believed that actions speak volumes over words. So with this said, I have come up with an updated version of that saying, which I find more applicable today (because no one actually talks to each other anymore): "You type your caption, but can you walk the walk?" Or, "You post your post, but can you walk the walk?" We post some inspiring Bible verses or motivating quotes, but do we back up our posts with our daily actions? Do our actions speak louder than our posts? Am I living in an inspiring way that would point back to the Bible verse I posted, or is my Instagram an entirely different character than who I am in "real life"? Do I post about patience when life gets tough, but then flip out in real life when things don't go my way? Do I post about being selfless, when in real life, I hardly ever give back to those around me? Do I encourage others to keep shining, when I am too self-conscious to shine myself? We are breeding a culture that is brave to post from behind a keyboard, but that bravery ends when we step out of the door. Encouraging social media posts, comments, and captions are all wonderful things, but too often that encouragement, love, and kindness end when we put down our phones.

Because I am 1,000% human, many times I'll tell God, "I'm tired. I can't walk the walk, so I am just going to sit here and text my walk, or post about my walk. It's gotten way too difficult to physically walk it all out. It's way more comfortable and less stressful to just encourage others with words, rather than my actions." My hope is that we would not just post inspirational quotes, but rather our social media would reflect the inspirational lives we are actually out living.

I encourage you, dear friends, to use your social media as your enjoyment, but not your self-worth. The amount of followers you have does not decide how amazing you are or how beautifully you were made, and it has no correlation with how you can impact the world with your God-given gifts. Some people's gifts are within social media, and that is won-derful! If that is you, then shine bright like a diamond with that awesome talent you were given. But if you feel like you are drowning in a sea of social media competition, and fight exhaustedly to keep up, then please, listen closely: followers dwindle, trends disappear, a new social media platform will be the next big fad in a year. What you see here and now is not the final judgment. If we value someone else's opinion more highly than God's, then that is a deep, hollow hole to fall into. Do not allow the dark traps of social media to capture your light. Do not allow what you see on a screen to define your reality. I am calling you to rise up and live for something more; find confidence in the purpose God created you for. A worthy life is not captured in filters, posts, or hashtags; it is in the everyday beauty of your great heart. When you get to heaven, God will not ask you how many social media followers you had because NO ONE WILL CARE. You may be the only "Jesus" that some people may ever come into contact with. It is our great pleasure to be something more than the world expects. Sadly, society is expecting Christians to start argu-ments, lead into conversations with pointing fingers, and cast judgment every chance we get. How about we stop comparing ourselves to others, realize the love we were given, cheer others on, throw "likes" around like confetti, and show the world something other than what they are expecting? We get to dream bigger, welcome in the lonely, love harder, show up when no one else does, adventure greater, and soar higher knowing that we are citizens of heaven, and social media is a fleeting pastime.

You do not need a stage, a pulpit, a million followers, or a microphone to lead change. Your everyday life is the biggest platform that you could ever stand on. Do not underestimate how much God can do with even social media when we change our perspective from #selfie to selfless.

Questions:

1. How many hours a day do you spend on social media (Twitter, Snapchat, Instagram, Facebook, etc.)? What would your life look like if you channeled that time elsewhere?

2. How do you feel after you have spent a decent amount of time scrolling through other people's social media accounts and photos? Better or worse than when you started?

3. When people look at your social media pages, what do you want them to think about you? Does the content you post match up with what you hope they would say?

4. Your social media accounts are through your perspective, but what drives your perspective? What are your motives?

#TruthToRemember → Always keep it real, but keep it focused on a very real God.

CHAPTER 3

Idol Issues

Flashback to 1992, in the quiet suburb of Irvine, California: *Kids Incorporated* was blasted so loud on my parents' TV, you'd think I was having a celebration. Well, I was having a celebration (even if I was the only one to attend), because my singing-n-dancing, big-hair-wearing, super 80s-styling friends were back in my parents' living room, and I completely idolized that show. (For any babies born after 1994: this is where Fergie and Mario Lopez got their starts as kids.) I would literally stand and stare at the TV the entire episode, hardly blinking, just wishing that I could teleport myself through the screen and join the kids in their "super cool" dance routines.

We've all been there; we have all idolized something, someone, or some place. Enjoying or looking forward to something is not idolatry, but idolatry is a sneaky thing, and it's not always a one-size-fits-all model. Sure, there are obvious idols that can be worshipped, such as large statues, designer purses, or even television shows like *American Idol* (I might be Carrie Underwood's biggest fan). But obvious titles, labels, or massive structures are not where idolatry ends. God has entrusted us with wonderful gifts and joys; some of my personal favorites consist of In-N-Out Burger, amazing heels, Instagram, genuine friendships, and sleeping in on the weekends, but it's when we start to idolize and abuse those gifts that life gets messy. In-N-Out Burger is one of my favorite treats, but it becomes an issue if that's the only thing I feed myself. Sleeping in on the weekends is one of God's greatest gifts (I am not a morning person, *#HelpMeJesus*), but life becomes difficult when I abuse that gift and sleep in every day, resulting in ridiculous laziness. I absolutely love Instagram (*#JudgeMe*), but it slowly becomes an idol if that is where I look to fill my self-worth. These simple joys can easily be abused and idolized without us even noticing we're worshipping a false idol! Our heavenly Father gave us these gifts to enjoy; but not so we would rely on them for our sole purpose or happiness. In 1992, I was pretty confident that *Kids Incorporated* did provide my happiness—until the show ended, along with my happiness. *These gifts are given to be appreciated, not idolized.* They're meant as the icing on the cake, not the substance of each bite to fill us up. When our mindset slips slowly into selfishness, we gladly take these gifts and become like a train leaving the station at full speed, with no sense of repercussions or if we are even on the right track. When I started to understand the valuable art of self-less appreciation, I cut back my own distress by a tremendous amount, but it has not been a flawless road.

I ~~Can~~ Can't Handle This on My Own

Over the past twelve years, dating kept me strapped to a roller coaster of emotions and uncertainty, but in an odd way, I found a great deal of joy in it. Every new date seemed like a new adventure. I loved forming new memories and experiences with someone (especially someone really cute!), I loved getting to know someone, I loved the attention, and honestly, I found dating amusing. In hindsight, dating became an idol for me. I had perfected the art of being selfish in dating, and I had unknowingly made it miserable for myself. We are fortunate to be given the freedom to date. Dating freely is a gift that many of us take for granted. For a large percentage of us, arranged marriages are not in our futures, so we get to mingle at our own pace, make our own decisions, and enjoy that wonderful gift of choice. But leave it to *moi* to take a gift, use it, abuse it, and lose it. I began to idolize dating, to look to it for attention, self-worth, and personal fulfillment. There is nothing like the high of the first texts, phone calls, and introductions. I loved "the game," witty banter, and the unknown. Abusing the act of dating for my own emotional stimulation became a regular behavior to me, and I had slowly transformed what was meant for joy into pain because I put dating on my throne instead of my heavenly Father. I was in a selfish state of mind and slowly unraveled until I realized I couldn't handle this on my own. There was never a time I would consult my heavenly Father with relationships that I was about to embark on, but I would consult everyone else around me. I would chat with my friends, my colleagues, my family, my roommates, and my classmates, but I forced God to take a back seat. I would decide that this was my life, my choices, my happiness—and I would control every ounce of it.

At the end of another failed relationship, I would cry (like, ugly cry where you're basically dry-heaving, your face shrivels up, your eyeballs hurt from squinting through the tears, and you nearly feel dehydrated from all the water that just left your body through your eye sockets), and I would blame God, question his love for me, and ask why he would let this happen. I started to fall down a dark hole, thinking, "He could not be a great God if he would allow hurt like this!" But one night, as I sat deeply brokenhearted, my world was radically rocked. When I was eventually out of tears, I was lying in the fetal position on my bedroom floor, and I heard God's sweet response to my deep pain. My heavenly Father gently whispered, *"Darling, you never asked my opinion until now. And now your heart is hurting. You walked down this road so confidently all by yourself because it was all about you. You never asked for my opinion. I do not want your heart to hurt. If you*

*would just let me lead you and if you could TRUST in me that
I have a better plan, then your heart would not hurt like this."*
That was a splash of refreshing water to awaken my thirsty
soul. I fully believe that he is speaking the same to your heart
about dating, or any other battle you are in right now. Proverbs
3:6 says, "Remember the Lord in everything you do, and he
will show you the right way." WOW, Thank you God. *#Hallelujah*

During my initial months in my selfishness detox, right after
the above breakup, I realized that two nasty habits had formed;
1) naturally trusting my man-made idols, more than the God
who created man, and 2) trusting in my God-given gifts, rather
than the almighty God who had given me those gifts. Hi, my
name is Kristen and I am a chronic idolizer, and the only medication to abusing my gifts is keeping my eyes on Jesus. There
is regular disappointment when I check my phone to no sweet
text messages from a significant other. Wedding invitations
have flooded my mailbox with no plus-one option. (Because my
friends knew that there was no way I had a serious boyfriend.
And they were right!)

On February 14, 2016, I literally ran the Los Angeles Marathon because I desperately needed a legal and pure way to
get my mind off the holiday. I figured, no better way than to
put yourself through so much physical strain that you cannot think of anything else besides the finish line and the pain
you're in—so much pain that you're not even thinking about
your handsome ex, who is happily celebrating this romantic day
with his new love! I needed the legal and healthy alternative
to a lobotomy—something drastic enough to get my mind off
my pained heart. Running 26.2 miles through Los Angeles did
just the trick. By mile 18, I was in so much pain. I am going to
sound nutty saying this, but it was the most incredible thing I
could have done. If I was wrapped up in a relationship, I never
would have signed up to run. If I was still idolizing the person I
shared a relationship with, then there was no way I ever would

have pushed myself. I finished the marathon in four hours and fifty-six minutes. (#PraiseJesus) I am *not* a usual long-distance runner. During my "training," the longest I had run consecutively was eight miles. (That's how I know Jesus exists; he kept me alive during those twenty-six miles.) I was in so much pain by the time I crossed that finish line that I had totally forgotten about Valentine's Day. My only dates lined up from there were my chiropractor, a massage, and my bed.

Detoxing yourself from an idol is not a walk in the park. (In my case, that detox is more like a killer marathon through the city.) Despite my best attempt at healthy distractions, I still had some very sad nights, but it was an exfoliation of my soul that I so desperately needed. I find myself still taking the reins of my dating life every now and again, because I consistently fall in the trap that it's all about me and my own security. I tend to idolize comfort or a relationship, but once I remind myself that God wants to lead me down a better path, then I get back on track.

Whatever idol you feel like you are detoxing from, or defeat you feel has captured you, let me assure you that you are not alone. God has been incredible to remind me that honesty is what this is all about; it's not about never messing up again. It's about what we do when we do mess up (because we will): we look to him, learn our lesson, shake it off (Hey, T-Swift), and keep moving. I know God has a husband for me, but I've had to learn relentless trust in every stage of life, that God will give me what I need when he knows that I am ready.

A.A.M.M.

God wants to bless you in the areas of your heart where you have desires, but he can't bless you if you are trying to bless yourself. You want big blessings? Then you need a big God, and it's required that you get out of your own way to allow that to happen. Often times, my own intelligence can be my idol. I secretly admire my opinion or strategy more than God's. I have a selfish habit of thinking I can "help God along." When my A.A.M.M. (All About Me Mode) takes over, I somehow believe that God needs MY help, because I know what's best. Am I insane?! This is the Creator of the universe I am talking about, and somehow I think that he needs my input because I know better? Imagine a little child "helping" her father mow the lawn. It's a beautiful, sunny Saturday, and the father is confidently leading the way with his legit, massive lawn mower. The child insists on joining, and because the father loves his child, he allows it for a little bit. The child trails behind with her miniature Little Tikes plastic lawn mower, imagining that she is getting as much done as her father. As precious as this image is, it makes me think. I am the child trailing behind God with my plastic lawn mower, thinking I am helping him get more accomplished! Sometimes God does not need our help. If we just get out of the way, God can get so much more done. I encourage you to check the idol within yourself, and realize you can't mow the entire lawn on your plastic Little Tikes mower. Step to the sideline and watch God do some incredible work in your life.

Surrendering to God's plan is not giving up; it's growing up. Once you can grasp that maturity, God will take those seeds of selflessness and plant incredible blessings in your life. If you truly desire pure joy, hope, and genuine love, it comes in the form of surrender and humility, which is why so few people have it, and millions tirelessly search for it. This godly concept goes against everything the world throws at us. Everything around us encourages us to stay in our way, to lead our own way, and to be our own way. The world takes our God-given gifts and tells us that if we were to use them for our own benefit to get ahead, to fight for ourselves, and idolize ourselves for our own cleverness, that will lead us to happiness. *Being selfish has never once led me to happiness. When I became _dismantled,_ I felt my purpose _discovered_.*

God doesn't enjoy seeing us dismantled, disheveled, broken, or helpless. He wants to see us fulfilled, hopeful, and encouraged, and then soaring! But we cannot soar if we have baggage weighing us down. It is impossible. Could you imagine if a glorious eagle tried to fly away, but had heavy sandbags hanging from its body, wings, and neck? It wouldn't happen; the eagle would be entirely weighed down, no matter how beautiful, strong, or intelligent it was. This stunning creature has the instinct to soar and finds so much joy in circling the clouds, but for some reason can't figure out why it can't get off the ground. God never ties us up with heavy loads. We did that to ourselves with self-centered behavior. Too many of us have our idols weighing us down in heavy loads, chains, and locks. But God tells us, "If you would simply hand over to me all of your control, your pain, your anxiety or fear, then that will lighten your load enough to set you free" (see Psalm 55:22). So many times I've held onto my own hurt and self-sabotage for way too long, and then had the audacity to get mad at God when I'm not able to fly how I want to. I have turned precious gifts into idols, and was deeply upset when they let me down. *I put all my faith and happiness in these gifts, but didn't trust the one who gave them to me.* God reminds me that it's not about my strength, it's not about my desires, and it's not about my control. All that is required is selfless release; then our chains are broken, and we can soar how we were created to.

As Christians, we need to take medicine DAILY to fend off the highly contagious I-Think-I'm-An-Idol-Perfect-Enough-To-Be-Worshipped Disease. The only antidote is *#AntiSelfie* Medication, and it's prescribed through the Bible. It also fights against other bacteria, such as Idolatry, Egotism, and Self-righteousness. If this disease is noticed early enough in the beginning selfish stages, it should not spread to the rest of the body, especially the heart and the brain. But please proceed with caution, because once it reaches those vital organs, then well, we have someone among us who is breathing, but not really living. The I-Think-I'm-An-Idol-Perfect-Enough-To-Be-Worshipped Disease has unfortunately taken over their body, and they are no longer living the life they were meant to live. They have officially been over taken with Selfishness; a very common but fatal disease that has caused an epidemic all over the world. Treatments should be handled quickly and taken with care. **In case of emergencies:** please remove their phone; quickly take away all mirrors and computer cameras. Force the diagnosed person outside to absorb something other than themselves. This should relieve their symptoms until further help arrives.

Let's not be a culture that is sick and ridden with zombies; people who are breathing but not really alive. Let's be a culture that is so alive and engulfed in Jesus and the love he gave that we can't help but be more obsessed with him than ourselves. Let's not allow for idol-worshipping or the Selfish Disease to hold us back from the life that we were meant to live. The entire world is expecting more self-obsessed, egocentric, self-righteous, condemning, know-it-all Christians. But what if we gave them a shock? Let's *shock the world with some selflessness.*

Questions:

1. Are there any gifts God has blessed you with that you know you've abused for your own benefit? Where did that leave you?
2. Is there anything specifically in your life that is tough to surrender to God?
3. What are some typical daily habits that you can do to keep yourself resistant to the Selfish Disease?

#TruthToRemember ➔ Every gift you are given is to be appreciated, not idolized.

CHAPTER 4

New CEO: God

There has always been something about working that has given me such satisfaction. (My parents were legitimately confused when I was a teenager with three jobs.) My first job was when I was sixteen years old, and I haven't stopped since. I loved challenging myself, hearing people's ideas (even if I didn't agree), making new friends, seeing a business grow. But every Sunday, I would leave God at church. I'd rarely invite him into my life, and least of all my workplace Monday through Friday. My career was all about me. God had his time and place, so he could have Sunday, but that was it. Whether I was volunteering or receiving a salary, at the end of the day, it was all about me. I was consumed with my fulfillment, my own happiness, and how everything affected me—if I was upset, if a coworker said something rude, if my boss treated me in a way that I felt was unfair. I rarely sat back to think about how I was affecting other people. My job was my identity that I had earned, that I had fought for, and God didn't have a hand in it, because I was the one who physically put in the hours, tolerated the driving (and the traffic; Hello, Los Angeles!), and the usual stressing. God seemed so distant, sitting on his magical throne with his feet kicked up. Why should I bring him along; I had it handled. (Looking back, I can insert a monkey emoji covering its eyes here.)

After living this way for ten-plus years in the workforce, with a roller coaster of satisfaction and dissatisfaction, I started to question it. There *had* to be more. There just had to be. Apparently I was not the only one that felt this way: Forbes.com released an article in 2014 based on a study by the Conference Board (a New York City based nonprofit research group) that revealed that 52.3% of Americans were unhappy at work. Over half of America was unhappy! The reasons for discontentment varied, but the fact remained the same; there was clearly something missing. I was part of that statistic many times—constantly searching for a bigger project, something more to conquer, and often times not even taking a second to bask in a job well done or giving thanks to heaven that I was able to complete that job. It was always onto the next task, almost before I finished what was set in front of me. I was consumed by the challenges, rather than by my true purpose. Selfishly, I was living for the promotion, status, or title, rather than living for God. I love working, I know that God created me to work, and I am not going to quit what I love to do (and I financially don't have the luxury of choosing to work or not; a girl has got to pay those bills!), but this roller coaster of discontent made me more confused than ever. It was not an unhappiness based off of salary or title or status. There was something burning in me that I couldn't put my finger on.

Never in my life have I been struck by a passage in the Bible as I was with Romans 12. It was that "Ah-ha!" moment when I feel God's spotlight on me, and he's saying *"Finally, Kristen! The light bulb turned on! It's about time. I've been waiting."* Romans 12:3 says, "Do not think of yourself more highly than you should. Instead, be modest in your thinking." Many days, if I'm honest, I was not modest with myself. I took credit where the credit was not mine, and I was quick to pat myself on the back when I had no business doing so. Romans 12:6 follows with, "So we are to use our different gifts in accordance with the grace that God has given us." We are meant to *use* our gifts and *SHINE*; that's why God gave them to us! He wouldn't have made you incredibly talented at something if he wanted to you be ashamed by it or keep it to yourself. He *encourages* you to use and share whatever talents you have, *BUT with the grace that God has given to us*. Therefore, may all the glory be to God, not ourselves. This was a tough concept for me to adopt. I figured, if I don't sing my own praises at work, then who will? Will all my hard work go unnoticed? If you keep God as your CEO, then your hard work will never go unnoticed. It will be praised and celebrated in heaven. You may not get an email from God saying "Great Job," but if you have a relationship with him, and not just religion, you will hear that whisper in your soul giving you more satisfaction than any earthly promotion could provide. Are we to stand up for ourselves when a job is well done? Absolutely. Are we to defy earthly bosses until we get our recognition? Never.

Having *grace* in the workforce does not mean *giving in*. Having *peace* does not mean you are a *pushover*. Being *kind* does not mean you are *blind* to whatever backstabbing is around you at work. Having Jesus in your heart does not mean your head is in the clouds, and you suddenly become immune to pain or hurt. When you are working for God, however, the moves that others make against you won't send you flying off the edge. If you have perspective of your greater purpose in life, then it makes it slightly less difficult to simply do your work.

There is no doubt that God put me in my profession in my city to be successful. God did not create his people with gifts, abilities, talents, and passions just for us to be boring and dull. Success is not a bad thing. Working hard is not a bad thing. Doing a great job in your profession is not a bad thing. It is an amazing thing! You should hustle, have grace, and shine to your greatest capacity. I love to see women working hard and growing exceptionally in their professions. We are not meant to be pathetic and timid in our vocations. We are meant to do our jobs with purpose, drive, dignity, care, and confidence. It only goes awry when we take credit for our own success. These gifts are not our own, so we must not take credit for them. Sure, we execute them well, but your work or talent is not about you—it is about God. Romans 11:11–12 is very straightforward in saying, "Work hard and do not be lazy. Serve the Lord with a heart full of devotion. Let your hope keep you joyful, be patient in your troubles, and pray at all times."

Godfidence

When I was twenty years old, I nearly sabotaged my own career. In many vocations, wise advisors mention, "You have to get out there and network. *It is all in who you know.*" That's all fine, but I didn't know anyone in the fashion industry! And I certainly did not come from enough money to buy my way into the fashion industry or to even pretend like I fit in. That is not a very promising start to a burning passion that I had within me. I felt defeated before I even began. I felt like saying, "Thanks God, what a tease this is. How the heck is this going to happen?" I quickly learned that the first half of the advice was true; I did need to get out there and network! I had to do my part, stretch myself, and take any opportunity that was offered to me, even if it wasn't paid. I then learned that the second half of that advice was also true; it was all in who you knew. *But the breakthrough came when I realized that I knew God. And if I knew God, and if he had truly created the earth and everyone in it, then I had the connection to know anyone he wanted to introduce me to!* Without even knowing it, I was underestimating God in such a catastrophic way. My blinders were on, only thinking about me and my capabilities. When I started to shift my focus to God's capabilities and trust in his connections to lead my career, everything changed. Opportunities fell out of thin air; people and connections came into my office that I never would have thought possible. I was being saved by a favor so great that only God could provide it. When I was first offered my position, I was sweating out of my little blazer. People in my company miraculously had confidence in my skills, even though I was so new to the industry and hardly had confidence in myself—I was honestly simply trying to keep my head above water. I was praying I wouldn't sink, but rather swim more fluidly than Michael Phelps. Some people call this luck or coincidence, but I refer to it as Godfidence. It's a good thing God knows all about the fashion industry, because he was the only connection that I needed to get going.

When I was growing up in the church, I believed that God gave favor or the best connections to those with honorable careers, like pastors, missionaries, or international volunteers. Those are extremely honorable careers, but what if your heart simply doesn't fit that mold? If he instilled a passion in your heart for an industry, he will flood you with the tools and people to get you started. Whether you are a blogger, chef, race car driver, photographer, wedding coordinator, school teacher, baker, lawyer, finance executive, or florist, God will show up in miraculous ways. I just encourage you to have the eyes to see these miracles, because likely you won't know that a miracle just happened to you until after it walks away. Whatever mountain is in your way with your current career, or the career that you long to have, God is waiting to give you your breakthrough. God loves you SO MUCH. Once your head and heart are shifted from your humanly fears, doubts, and capabilities and surrendered to heaven, then I encourage you to buckle up, because you've just signed up for the ride of your life.

Work Hard, Pray Hard, Play Hard, Slay Hard

So many people I meet want the "play hard" lifestyle without the "work hard" dedication, but they are a package deal. The slaying will not come unless the praying has come before it. No matter what your final goal is, every road that leads to something incredible will be filled with doubt, fear, and angst. But ironically, that is when you are on the right path. Remember that enemy that I spoke about before? Well, wherever God is providing something amazing, that good-for-nothing enemy is not far behind, providing something dreadful, worrisome, or fearful in your path. But rise up, and do *not* be intimidated. If the Lord has called you to something, then there is absolutely nothing in this world that will get in your way. There are things that may make you worry or doubt, but do not let those speed bumps flourish into mountains within your path. Make that enemy so small that he fits under your knees at night when you kneel by your bed to pray.

You can ask anyone; I have always been a rambunctious, curious, outgoing Energizer Bunny, but when I was navigating my way into the fashion industry, there was about a two-year period where I did not have one day off except Thanksgiving and Christmas. I was working five days a week as a retail manager to pay the rent and learn more about how a business works, I crammed all my college courses into two days a week, and I picked up any freelance styling work I could get my hands on. A schedule like that would destroy even the strongest Energizer Bunny. Literally, there were times when I had more coffee in my body than blood. I would use my vacation time from work to pick up a styling shoot, or miss a class here or there if the lecture wasn't crucial or I knew we had a substitute. I am not suggesting that anyone take on this psychotic schedule, but I am so thankful for the hustle that I was able to endure. God really allowed me to be stretched, to understand what hard work meant, and to sweat and cry a little bit along the way as I figured it all out. But the downside was that this Energizer Bunny started to become a slightly angrier person because I had no free time to hang out with friends or family. My sweet girlfriends would call me and say, "Hey! Do you want to go to the beach today?" And I would respond with a bitter "I *can't* go to the beach today. I have to work." Click. (#*BlessThisMess*. My friends are literally angels on earth for not deserting me years ago.) During what I refer to as my "sleepless years," I understood the art of sacrificing the things I wanted to do, versus the things I knew I needed to do. What I *wanted* to do wasn't going to get me anywhere, but what I *needed* to do was building the cement foundation for my future. The beach will always be there, but certain opportunities will not. I had to start shifting my eyes off the immediate gratification of fulfilling my selfish desires to fulfill my greater purpose. Even though I was still working toward a goal that was my own, I have no doubt that I was taught numerous selfless life lessons along the way that I will never forget. I learned to never show up late and to be grateful for every learning opportunity; that a positive attitude is not naïve, it's leadership; and to be open to criticism if I do make a mistake, but have grace on myself, because no one is perfect, not even the boss! There was a quote on social media floating around that read, "The dream is free, but the hustle is sold separately." Can I get an amen?

Miracles Come in Many Different Packages

A very wise pastor at my church once stated in a service, "Work is not 'a blessing and a curse.' Work is always a blessing. It only becomes a curse when you leave God at home."[1] That stuck with me. It rocked my world to uncover that even the tough times at work can be a blessing. Everything with God's name on it is a blessing. James 1:2–3 (NIV) says,

"Consider it pure joy, my brothers and sisters, whenever you face trials of many kinds, because you know that the testing of your faith produces perseverance." OK. Hold. Up. Did I just hear that right?!? "Consider it *pure joy* . . . ?" Sorry I'm not sorry, but that sounds absolutely insane! Sorry Charlie, but sometimes I don't think I can accept that I should be joyful whenever I face trials, because trials are tough! That's why they are called trials! Should I put on a fake Christian smile and say, "I am so thankful for that idiot at work because he is a 'trial,' but thank God for him because that idiot has brought me great joy"? No, we are not supposed to say that. Nor does God expect that of us. He created us! He KNOWS how our minds think, how they get ticked off, our trigger points, what can give us peace, etc. The God I know is realistic, but he is also realistic in letting me know that what I see here on earth is not all there is.

I love seeing God work in my office. The miracles, big and small, that I have seen him handle give me chills. There is one specific story which might sound silly to most, but I am going to tell you about it anyway. I had a client who needed a tuxedo because he was attending a massive red carpet event in Europe. I didn't have the exact style in his size, so I ordered one from Dallas for him. The timing was tight, but it was due to arrive the day before his flight. For whatever reason, when UPS came to drop off the package to my office, they tried to deliver it through the back door. From where I sat at my desk, the back door was on the opposite end of the building, so there was no way that I could ever hear someone knocking there. As I was busily working away that morning, the driver had come by three times, but there was no answer to all three attempts. Meanwhile, I noticed the time and thought it was strange that I hadn't received the delivery. By chance, I checked the back exit door and found three UPS notices stuck there, notifying me of the three attempts. The delivery man needed to move on with the rest of his stops, but would try again the following day.

In this specific scenario, I could not have him come back tomorrow. *Tomorrow* was not an option for me. I needed that tuxedo that day, as my client was leaving on his flight in less than twenty-four hours. Panic set in. Instantly, I got on the phone with UPS to sort out the dismal situation. The kind lady on the other end of the phone tolerated my fear, and she was doing all that she could to help my desperate situation. She told me that she could not get ahold of the driver, but was familiar with his route. With this sudden glimpse of hope, I told her I didn't care where he was; I would meet the truck at one of his next stops. He was due to go to downtown next, which was a solid thirty- to forty-minute drive for me each way, but at that point, I did not care. I would have ridden a skateboard anywhere in the city if that's what it took. As anxiety took over, sweat literally started to creep from my forehead. The UPS operator told me that she was going to try to call this man just a few more times, and she would need to call me back. My sweaty palms reluctantly put down the phone, and I just sat there and stared at my computer. *This tux is totally lost*, I thought. *What the heck am I going to do? What am I going to tell my client? They will never want to come here again. How could I let this happen?* It was at that moment that I bowed my head to pray. I probably should have done that first, but better late than never.

I always felt justified going to God with "honorable" prayer requests, like a friend's sickness, a family member's hurting heart, financial stability, etc. I felt as though God was more inclined to answer "honorable" prayer requests, and the rest got taken care of whenever he had time. I did not feel justified with this prayer. I thought God would see my angst as frivolous and silly. Why would God care about a lost tuxedo? I was not helping the sick; I was dressing actors for the red carpet!

But I thought, what do I have to lose? Sitting at my desk, anxiety driven and totally out of hope, I came to my heavenly Father and said, "God, I know this is just a tuxedo. There are people dying and I feel really stupid coming to you with this request, but I know you see what is going on, I know that you love me, I know you blessed me with this job, and I know you are cheering for me to succeed. I would be so grateful if you could help me. I know you know where that truck is. I know you know that truck driver's name. I know only you can turn this mess into a victory, because I have tried all that I can, and I can't fix this, Lord. This is totally out of my hands, so I am putting it in yours." After that moment of silence, I continued working for maybe another two minutes. Then the phone rang. I thought to myself, *Thank you Jesus, this is the phone call where my UPS operator friend will tell me that they found the driver!* I was very wrong. The news she delivered was the exact opposite. They still could not get ahold of the driver, and could not guarantee that he would be going downtown next, so she advised it would be useless for me to go all the way down there. I was defeated. *But I JUST prayed,* I thought. *But it's alright. Why would God care about a silly tuxedo, or my silly fashion career?* I sunk back in my chair and tried to think of back-up plans A, B, and C. Then, the unimaginable happened. I got a call from my team members downstairs saying that a box had just arrived for me.

It's the tux! It's the tux? It is the tux. I quietly mouthed those four words repeatedly, not sure what tone to pair with the end of it; I felt like questioning this miracle, I wanted to rejoice with happiness, and I was simply trying to grasp what just happened. I could not believe my eyes. I stood there and stared at the cardboard box for probably a solid sixty seconds without blinking or saying a word. My colleagues probably labeled me as insane that day, because 1) I am never that silent, and 2) my body was frozen in a shocked stance, mouth open and all, staring at a tall cardboard box. But I didn't care. I had chills running up and down my spine. Did this seriously just happen? This tux was gone into the abyss of Los Angeles traffic! The driver could not be contacted! How did the driver just happen to make a fourth attempt for delivery that day? This was not a coincidence; this was a miracle from God. A tuxedo miracle! HAL-LE-LU-JAH.

I instantly felt so loved and adored by my heavenly Father, that he would hear that prayer and honor it. Isaiah 43:1–2 says, "Do not be afraid—I will save you. I have called you by name—you are mine. When you pass through deep waters, I will be with you; your troubles will not overwhelm you. When you pass through fire, you will not be burnt; the hard trials that come will not hurt you." It became so clear to me that day that God cares about us so much that he wants to take care of our needs, even when we face times of trouble in the workplace. God doesn't only love us on Sundays when we attend church service. If we just invite him, he will help us when we need it most, even in our daily jobs. God took a situation that could have very much been a "curse" and turned it into a blessing. In Isaiah 46:4, God says, "I made you and will care for you; I will give you help and rescue you." God doesn't always have to be rescuing from cancer, or divorce, or even wars; he wants to help us even in the workplace, when we need to be rescued from a stressful situation. It was like he was waiting up in heaven, watching me from above, simply standing there, and waiting for me to ask him for help. And holy enchilada, did he deliver! (No pun intended.)

What are the "lost tuxedos" in your life or in your career—that is, what things do you need to completely surrender to God, so he can show up and do his great work? If you are anything like me, work can start to consume you; sometimes consuming out of passion, sometimes consuming out of projects and deadlines, and sometimes consuming out of fear.

Whatever the case may be, if you do not surrender your work life to God, you are withholding a massive chunk of your head and heart from the One who wants to help you, guide you, and be your sanity in an insane world.

Sometimes what we need to surrender the most is what we keep guarded the most. I would think to myself, *Fashion is my thing. I'm sure God is more concerned with world hunger and deprivation. Why would he care about THIS job? I've got this covered.* How dare I cut down the capacity of the all-knowing, all-loving God who created me? God is very clever to reveal to us how wrong we are, in ways that we only we would understand. Please remember that a relationship with God is not a one-size-fits-all model. You are unique, so the heavenly Father will speak to your heart in unique ways. God allowed me to make many, many mistakes, to fall flat on my face, and to be greatly humbled. Even after seven years of working for a company I love, in an industry I adore, I am still humbled daily. Growth does not come without growing pains, and boy, did I have some growing pains in my career. I have learned boatloads about the fashion industry. I would like to think that God entrusted me with the skills to be good at my job, but I have never stopped learning. If I stop learning, then what else is there to life? To think you genuinely know it all? Where's the fun, mystery, or discovery in that? God gave me a heart for the fashion industry for a reason: to do great, honest work for his glory, not my own.

No Corporate Ladder in Heaven

Whatever job you have or profession you may be in, remember God has you there for a reason, and that reason may never be clear to you. God doesn't believe in hierarchy; that was something we brilliant humans created. He does not look at the corporate CEO any more highly than the Subway sandwich employee. He wants to make you shine right where you are. Whether you have been called to do missionary work in

Uganda, continue to attend school at an American university, or become a nanny overseas, if you work with purpose, God will bless you wherever your calling leads. My mother ran her own at-home daycare for more than twenty years. She had a bachelor's degree in child psychology and a state license to watch up to six children per day in our home. Beyond just raising me and my two brothers, she would thoughtfully teach and care for little children under the age of four full-time. This was very thankless, tiring, and far from glamorous, but she did it with care, purpose, and love. She watched those children like they were her own. Years later, many of those children are now grown up into their teens and into adulthood, and I see the immeasurable impact that she had on their young lives. My mother saw her purpose and worked at it every single day.

For many, many years, my father commuted two hours each way to work, just so he could provide for our family. Then for another few years, he commuted from Southern California to San Francisco every single week, just so our family didn't need to be uprooted and I could continue at my school with my same friends. My mom and I would routinely pick Dad up from the airport on Friday night, and then drop him back off Sunday night. He was extremely sacrificial and unappreciated by his unknowing children. Looking back as an adult, I don't know how he managed. Somehow my father worked tirelessly with poise and discreetness, and along the way instilled in me a work ethic that I am beyond grateful for. He worked for his purpose, and he did a really good job at it, even when it wasn't easy.

I know there are millions of people out there who work around the clock for little to no acknowledgement. They struggle and hustle just to get by. (Trust me, I get it, the struggle is real. Not many months pass by before bills stack up and I am forced to eat nothing but ramen and oatmeal until the next paycheck.) Whatever your career may be, work at it with the idea that God is your CEO, and his bonus structure and promotion scale is unlike any you've ever seen! Of course, we have human bosses that we need to respect on earth, but if you know that your job is so much more than the title, the paycheck, or the business card, then the most mundane, seemingly useless tasks will suddenly have great purpose. You were chosen to do your task in your location. If you serve up French fries, do it with purpose and joy. If you fold clothing in a retail store, then fold with kindness and enjoyment. If you bag groceries at a grocery store, then greet those hundreds of customers you see every day with happiness and warmth. If you do digital marketing, then execute every project with diligence and delight. If you are a stay-at-home mom, then raise your children with dignity, compassion, and care. When you keep your eyes on the Boss of all bosses, the King of all kings, the Lord of all lords, then you can expect raises, promotions, transfers, opportunities, and introductions that you could have never done on your own. Once you shift your eyes off yourself and glance to your Father in heaven who wants to guide you, then miracles will start to happen. 1 Timothy 1:12 says, "I give thanks to Christ Jesus our Lord, who has given me strength for my work. I thank him for considering me worthy and appointing me to serve him."

Heavenly Warning

Caution: keep your eyes peeled for what God might do, because it will likely be in a way that you would never expect. The miracle might not even be in your workplace, but in your personal life with a family member or friend. Once you can genuinely find joy from shifting your eyes from yourself to your heavenly Father, then that same happiness, love, and security will boil over into other aspects of your life besides work. The more you give him what you have, the more he will entrust you with incredible blessings, because he knows he can rely on you to carry them out.

So many people work to retire one day. But our life purpose is not to retire. Do you honestly believe that you were placed on earth to work tremendously hard for thirty, forty, fifty years, just to one day sit back and enjoy your benefits package? There is so much more to life! Whether your work is volunteering on a committee or at an animal shelter, running a start-up, or creating a TV show, when you live life for God, your work is never officially done. 2 Thessalonians 3 emphasizes the importance of work, adding, "We say this because we hear that there are some people among you who live lazy lives, and who do nothing except meddle in other people's business" (v. 11). As long as you have oxygen in your lungs and an able body, then your time living for your greater purpose isn't done! As Dr. Seuss brilliantly puts it: "You have brains in your head. You have feet in your shoes. You can steer yourself in any direction you choose." But I am going to put my *#selfie* to selfless twist on it and say, "You have brains in your head. You have feet in your shoes. You can put your faith in God, and your direction? Let him choose." Allow God to steer your direction into a meaningful, legacy-leaving life. Your number-one job is to be an employee of the King of the Universe: to be an ambassador, to do your job well, and to please your boss in heaven. Once we realize that our job security is in him and not in ourselves, we are set free.

Questions to Ponder:

1. If you worked with the mindset that God is your CEO, what are little changes that you would make in your everyday work life?

2. If a friend walked into your office and asked any of your coworkers if they thought you believed in Jesus, what do you think they would say?

3. Has anything incredible ever happened at work, and when other people credited it as "good luck," you knew that God was the one behind it?

#TruthToRemember → Whatever your career may be, work at it with the idea that God is your CEO, and His bonus structure and promotion scale is unlike any you've ever seen!

CHAPTER 5

Relationship Revival

Please don't roll your eyes at me, because I am going to be cliché anyway: relationships are a gift. (I saw your eye roll.) Some are more challenging gifts than others (and often I wish there was an exchange policy or a money-back guarantee on these "gifts"), but God created us to not live life alone. He has instilled a longing for relationships since the very, very beginning: God created Eve because he knew Adam shouldn't be alone. Additionally, he made it possible for them to create more life together, so they would flourish in reproduction and eventually be surrounded friends and family. If Adam and Eve had succeeded in their relationship, obeyed God, and eventually reproduced, I imagine the Garden of Eden basically being like *My Big Fat Greek Wedding*: family that celebrates in community, and community that lifts each other up through song, dance, and overwhelming love, whether you like it or not. Sadly, we all know how that story ended; Adam and Eve disobeyed and ruined the party for everyone, leaving humanity with the massive issue of relationships to work on for the rest of history. (Thanks, guys.) From literally day one of humanity, we are shown how important relationships are to our survival, and how we treat relationships affects generations to come.

Independent Women

Hard work should be expected from every human on the planet, and women should be encouraged to be liberated because they are capable of great things. But let's get one thing clear: independence doesn't mean that you say "Girl Bye" every time someone meets you with opposition. Instead of screaming #GirlBye, how about we start being a generation of women that asks #GirlWhy? In today's world, we are told through marketing tactics, music, movies, books, and even close friends and family that if we have any self-respect, then we need to live life independently and basically leave a path of blazing destruction until we get our way. We are overtly told that if a friend hurts us, we should burn that friendship and never look back. If a company you work for makes a decision you feel isn't fair, then do all you can to get your revenge right before walking out the door into the next opportunity. I am Italian, with a fire inside of me so feisty that I would burn those around me with just a few words. For years, I took so much pride in being independent, but I viewed independence as a "don't mess with me" shield and looked down on others who didn't do the same. Take it from my personal anguish: living life this way only leads to destruction and so much pain.

Relationships are not about us! Of course, there are always exceptions (I would never want you to stay in a harm-ful work environment, or tolerate a destructive relationship), but often, half the problem is ourselves. I was once told, "You can never change another person. The only person you have control over is yourself, so why don't you check your own heart, re-evaluate how you speak and what you're saying, and get your eyes off yourself. Once you alter yourself in such a way, the other person will have no choice but to respond dif-ferently." If the laws of physics apply to other areas of our lives, and with every action, there is an equal and opposite reaction, then why don't we try altering our own actions to be slightly more loving, to see if we get different reactions? And if you feel like this still isn't successful, then the good news is that we have the almighty God on our side, and he loves justice, so he will bring that justice when he sees fit. Having this discretion when it comes to relationships is crucial. If God tells you to walk away and love from afar for the safety of your heart, then always do what God tells you. Until then, we are called to take our eyes off ourselves and simply love in these relationships.

There are specific seasons when people will come in and out of your life for a purpose. We are not meant to be best friends with every single person that we get to know. If someone becomes destructive, then there are ways to seek help and love from afar. When a male and female friendship teeters on the verge of something romantic when it is highly inappropriate, then there are times to step back and love from afar. I would hope you understand there are exceptions now and again, and I am not going to waste your time with listing every single scenario it is appropriate to back off from a relationship, as matters of the heart are not always black and white. But I encourage you to PRAY, listen to what God is telling you, get out of your own way, and remind yourself that it is not about you! Life is about an amazing God who wants to lead you to incredible relationships to grow your heart while on earth.

LOVE: An Action, Not Just a Description

Loving people was so important to Jesus that he called it the second most important commandment. Not the sixth or the eighth, but the second. But the command to love people has not always sat well with me. I have had many conversations with God where I say, "Hold up—you have got to be kidding me. You want me to LOVE them? Did you not just see what I saw?" And honestly, I am sure that other Christians have said the same about me in my BC (before Christ) days. Some days, I was as cuddly as a cactus, but somehow people in my life still managed to love me. This gives me the faith that I can do the same. We are not called to "love people *and* their actions," but we are called to love people, despite their actions. As we love them and call them to higher actions, that love, hopefully, will permeate deep into their hearts and lead them to better actions.

Jesus makes it very clear that we are called to "love our neighbors as ourselves." I don't know about you, but I love myself a lot—a little too much most days. If I was half as concerned with those around me as I am with what am I going to wear, how someone never texted me back, and my weekend plans, then I would have a lot more room to be a more selfless friend, sister, daughter, aunt, and colleague. A life lived with selfless love is so much more rewarding and exciting than living in a selfish bubble. But I understand that living in a selfish bubble is safe. No one can hurt you there. You are comfortable in your bubble. Well, sorry sister. On behalf of God, I am here to burst your bubble, because God did not create you to be safe in a bubble. You have gifts, talents, and love to share with the world, and I will not allow you to sit there and let everyone else live the life that you are supposed to be living. Get in the game, girl! I have never heard of anyone who sat on their death bed and said, "You know, I am really glad that I was so selfish my whole life. I am just really thankful I stayed in my bubble. I don't really mind that I burned all those bridges throughout the years, because I was more interested in my own comfort. I just feel so fulfilled." YEAH, RIGHT. The reality is that all our bodies will one day fail. But will your legacy die with you? Or will you pour into people's hearts with every breath; to create so much love that it literally can't die with you? No one is perfect, but every time they bare their flaws, remember their amazing features. Being selfless starts with our friendships; there is no such thing as a perfect friend, but there is such a thing as a selfless one. You are so loved, and you were called to love. We are shaped to value those around us that God has placed in our world.

There is nothing greater on this earth than solid relationships and quality friendships: Those people who love you to very core, even though they've seen your dark side (and terrible middle school outfits!). Those friends who turn into family, no matter how opposite you may be. I have a very best girlfriend I have known since first grade. Her name is Molly. We are opposite as opposites can get. Molly is blonde and petite, played soccer in high school, excelled at every academic course she took, is naturally more reserved, and can cook like I've never tasted before. I am brunette (despite my artificial coloring), was the captain of the dance team in high school, did not excel at any academic courses (except English, when I tried), know no strangers, and cannot cook to save my life. I challenged nearly every rule, and Molly was much more obedient about following them. Molly is dedicated when it comes to dating, and long-term dating never appealed to me. When an interesting opportunity would arise, she would ask, "Why would you do that?" and I would reply, "Why *wouldn't* you do that?" God could not have created two more opposite humans, but we love each other as deeply as it can get. I don't have any sisters, and neither does she, so I have a theory that God gave us each other to practice what it would be like. We have fought, pushed each other emotionally, and expanded one another's horizons. There is nothing I wouldn't do for that woman, but we never would have gotten to this place if we didn't sincerely love one another with a selfless love and allow our differences to keep us growing, rather than fighting. Our differences are what I love about us!

Sure, I benefit and grow from my relationship with Molly, but once again, I've come to find out that relationships are not about me. After loads and loads of prayer, and a trail of making mistakes, I have come to ask the questions "Can I still choose to love this person, even when I don't *feel* like it?" and "How can God use me to be a support to this other person?" You know you are living a life to honor God when you can encourage those around you, even when you are losing courage yourself. Or when you take the time to listen to one another, when all you feel like doing is watching Netflix. Or when you physically show up for one another, when all you want to do is be alone. I have found that a simple text, compliment, or hug goes further than we might ever realize. Many times, the more we overwhelmingly pour into others, the more they will pour into us. And if they don't, which has happened to me, then that's absolutely fine. At least I gave it my very best shot to love them the most genuinely that I possibly could.

Someone in your life could be going through some pain that you might not have any idea about. I really wish that I had X-ray vision for the heart. It is not about what your two eyes can see or how you feel; it is about how your loved one feels. To be there for a loved one during a time of hurt is one of the most incredible things you can ever do for them, even if you can't figure out their hurt yourself. It is not up to you to decide what is hurtful and what is not. It is not about you! Being selfless in a selfish world is about showing up when no one else does. It is about those around you whom you are meant to comfort, support, and encourage.

A dear friend of mine modeled this a couple years ago, and it left a mark on my heart that I will never forget. After enduring a really, really hard breakup, I was going through my usual routine of "staying strong," throwing myself into work, swapping between Taylor Swift and Beyoncé on repeat, making any plans to keep myself distracted from my shattered heart, praying a lot, and doing my best to march forward. I needed to get the heck out of Dodge, so I hopped on the train down to San Diego to visit Tenley, one of my very best friends, for the weekend. I needed some quality girl time, I needed to get out of the city, I needed more Jesus, and I needed a margarita (not necessarily all in that order). After settling into my friend's apartment and chatting so quickly I'm sure only birds could understand us, we finally paused, and she asked me, "How are you?"

I said, "I'm fine. I am getting through it. I know God is good, and that guy wasn't for me, but I am still hurt."

She simply responded, "Kristen, God IS good, and you're right, that guy was not the guy for you, but it's OK to be sad." With those few words, "It's OK to be sad," I completely lost it. The floodgates opened and I could have saved California from its drought with all the tears that came flooding from my eye sockets. It was OK to be sad, but no one had reminded me of that. Any normal person's first reaction is to offer helpful or cheerful sentiments when loved ones are hurting, in the form of "you will find someone so much better for you," "you have so much going for you, don't waste your tears on him," or "forget about him; he's a jerk." Every single one of those statements were true: I would find someone so much better for me, I do have a lot going for me, so I shouldn't waste my tears on him, and yes, I absolutely need to forget about him because he was kind of a jerk. Every supportive effort from friends and family was very sweet, but the one that changed my heart was the one that met me where I was at, didn't try to coach me through the moment, but just sat with me in silence while I cried. Sometimes, it's the things we don't say that matter just as much as the things we do say. And to this day, because of what my friend said to me, I have tried to alter my own reactions when my friends have broken hearts. It is way too easy to jump in with our own advice, our own disastrous heartbreak to make them feel less about theirs, or a rambling pep talk. The truth is it's not about us! It is about a friend who is hurting. We want to give hope to a hurting friend, but sometimes they just need to feel the depth of their hurt before they can see the hope. Even though we may see the full forecast—that the rainbow comes after the storm—their broken heart is still in the storm, so we have to dance with them in the rain until their sun starts shining again.

Sure, God gives us loving relationships for our own enjoyment and pleasure, but that's not the entire purpose. It's about loving people around you in the way that Jesus loves us, so selflessly and without ceasing and without judging. I am far from the friend that Jesus is, but I know that's my goal. It might take me my entire life to strive for that goal, and I may never fully get there, but it's the effort that God sees. And not only will God see our efforts, but our relationships will be healthier and stronger.

Drop the Gavel—You Are Not the Judge

Many times, I have allowed my own judgment to completely sabotage a friendship or relationship. My own eyes allow me to pass a verdict on other people's lives; whether at work, at church, with my closest friends, or even with family. Proverbs 11:27 says, "Anyone can find the dirt in someone. Be the one that finds the gold." And here is a friendly reminder to Jesus followers everywhere: We are not here to judge anyone, save anyone, or treat any person on this planet as a "project" because we somehow think we (as Christians) have figured out all the answers. Do not shower friends with pity; shower them with selfless love. Yes, Jesus is the way, the truth, and the life, but that doesn't entitle us to peer into people's lives and obstruct when we aren't meant to. This is not about religion, race, background; this is an even playing field called life. God created me, just like he created you, and your child's teacher, your yoga instructor, the cashier at the grocery store, and the woman in Uganda. John 3:17 says, "For God did not send his son into the world to be its judge, but to be its savior." Unless you lived a sinless life, died brutally on a cross, and then rose from the dead three days later, then you are imperfectly human, just like me. You are not God; you do not do the saving. God does the saving, and you do the LOVING (#WelcomeToTheClub). Allow me to repeat; you don't SAVE, you LOVE. You may have a calling, but humans are not your projects, and *you* cannot save anyone; only God can do that. Our heavenly Father is so incredibly good to remind us in Matthew 7:1–5 how much he despises human judgment: "Do not judge others, so that God will not judge you, for God will judge you in the same way as you judge others, and he will apply the same rules to you as you have applied to others. Why, then, do you look at the speck in your brother's eye, and pay no attention to the log in your own eye? How dare you say to your brother, 'Please let me take that speck out of your eye,' when you have a log in your own eye? You hypocrite!" Dang; if that isn't clear enough, then I don't know what will be. Drop the microphone; we can all go home now. . . . Just kidding, God's not done yet, therefore, I'm not done writing.

I love the saying "You have to earn the right to be heard." You are a lot more effective if you spend quality time to get to know someone, invest in them (the good, the bad, the ugly), commit to being their friend, and just love them for who they are. Once that foundation is built, someone is so much more likely to value what you are saying. They might actually listen! Many times, we become "fixers": we observe their life for a hot second (or through what they post on social media!), then with the best intentions of passing on "words of wisdom," we drop atomic bombs of what we think they are doing right or wrong in their journey of life. (Hey stranger, nobody cares what you think! If you don't agree with what they are posting, then stop following them. Please, please, please stop berating people with such hurtful, vicious comments on social media. Trust me when I say this, their deep decrease in followers will be a lot more heart-wrenching, rather than any rude comments you may write.) We, as mere humans, are not here to save or judge ANYONE, no matter what their race, religion, background, skin color, family, or residence. Jesus already saved the world, and God is the only one with the credentials to judge. We are simply here on earth to ensure a relationship revival of love, hope, and joy, based not off our own strength, but that which God has given us.

Relationships within the Church

Ironically, the church can be a tough place to love people, due to the fact that our expectations of people are much higher within the church than they are in other aspects of life. I may hold my friend from small group to a much higher standard than I would my anti-church personal trainer. Or I hold the church coordinator to a much higher standard than I would my professor or teacher. I validate this thinking with thoughts like, "Well, they know the Lord. They should know better." I believe as a church we are here to encourage each other to strive for a more Christ-centered life every day, but when do our personal expectations surpass the reality of human flaws? There is holding someone accountable in a loving manner, and then there is the bar so high that no one could jump across, even if they had a bungee, trampoline, and Pogo stick combined. Are we setting up our church to fail or succeed? We are not the ones to play police officer, because yet again, it is not about us. We are here to love, not judge our friend on their struggles or condemn someone for being authentic.

Relationships within the church never really appealed to me because I found the church to be hypocritical, judgmental, righteous, or just plain phony. I really loved God, but I didn't really care for the church. Why would I ever want to sign myself up to go hang out with people who didn't genuinely seem interested in me either? It all seemed so forced. I would go to church for God and God only; I left no room in my heart or schedule to care about his people. Then one day, God spoke so clearly to my heart. He said, *"Kristen, BE the change you wish to see in the church."* Wait, the church? I thought the quote was supposed to end with "world." Well, not this time. My soul was stirred to question, "How am I supposed to be lovingly selfless in the world, if I couldn't even be lovingly selfless to my own church and its people?" Be the change you wish to see in your church. Do you think that most of your church is really unfriendly? Well, then, go find someone sitting alone and introduce yourself. Be as friendly as you could possibly be (again, without being phony). Do you think that the congregation gossips? Then be the example of the woman who chooses to not gossip. Do you think that your church is phony or fake? Well then, be the first person to share your struggles, and leave the door open for them to be honest about theirs. Be genuine, be encouraging, and be selfless in honor of one another. Be the person you wish you had at church.

Everyone should be important to the body of Christ. *Everyone*. (Did I stutter? No, I did not. Everyone means everyone.) But what about Joe White, who always seems to sing too loud during service and disrupt others? Joe is important, and he is loved, and he was placed in your life for a reason. Well, what about Katie Smith, who cannot seem to take a cue that you are tired and just want to stop talking? Katie Smith is important, and she is loved, and she was placed in your life for a reason. But that Sarah Jean is just so annoying with her "problems" that really aren't even problems; she just needs to get over herself. Sarah Jean is important, and she is loved, and she was placed in your life for a reason. (I think you get the pattern now.) It is not about you! If we aren't even demonstrating grace, peace, forgiveness, and patience within the church, then how the heck do you expect to have loving relationships outside of church?

Everyone should feel accepted at the church, because we all have a job to do. Let's be clear: you are not called to be best friends with every single person at church. That is physically impossible (unless your church consists of four people). It is healthy to have a couple very close friends to confide in, a small group to share life with, and the church body to genuinely love. We are called to love some people from a further distance, but regardless, we are called to love them. Katie Smith might be extremely aggravating to you, but she has an incredible gift in serving the children's ministry. Joe White may make you irritated beyond repair, but he serves in the church parking lot week after week, even when no one else is willing to help. Sarah Jean's attitude may tempt you to pull your hair out, but she has organized multiple mission trips all over the world, which have led so many people to Christ's love. We all have bad, ugly, annoying flaws—and incredible gifts. Those personal gifts were meant to be contributed to the church and accepted and celebrated as a body of Christ. We cannot pick and choose what parts of people we want to love. God cared about them enough to create them, so we must honor God and care about them too.

Last but not least, let's please remind ourselves that whenever there is something amazing happening in the Lord's name, the enemy is not far behind. (He is like a mosquito that will just not quit!) The chances are that something incredible is happening within your church walls, and the enemy doesn't like it, so he plans to destroy it. And what is the quickest way to destroy something amazing within the church? The people! It's not rocket science. If the enemy wants to distract the church, all he has to do is divide the people to the point where relationships are unmanageable, feelings are deeply hurt, and pain manifests in a place where there should be healing. The people within your congregation aren't your problem; the enemy is your problem! Walk boldly, don't be fooled, and once again, repeat after me: "Not Today Satan!"

Church Anatomy

1 Corinthians 12:14–20 says, "For the body does not consist of one member, but of many. If the foot should say, 'Because I am not a hand, I do not belong to the body,' that would not make it any less a part of the body. And if the ear should say, 'Because I am not an eye, I do not belong to the body,' that would not make it any less a part of the body. If the whole body were an eye, where would be the sense of hearing? If the whole body were an ear, where would be the sense of smell? But as it is, God arranged the members in the body, each one of them, as he chose. If all were a single member, where would the body be? As it is, there are many parts, yet one body."

Once you find a church home, you are a part of a body. The church body should actually function quite similar to the human body. You are needed, and you will need others. I know "needing others" is a tough pill to swallow, but sister, once you accept this, I promise you that your life will sincerely start to shift. I always thought that "needing others" made someone look weak, like they were incapable so they needed someone else to make up for their lack of capability. God did not create a weak human when he made you. He did not create a weak person when he created me. But we are not perfect. I have gifts other people might not have, and other people in my circle have incredible gifts I don't have; that is why we need each other. It is not because we are weak; it is because we learn from each other and lean on one another. Personally, due to my selfish independence, I have built up quite a wall. I prefer to help *others* when they need it. A burden is the last thing I would ever want to be to someone, but needing some help or back up is not the same as being a burden.

For the human body to function properly, the muscles, bones, nerves, circulation, and arteries need to work together. If a person's human body does not function properly, then it is quite difficult to live the life they want to. It is not always impossible, but quite difficult. The same goes for the church; if everyone doesn't work together, then it is quite difficult for them to be effective the way that they were intended to be. It is not impossible—just far more difficult.

One day, I was helping my brother's family move into their new home. My three-day stint at the gym suddenly gave me the inspiration that I was now the Hulk, so I offered to help my brother carry a very heavy wooden dresser. My arms were fully extended, my fingers gripped the edge so tightly that my knuckles were turning white, and I was shuffling my feet along, barely lifting this heavy mass of wood so it didn't scratch their new floors. I took a wrong step, missed a stair, and dropped my end of this monstrous dresser on my big toe. At that moment, all sorts of cringe-worthy words flew out of my mouth before I could even think. The toe was instantly THROBBING, and for some reason, I thought cursing like a sailor would relieve the pain. (It didn't.) But I thought to myself, *Thank God it was just my toe. It wasn't my entire foot or leg, and I will be fine.* Oh man, I was wrong. If you ever hurt a toe or finger, you suddenly realize why God gave them to us, because we need them! For the next week and a half, every time I walked, my right big toe pulsated an insane amount, to the point of pain and discomfort, no matter what shoes I wore (and I have A LOT of shoes to choose from). There was no escaping it; my big toe was severely bruised, and I had to face how much I really needed to value my big toe! I always thought of our big toes as somewhat dispensable, but my dear friend, if you learn nothing else from this book, please know that our big toes are there for a reason! They steady our balance and keep us walking forward.

Sarah Jean, Katie Smith, Joe White, and every person in the church has a God-given gift and reason to be there. If you think of your neighbor as a useless "big toe," please remember my story of how painful it was to walk with a hurt big toe. You need to cherish that big toe before it gets hurt, or your church will be forced to limp along until things get better. The church body will get injured if you look at people as dispensable, and your walk with God will suffer as a result. God values each person enough to give them breath every day, so you have no choice but to value them for who they are. Continue to stretch yourself to all new levels of selflessness, even if that simply means loving the "big toes" in your congregation. Spoiler Alert: you don't determine whose gifts are more valuable than others'. It is not about us! We are all needed and called to contribute something unique.

God created each person strategically and individually. He took his time. God was clever and thoughtful when he created you, so that you could be different from your neighbor. How boring, mundane, and awful life would be if we were all alike! I get nauseated just thinking about it. It's like having plain chocolate ice cream every day for the rest of your life. Sprinkles are not an option, caramel is nowhere to be found, and whipped cream is like a daydream. You might have a different upbringing, hair color, or way of dressing, but that's great because God intended his people to be diverse. He gave you your clever brain to be unique to your neighbor. And he created your neighbor to have some different opinions or insight— possibly to help you see things from a different perspective. *Diversity should be insightful, not intimidating.* We are meant to cultivate diverse relationships that are surrounded by the love of God. As a church, we are here to value opinions, be slow to talk and quick to listen, and remind ourselves that it is not all about us! It is about the incredible, insanely loving God who created your fellow churchgoers. You didn't create everyone, so you will probably not understand everyone. That is OK; you are not meant to understand everyone, because it is not about you! The church body, and how it functions, should be something that people are drawn to, not scarred by. What are you doing in your everyday life to draw people to the church?

Family Policy: No Exchanges or Returns

There's a quote that says, "You're either a blessin', or a lesson." Many people might reflect on their own families as lessons, "lessons" that we cannot avoid due to shared blood or the same last name. Our families, whether you like to admit it or not, have largely shaped the people we are, whether that is for better or worse. Whatever family background you came from, this was the first glimpse you saw of what a relationship is and likely influenced how you handle relationships yourself. If your parents abandoned you, you may view relationships as abandonment. If your brother, father, aunt, uncle, or mother abused you, you might see relationships as hurt and pain. If your parents were physically around, but mentally and emotionally neglected you, you could view relationships as neglectful. If your sibling tortured you growing up, and still continues to do so to this day, then you may view relationships as torture that you can't escape. If your parents split in a bitter divorce or adultery, you may see relationships as hate and lies, or even conclude that nothing lasts forever, so why try anyway? If your mother or father constantly judged you, then you might view relationships as entirely judgmental. Whatever our young eyes and hearts were exposed to likely formed how we view relationships. And this isn't only applicable to romantic relationships; I am referring to relationships as a whole. Whatever we grew accustomed to with our family relationships has a likeliness of spilling into every other relationship in our life.

You may still be secretly bitter with God for allowing you to witness interactions in such a volatile form at a young, impressionable age. Please let me say that I am so sorry for your pain. I am so, so sorry. Sadly, because of the sin from the very beginning with Adam and Eve, relationships have been flawed almost since day one. But please remind yourself that this unhappiness is not where the story ends! In Jeremiah 30:17, God says, "I will make you well again; I will heal your wounds." In this verse, he is speaking to the Israelites, promising to restore them to their lands after near destruction. He has the same promise for you: he will restore your hearts and minds to wholeness after any destruction your family has caused. Do not let the enemy win by capturing you with your impression of how relationships function. The enemy will do whatever it takes to hold you down with pain and sadness from the past. He will gladly lock the chains to your past and throw away the key. With God's hope and love, he rips through those chains that Satan tried to lock on you. In my times of desperation, when I know God can free me from my chains, I turn to Jeremiah 17:14, which says, "Lord, heal me and I will be completely well; rescue me and I will be perfectly safe; You are the one that I praise." God is so gracious with rescuing if we allow him, but he never promises that we will forget the painful things that happened to us, or forget what we saw or heard. Once we are healed through Christ, we have the opportunity to take pain that held power over us and turn it into power we can use for good. Your past experiences are your most powerful testimony; more than any good deed you could do, your story of survival and God's strength could change hearts. You have the power to use your own relationship trials with your family to help someone else. God will never waste a hurt, but the question is, will you? Will you allow yourself to be chained to the destruction of past relationships or family memories? Or will you be selfless with your stories and share your pain, so others can be healed too? You were created to be exactly who you are, where you are at, and God is going to use your relationship stories in incredible ways, if you would just allow him to. Just in case no one has ever told you: you are an overcomer. You have the choice to be selflessly enhancing toward others or selfishly hostile, but the choice is entirely yours.

Why is it so much easier to compare families than appreciate what we have? We, as women, are so hard on ourselves, and sometimes those around us. Comparing seems to come so naturally that we think that it's healthy.

I strongly encourage you to never compare your family to your neighbor's, colleague's, or friend's family. You never know the truth behind those relationships—the pain they've endured or the trials they are currently facing. I grew up in one of the most beautiful, well-kept, safe places in America, yet devastation found its way into my friends' homes many times. Families hid behind tinted windows of gorgeous SUVs to distract anyone from the reality that the husband had just lost his job. Mothers would strategically and sneakily vie with each other at school board meetings by flaunting their children's achievements, instead of truly supporting each other. No one is perfect, no relationship is perfect, and, therefore, no family will ever be perfect. But hallelujah; through love in Jesus Christ, there is a hope for a better tomorrow for your family relationships! Even when you think to yourself, "Oh heck no; my family is way too far down the drain for recovery," that is exactly when God likes to swoop in and show off. If your eyes, ears, and heart are open to him, I know that he could really amaze you with relationship renewal and revival. Even if you never get the apology you've been waiting for from someone who owes it to you so deeply, if you allow God to work on your heart first to renew that relationship, then you're already ten times better off than you were bitter!

Fight the Good Fight

In the modern world, we are very busy, rushing from one appointment to the next. Whether it's a workout class, a career, kids, a husband, a wife, dating, school, volunteering, church, hobbies, carpool, or traffic, there is always something keeping us from maintaining valuable, nourishing relationships. Here's a secret that I've come to find out, and I'll share with you, free of charge: Many times the enemy disguises himself really well—so well, he comes in the form of a massively filled schedule. When we are spread so thin, living life by our calendars, we miss out on the very thing that God placed us on earth for: fulfilling relationships and community with one another. These relationships around us are God's precious gift to us; we must fight to maintain them, cherish them, and grow them, even if that means slowing down to appreciate them. Valuable, soulful relationships do not just grow on trees. They have to be fed with time, watered with love, and nurtured with care. We must actively forgive, we must actively prioritize, and we must actively pursue.

You must fight for your relationships, because there is a very real enemy who is fighting against you! Let's make this clear as crystal: the enemy will do anything to tear you down, and that starts with your relationships. If he really wants to get to you, all he has to do is mess with the ones you love most: cause chaos with your best friend, plant awful seeds with your boyfriend, or wreak havoc among your family. He usually has a very decisive divide-and-conquer tactic. Anything good has a target on it for his arrow to pierce, so if you have wonderful relationships, get ready to protect those, because those are usually the very things he will go after first.

We are created to fight for our friendships, fight for our marriages, fight for our children. God did not create his people to be timid, easily scared, or puny when it comes to love. God has never given up on us, and he never will, so why would we so easily give up on those around us? I know that I've definitely disappointed or hurt some close to me, and they never walked out or gave up on me. Whether we mean to or not, when our eyes are on ourselves, it become extremely easy to hurt those around us. When we are careless or self-centered, we stop paying attention to our relationships nearest and dearest. This behavior runs an extremely high risk of hurting someone dear to you, whether you mean to or not.

The greatest part about relationships is that it all starts with God. I have noticed a pattern over the last several years: when my relationship with God is intact, the rest of my personal relationships seem to follow. It is nothing magical and nothing coincidental. When you put God at the center of your world, then suddenly the world seems so much clearer, even in uncomfortable, discouraging situations. There is a peace that surpasses all understanding. Life does not suddenly get easier, but we get easier on the relationships around us, because we can clearly feel and taste such an incredible love and peace that was given to us from above. We can't help but pour that back into the earthly relationships around us. It's like when you are filling a water pitcher, and the water level creeps up the sides, looming toward the top, and then when it reaches the very brim of that pitcher, it can't help but overflow into the surrounding area. When our relationship with God is at our best, then we can't help but overflow. Whenever I am at odds with someone, or I feel as though I am feeding bitterness toward someone near me, God has been good to train me to look inward first (this is still a work in process). Before I point the finger at how annoying that person is, I feel God gently tap me on the shoulder to hold the mirror to my own relationship with him. Right as I'm about to go in for the first punch at someone else, I literally have a vision of God grabbing me by the arm like a good friend at a bar while saying, "Hold her back! Hold the woman back!" Metaphorically speaking, God takes me outside of the situation to cool off, talk some sense into me, and tell me to calm down. When I remind myself that, once again, it is not about me but about my relationship with God, my surrounding relationships become so much more clear.

Questions:

1. Is there anyone in your life right now that you need to forgive, whether they asked for your forgiveness or not?
2. When have you had to fight to maintain a close relationship?
3. Who, within your church, have you wrongly judged, and how did that situation turn out?

#TruthToRemember → Don't waste time fighting *within* your relationships; invest your energy in fighting *for* them!

CHAPTER 6

Anger Is So Last Season

"Did you see what she did to me?"

"I cannot believe that he would just abandon me like this!"

"Did you hear what she said about me?"

"They are THE WORST DRIVER EVER! Pick a lane!!" (That one is for all my Angelinos)

In this world, there is so much to be angry about: unnecessary deaths on the streets, people backstabbing at work to get ahead, terrorist attacks on innocent lives, parents that abandon their children. The list could go on forever. I know I get angry. It's hard not to!

One of my favorite pastors, Rick Warren, once summarized it in a service: When we realize it is not all about us, we are able to recognize that because of God's love, it's possible to be joyful *in* all situations, but not necessarily joyful *about* all situations.[2] This was a lesson that I will never forget. God is just as angry about the sin in the world as we are. God does not like cancer, he doesn't like watching us grieve, he hates when people hurt each other, and he isn't excited about poverty or pain. As Christ followers, we don't need to be thankful *for* a situation, but we can still give thanks *in* every situation, because of the hope and love that we have in our heavenly Father. When we are able to get our minds off ourselves, even in anger and pain, miracles start to happen, whether we realize them or not. You are not meant to live a life defeated by anger, resentment, or hurt from the past; you were created to be an overcomer in your pain, because you know that your heavenly Father has already overcome death.

When Your World Is Rocked

Back in 2010, I got a nerve-wracking phone call. My mom said she wanted to meet me to talk about something. Any time someone says that they "want to meet you in person to talk," it's either really incredible news, or it's an awful delivery of information they can't bear to do over the phone. Judging by her tone, I had a gut feeling it was the latter of the two. To make matters worse, she was very vague and refused to reveal the subject over the phone. This was bizarre because my family is very close, and we can hardly contain secrets, even over the phone. (Like I mentioned, we *are* Italian! We know no secrets.) My mind went racing: *Are my parents getting a divorce? Are my brothers OK? Is everything OK with Grandma?* I was looking forward to getting some answers when we met just a few days later at a Starbucks in San Diego. Sitting at the small, circular table, my mom told me that she was diagnosed with a brain tumor, and they found out that it was cancerous. I felt my heart sink to my stomach, and unimaginable scenarios whipped through my mind, then everything went blank. *Did I just hear her correctly?!?* I mustered up the little strength to ask my mom how this happened. Apparently it was a slow-growing tumor, which was a good thing, but it had been growing subtly for about ten years, and was only detected because it was starting to affect her eyesight. Behind the tears that flooded my face, and the uncertainty of our family's future, I was PISSED. *I was so mad at God.* I was hurt. I felt like God had sucker-punched me in the gut. I wanted a refund on this whole Christian thing! Didn't following God give me a free pass on the whole cancer front? HOW could he let this happen? There had to be a mistake. My mother was literally an angel on earth. She loved the Lord with all her heart, worked tremendously hard alongside my father to make sure we three kids were taken care of, hosted youth group at our home when we were younger, and enjoyed mission trips to Mexico and Haiti. Of all people in the world, WHY my incredible, giving, selfless mother?

Shortly after that, her brain surgery was scheduled, but it was the weeks leading up to it that were some of the toughest. One night, we went to our church and a prayer group took us into a separate room to pray for my mother and our family specifically. I was livid with God—yes, I went to church fuming. I don't think I've ever cried so much in my life as I did during their incredible prayers. I wasn't crying because I was touched by their prayers or the power of God. I was crying because I was angry! I was hurt! I felt totally abandoned. Every ounce of me wanted to advise these sweet Christ followers to stop wasting their time on these prayers; my mom had prayed for thirty-plus years, and look where it got us. It was almost like I'd be doing them a favor, like don't waste your breath; "it" doesn't work. I felt like screaming out, "God, where are you NOW? I'm completely sinking, yet aren't you the loving one that is meant to save me? We shouldn't even be here! My mom should be healthy. I should be living life as a carefree twenty-year-old, and none of this should be on our radar!"

The day before her surgery, we tried to maintain some form of normalcy without thinking too much about the possible outcomes of the looming surgery. We went to the movies and even popped into a photo booth at the mall. Despite our smiles, there was heaviness in the air. We held hands tightly as we walked, and I tried to memorize my mom's every facial expression, every movement, and every smile, as we weren't guaranteed those things would happen again.

Her surgery was an eight-hour process. God bless those surgeons, their hands, their knowledge, and their patience to perform something like brain surgery. The surgeon had warned me the night before the surgery that even if she did come out alive, there could be extensive nerve damage, which could result in loss of speech, memory, movement of her limbs, sight, hearing, etc. As I sat there nervously in the waiting room, there was a very real possibility that even if my mom came out alive, she might not remember me. Or she might not be able to talk. My anger and frightful flashes returned: Who would help me get ready on my wedding day? Would future children ever get to meet their incredible grandma, or would she have to watch down from heaven? Who would I call when a cooking recipe went up in flames, and I was trying to salvage it so I could feed myself? The amount of thoughts, stress, doubt, and fears that go through your mind during a surgery like that are unimaginable. I wish I'd been braver, and could tell you that I sat in that waiting room confident, knowing 1,000% that God had this. My mom would come out alive, and we would all be fine. But I was scared. I was *terrified*. And I was mad we were even in the hospital waiting room.

As the surgery came to a close, the surgeon appeared in the waiting room, where my brothers, my dad, and our dear family and friends had gathered to pray and wait with us. The surgeon took my dad out into the hallway, and we all watched impatiently for any facial expressions. Finally, my dad turned around, the biggest smile on his face and arms raised in the air, as if the touchdown of his life just happened. The surgery was a success! This was the beginning of a long, tiring road to recovery, but I got to keep my mom. After multiple face and eye surgeries to correct nerve damage, and three months of radiation five days a week, my mother is a walking miracle.

God allowed my mom to stay on this planet, but I know not everyone has had the same fate as me. I will never understand why God makes the decisions he does. (Trust me, I have a massive laundry list of questions that I cannot wait for God to answer when I get to heaven.) But looking back, through the pain, the fear, the uncertainty, there were miracles: The doctors and surgeons she was able to seek help from. The way it brought our family closer than we thought possible. The opportunity for my mother to speak about her faith to the radiologists that she saw nearly every day for three months. It brings chills to think that God was there through it all. I see him sitting with us when my mom first broke the news, in that Starbucks in San Diego. I see him hugging me during that prayer time at church. I see him holding hands with me and my mom the day before the surgery. God was in the operating room, gently guiding those surgeons' hands. And he was with us in the waiting room. He draws near to the brokenhearted. God took an incredibly scary, awful situation and made something beautiful from it. When the storms of life seem to be relentless, and refuse to stop coming my way, my greatest weapon is giving thanks. Without a grateful heart, you've already lost your battle, and we were not created to be defeated!

If I kept my eyes on myself, I could walk away from that scenario saying, "Gosh, what a terrible time in my life that was," and let that be the end of the story with anger buried in my heart. But since God has shown me that it's not about me, but about his miracles and his love, I am able to reflect on that time as one of the most central to forming my heart to be the way that it is. I am not joyful for the fact that my mom had cancer, but I *am* able to find joy in all that the journey was and the way it allowed God to work in our lives. When I glance to God in heaven, I am reminded of the promises written in the Bible: "'He will wipe every tear from their eyes. There will be no more death, or crying, or pain, for the old order of things has passed away.' God who is seated on the throne said, "I am making everything new!'" (Revelation 21:4–5)

Not an Easy Stroll

Where in the Bible did God ever say that life on earth would be easy? Life with God is hopeful, but easy was never a part of the deal. My Bible promises that God will give rest, shelter, and peace beyond any understanding (Matthew 11:28, Philippians 4:7), but never that life will be painless. God actually promises to give us rest, shelter, and peace because he *knows* life on earth gets really, really difficult, and we need that safe place of shelter when the storms of life blow through. Before I fully understood this concept, I used to think, "Gosh, God is just so cute; offering mini getaways to rest and relax. Dang, God just spoils me so much." Then life started smacking me across the face, and I finally understood why God offers us rejuvenation to begin with. LIFE IS HARD! He offers us rejuvenation so we can get back into the ring and continue to fight the good fight. It's like boxing: two athletes are fighting so hard, but when the whistle blows, it's their "safe time"; they go sit on their tiny chairs for some quick comfort, pep talks, renewal, and to refocus so they can get back into the fight. During our tough life battles, God blows the whistle and allows some sacred time to get refreshed in him. I used to get so angry with God when I had to fight the good fight, but I was really happy with him when he provided restful shelter. I later realized that I only appreciated the shelter so much because he had allowed me to stretch myself further than I had felt comfortable.

From Painful to Powerful

The Lord saves his hardest battles for his strongest soldiers. As inspirational as that statement is, I am constantly feeling like it is an unfair duty to give someone. During many painful times, I have wanted to yell, "I am tired of being strong! I am still mending from the last pain, and I'm tired of trying to understand." But once I take my eyes off my hurt long enough to focus on God's face, I find unrelenting peace. I have learned the power in allowing God to transform any pain into passion, and consented for God to use my pain-filled story to help someone else who might be going through a similar situation. I have met more people with cancer than I ever thought possible, and it is a beautiful gift to be able to comfort someone with my experience when they start to feel alone.

Take a moment to reflect on your own painful times. Maybe someone you love went overseas to war and never came home. There are thousands of other mothers, wives, and daughters who are desperately seeking a friend that can understand. Maybe your husband left you. There are hundreds of other women within your city going through the exact same heartbreak. Or maybe you can relate to being jobless—hopping from interview to interview, pinching pennies, stressing about provision, and anxious about whether a job will ever be offered. There are thousands of people out there who are facing the exact same scenario that you endured, and they could really use some encouragement and help. God will never waste a hurt. Whatever grief you've had to endure, God has the capacity to make all things beautiful. We just have to be open to it. Don't let your pain and hurt conquer you.

I don't want to brush over anyone's pain. These words that I am writing are just text on a page, but I know that your pain is very real and runs to your very core. God sees your pain, and he wants to free you from that hurt, but that can only happen when you take your eyes off yourself long enough to lay that pain at God's feet and admit, "this is not about me. I deliver my pain to you. You handle it, God, because I know you can." This one remarkable step will not suddenly make everything OK, as the physical, emotional, and mental pain may linger for much longer, but it's the first step to freedom from a painful past. There have been days when I burst into tears suddenly months after a breakup because a memory comes flooding back. If you have ever felt this way too, let me tell you, you are not crazy. Just because we lay down our pain, hurt, anger, or sadness once, doesn't mean that it's all deleted. We must be relentless with letting go over and over and over again as the healing process takes it course. Going to physical therapy once for a hurt muscle will not cure the issue. It takes time and repetition to make a full, healthy recovery. With every submission to God with your pain, you get closer to freedom from the past hurt. I encourage you to rise above, put God on the throne of your life, stay encouraged to be the warrior I know you were meant to be, and let the enemy know that he messed with the WRONG person.

Many people search endlessly for justifications, answers, or any reasoning when they are angry or hurt. They assume that finding the answer will fulfill them or take away the pain. An answer or slight understanding might ease the pain, but it won't remove it. I'm sorry to break it to you, but it's not about you, the answers you receive, or the justification you may never get. You need God, who is ready to pour unconditional peace that surpasses all understanding, if you would just allow him to work. My mom was diagnosed with brain cancer. Well, good to know what the issue was, but that knowledge didn't bring any peace. I knew that she had to have brain surgery to remove the cancer, but that answer didn't give me hope or peace, either. I battled with pancreatitis years ago: I endured excruciating pain, and then searched for answers with doctor visit after doctor visit. When I was finally diagnosed, it answered a burning question, but did not give me relief, peace that was unshakable, or joy that I could be healed. I was angry; I got an answer, which I hoped would solve my hurt, but my heart and soul were still searching for something greater to give me joy again. Boyfriends have left me, breaking my heart in the wake, yet even if I heard their reasoning or explanation, it still hurt to the core. Yes, finding out the main issue or problem is crucial to any healing process (whether emotionally, physically, mentally, or spiritually), but simply having facts and doing specific exercises are not going to restore your joy.

Forgiving the Unforgivable

Slightly before Thanksgiving of 2012, a young boy brought his father's gun on a school bus in Miami. The boy thought that the gun wouldn't go off, but he accidentally shot and killed one of his close friends on the bus. A mother lost her precious little girl that day. The victim's mother did the unthinkable in court. Even though she was still visibly shaken by the loss of her young daughter, she suggested to the court a lenient sentence for the killer, with more opportunities on educating this young boy about gun violence, and giving him a second chance at life. Then to follow, this ordinary, grief-stricken mother actually gave the boy who killed her daughter a forgiving embrace! I personally pray for strength and faith of that capacity. This shattered mother, whose world was just crushed by the death of her daughter, was given confirmation they had her daughter's killer in custody, but that validation didn't give this devastated mother any rest. She didn't allow anger, hurt, or pain to consume her life; she knew that her daughter would have wanted her to live for more. She didn't focus on facts or justification. Making this young boy's life hell was not going to bring her daughter back. She knew she needed peace and forgiveness to move on.

Hurt and anger can come in many different forms. We all have deep gashes from hurtful scenarios and scars that people left on us: unexplainable breakups, unemployment, loss of a child, loss of a spouse, addictions, rape, car accidents, human trafficking. Anger usually leads in one of two directions: spitefulness or depression. With spitefulness, anger can cause someone to work viciously to prove their point, driven by pure revenge. Depression is usually the other side of the pendulum: giving into your pain and wounds, never really letting them heal, so you can always be reminded of the scars of where you came from. My prayer is that you would not allow for any scabs to stay on your heart.

But fortunately, with God's love, and when we realize the impact of going from selfish to selfless, there is a third option that anger can spur into. When God takes over, anger can turn into peace. When anger gets laid at the cross, it becomes God's problem and not our own.

When I have dealt with the anguish of pain or anger, my mom would often remind me, "Pray hardest when it is hardest to pray." I would smile and nod at her reminder, but secretly, I would wrestle with the feeling that praying was the last thing that I wanted to do during this time. When I witnessed an injustice, the feisty Italian in me would rise. If a person was just plain ol' mean toward someone else, my retaliation plans would start to form. My first reaction was never to pray; I did not want to calmly sit in peace and quiet with God while the battle raged on. When the fires started to blaze, the last thing I ever wanted to do is pray. Instead, I was eager to take physical action; I would want to argue back or text a mean reply. I wanted to fight fire with fire. Whatever blaze someone brought to me, I wanted my blaze to be bigger or more powerful, with hopes to put theirs out. But one day, after being burned way too many times, I realized how foolish I had been acting. When firefighters arrive on the scene of a catastrophic blaze in front of them, they don't bring more fire with them to put out the flames; they bring water! But I found water itself to be such a dull substance. It's so plain, ordinary, non-threatening (in most scenarios), and boring. Take a glass of ordinary $H2O$ for example; you can casually hold it in your hand and drink it to be refreshed. But the second you pour it over a small fire, this calm substance magically puts out this complex, threatening element known as fire. The heat and flames are suddenly gone, and all it took was a calm glass of water. Prayer is like water in the fires that we face. Prayer gives life, sustains, and allows us to grow; it is simple yet powerful enough to put out even the biggest flames we face. Everyone needs it, and everyone should use it. Sometimes, when facing the greatest battles or fires of life, I have found that I fight better from my knees, in a position of prayer, than I ever could have standing on my own two feet. And I always have to remind myself: water may seem harmless, but water can put out a fire. Fire cannot destroy water, and the flames in your life cannot destroy you if you continuously coat them with prayer.

Spoiler alert: there is a very real enemy who will keep fires flaming as long as possible, so a crucial part of finding that peace is recognizing who the real enemy is. In Ephesians 6:12, Paul says, "For we are not fighting against human beings but against the wicked spiritual forces in the heavenly world, the rulers, authorities, and cosmic powers of this dark age." When I first heard this verse, it came across as some aggressive sci-fi talk, but after I researched further, I learned that the core of this verse is to remind us that other people are not our problem. There is a very clever enemy playing with humans' puppet strings, turning their hearts, thoughts, and actions against each other. When I get in my selfish mode, I forget this verse and start to run my hamster wheel of fighting against the wrong thing; I am fighting a battle while forgetting who my enemy is. My enemy is not the person standing in front of me; he is invisible, deceiving, and cunning, and has been orchestrating this hurt, destruction, and chaos the entire time. When I lift my eyes off myself and gaze toward heaven, the battle becomes so much clearer.

As long as there are people in the world, there will be sin and hurt. If God wanted to wash away all the sin in the world, he would have to wash away the human race, because WE are the ones who are causing all this destruction and pain, large or small. I know I have been very guilty of causing others pain. How many times have I talked behind someone's back to make myself feel better? How many times have I let someone stand in the corner alone, while I happily let them feel uncomfortable with no one to talk to? How many times have I cursed and lost my temper? How many times have I delighted in watching someone else's pain because of the pain they had first caused me? How many times have I pointed the finger without giving it a second thought? I have been impatient, unforgiving, vengeful, and angry! I am very human, and thankfully, God is well aware of this. Because of God's grace, he does not expect me to be perfect, but he does expect me to strive to be a better version of myself through the love he graciously offers. That includes passing this grace on. I pray that we become a generation that doesn't just tolerate, but actively loves and pours out grace. Tolerating has never radically changed the world, but intentional love and grace has.

When I am at the height of my personal "It's all about me" phases, I hold onto anger. I hold onto it by rationalizing, "I deserve to be still be upset. Do you know what they did to me?" or "I am so angry, I am never forgiving them," or my daily anger "Why can't anyone drive in Los Angeles?!" When I step out of my own world, it's humbling to see the possibilities that I might not be aware of. Maybe that woman is driving terribly slowly because she recently had a surgery, and is cautiously driving to the pharmacy to pick up her medicine because no one else around her can help her. Or maybe that person cut me with their words the way they did because of some pain buried in their heart, and I somehow yanked on a string provoking that without even knowing it. One day, I was trying to get ahold of a friend, and she just wasn't returning my phone calls or texting me back. I was getting so annoyed because I needed an answer from her, so when my phone finally rang, I was ready to hastily question why she took so long. My friend told me that she had to take her mom to the hospital because she got sick again. I instantly sunk back into my bed and felt a pit forming in my stomach. Wow, what a wakeup call that was. It is not always about what we see and what we don't! It is not about us.

Hurt Doesn't Need to Keep Hurting

When you hold onto anger and resentment for a long time, it only hurts you! Anyone who has ever abused you, hurt you, or cut you down in the past is likely not thinking about you and what they did—otherwise they would have apologized by now, or attempted to make it right. It feels as though we are letting that cruel person off easy if we forgive them; like if we hang on to hatefulness towards them, it somehow hurts them. It doesn't hurt them. They don't care. It only hurts you. By forgiving someone, you are not saying what they did was right, but you are making a change to live the right way: in freedom. From my experience, the most effective thing you can do with your anger is lay it at God's feet and let him handle it. I know it is so *difficult*, but we can't afford to hang onto anger. God hates injustice, and he will fight for you, but he's not going to fight *with* you to hand over your pain. He is longing to break your rusted chains and set you free from anger towards others! Sometimes you will see the fruits of God's revenge, and other times you won't. But again, I keep reminding myself that it's not what I see or hear, but what God does. He will always have the final say. I can honestly say that I have regretted holding onto pain for too long, but *I have never regretted forgiving someone.*

> Never take revenge, my friends, but instead let God's anger do it. For the scripture says, "I will take

revenge, I will pay back, says the Lord." Instead, as the scripture says: "If your enemies are hungry, feed them; if they are thirsty, give them a drink; for by doing this you will make them burn with shame. Do not let evil defeat you; instead, conquer evil with good. (Romans 11:19–21)

Questions:

1. Is there a time in your life when you have been angry with God?
2. Is there someone in your life you haven't forgiven?
3. Has anyone ever forgiven you even though you really messed up and didn't feel worthy of forgiveness? How did that make you feel?

#TruthToRemember → Forgiving someone doesn't make what happened right, but it makes you free.

CHAPTER 7

The Volunteer Mirror

Everyone volunteers for a reason, but it's best that we take a hard look in our Volunteer Mirror to get a good glimpse of our motives. Some people genuinely want to give back to society in some way, and others solely want those "positive vibes" from helping someone else. Some want to clear their conscience of a wretched past, so they dance around their past to concentrate on someone else, while others simply want to be seen "being charitable," and still others don't have a choice because the law is forcing them to make up for something bad. Although the motives vary, the main question stays the same: are we volunteering for ourselves, or volunteering genuinely for the happiness of someone else? I have had to check myself out in my 'Volunteer Mirror' multiple times to gauge my heart's state. You check a normal mirror for something that might be wrong on your face, but you check your 'Volunteer Mirror' to check if there is something wrong in the motive of your heart. Just like unwanted food gets stuck in your teeth, unwanted motives of selfishness might get stuck in your heart, and if you don't check the reflection every now and again, then you don't realize that it's there!

About six years ago, I was fortunate enough to have my job move me to one of my favorite cities in the world: Los Angeles. Many call it "Lost Angeles," but when I moved here, I felt found. As I have mentioned before, I work in the fashion industry, and I was thrilled (and beyond scared) to be getting my opportunity to do what I loved. After about a year of working relentlessly and getting settled into West Hollywood, I still felt uneasy, like there was an itch that needed to be scratched. My career was going well, and I had a great apartment with a roommate I easily befriended, so I didn't understand my angst.

It's probably crucial to note that during this time, I had also taken a break from God. Looking back, he was definitely still there with me, but I didn't invite him or acknowledge him. It's not like God and I had some sort of dramatic breakup, but I simply didn't have the time to spend with God! What was once cherished time spent with my heavenly Father quickly transformed into a checklist of obligations I had to get to (which I failed most days), and there was no way in heck that I had time to go to church! I justified a schedule that was too busy to maintain a relationship with God for the time being, and adopted the attitude that I would circle back to God after I was done getting settled into my new life. I had bills to pay! I had a pressing work schedule! I had a social life that required attention! Well, I quickly found out God does not care about schedules. God cares about purpose. He allowed an anxious, unsettling feeling to reside in me until the feeling was so irritating that I had no choice but to turn to him and say, "What do you want?!? Why am I feeling like this, and why aren't you making me feel fulfilled?" *In that moment of frustration, God was ready to give me restoration.* In hindsight, I know God was pleased to finally have my attention again. It was that moment of desperation to rid myself of my anxiousness that I felt strong enough to take my first step to change my ordinary life and schedule: find a new church in Los Angeles where I could build community. I found incredible friendships and community in the remarkable church Oasis. After I joined a small group (or Bible study), friendships built and I experienced worship in Sunday service like I never had before (those people can WOR-SHIP! Holy Moses, it's like a glimpse of heaven); it opened my eyes to what God is really doing in my city and revitalized my little seed of faith.

A few months after getting settled into this strong, relevant, loving church community, I STILL felt like God was tapping on my shoulder and gently whispering to my soul that he wasn't finished yet, and he wasn't going to let this anxiousness inside of me dissipate. Through many nights praying, questioning, and seeking, it became apparent to me that God wanted me to volunteer. Volunteer?!? When I was growing up, I had already clocked my time volunteering so it would look good on college applications, but I was far out of college at this stage, so I suppose I could only get by on my childhood volunteering for so long. (See, I've literally perfected the art of Selfishness. I wasn't kidding. Even since I was a kid, I volunteered for my own benefit.) But I started thinking, *Why did I need to volunteer? Who was I trying to impress?* Eventually, I understood that God will never use us to impress; he will use us to influence.

I was a Caucasian, mid-twenties woman from a stable home in Southern California. I'm going to be brutally honest; I was a walking stereotype. I knew the LAST thing this city (or any city) needed was another young Caucasian girl who worked in the fashion industry and seemed to care about nothing but her work, her yoga class schedule, or the next guy she would date. All of those things are not bad, but they don't define a life, nor do they accumulate to a fulfilling one. I just KNEW there had to be more to my story, especially in such a large city. But where would I even begin? In a world and a city that is so beautiful, yet so broken, the possibilities to volunteer seemed endless and even overwhelming at times. When I got to a point of hopelessness that I could never make an impact, I felt God gently put the youth of Los Angeles on my heart. He wanted me to volunteer with kids.

With that assignment from God, I did what any other twenty-something would do when they get an idea that they don't know how to handle: I Googled "Volunteer with Children Opportunities in Los Angeles." Instantly dozens of groups popped up, but one that was reoccurring was Big Brothers Big Sisters. I knew friends that had been a part of this organization, and I had heard great feedback from them. I thought, *This is it, God. I am going to apply, and I am going to be paired with an awesome girl that you have set aside for me.* (Feel free to laugh at the previous sentence, as I was clearly instructing God on what was about to happen. Insert embarrassed monkey emoji covering its eyes here.) As I filled out the online application and paid the twenty-five-dollar background check fee, my heart was flooded with possibilities. I felt like my purpose for being in LA was coming together. I started to imagine fun outings to get ice cream, movie nights, guiding her along the first steps to apply for a job, etc. My imagination had taken flight. I felt so passionate about the life lessons and joy I could share with my potential "little sister" and simply couldn't wait to get going.

A few days later, I received an email from the organization alerting me of my scheduled meeting time in Downtown Los Angeles, so their coordinators could assess my personality, make sure I wasn't going to do any harm to this child, and see which young girl could be the best personality fit. That night I went to my small group at church and was SO excited to share what (I thought) God was doing in my life. I let them know that my meeting with the organization was scheduled to be in three days, and I requested that my small group lift my future 'little sister' up in prayer. I was so eager to meet her and begin this journey I was confident God had for me. My sweet friends promised to pray.

The next morning I woke up to another email from the organization. *That's odd*, I thought to myself. *Maybe they are emailing parking instructions, or advising who I should ask for when I arrive for my meeting.* I happily opened the email, only to find the exact opposite in the text. It was actually an email letting me know *they did not need me at this time.* They had recently reached capacity with female volunteers, with not enough little girls to go around. (But they did add that if I knew of any men that wanted to volunteer, they had plenty of young guys that needed mentors. Let's just pour some more salt into my sad little wound. I had never considered pulling a "Mrs. Doubtfire" until that moment. Judge me.)

I was crushed. THEY DIDN'T NEED ME?!? Before I could have snapped my fingers, I flew into self-centered mode 1,000%. I ran through a (ridiculous) mental checklist in my head of reasonable traits to make a quality mentor: "I am a college graduate. I have life experience. I have made good choices, I am responsible, and have made some mistakes, which I have grown from. I love God, and I am ready to shower this little girl with adoration and fun experiences. THEY DON'T NEED ME? WELL I DON'T NEED THEM!" I couldn't believe that *I just got rejected from volunteering!* My ego burst more quickly than balloons around a cactus. Who gets rejected from trying to help? Well, me apparently. I got rejected from trying to help. I was confused and mad at God. I was only trying to do what he wanted me to. What kind of sick game was he playing with my emotions, time, and faith? I *tried* to follow what I thought was right, and he slammed the door.

After I cooled down, I called my mom. God bless that woman. God bless all mothers. I believe my mother has hidden wings and a halo somewhere, because when I called her to rant (basically moan about my ego being smashed by a charity organization), she spoke the perspective I so desperately needed. She reminded me that, first, it was not about me, who accepted me, and who didn't. I was genuinely trying to follow God's path and the longings he placed in my life, and as long as I did not make it about me, then God would honor my efforts and open the doors where I would be needed most. And second, I should have been praising God that all the female youth were accounted for by loving volunteers who wanted to mentor them. What an answer to prayer that was! I should have been thankful there wasn't a line out the door of young girls needing to be paired up with a mentor. Wow. All it took was an outsider to shift my focus from me to the actual need in the world, and how that need was being met. When truth is spoken in love, it can be so powerful.

I quickly realized that volunteering was not for the faint of heart, and even the process of finding the right place to volunteer was not always an easy task. God gently reminded me that if he closes one door to an opportunity, then it's best to put on your gloves to protect those knuckles, because he may have you go knocking on a thousand more doors before he reveals what is best for you, even when it comes to volunteering. Not every experience volunteering or trying to help was going to be magical, heartwarming, or tear-jerking. Sometimes God allows us tougher experiences to prepare our hearts, and even test our hearts to make sure we don't give up at the slightest setback.

The following week, I went back to my small group, still entirely confused with what God's plan was, but I was somewhat more at ease with the situation. Still feeling the rejection from the volunteer organization, I felt somewhat defeated and didn't know where to try to volunteer next. I was back at square one. My sweet friends eagerly asked how my meeting went, and I had to come clean about how I basically got rejected and how it wouldn't happen at least for the next six months. A woman from my group came up to me when we dismissed and told me about this organization her friend runs with inner city foster youth in the city of Hawthorne on Wednesday nights. She said it was a much smaller, relatively unknown organization, but they were always looking for volunteers. I thought, *Sure, why not. What's there to lose? I've already been denied by one organization—can't go anywhere but up from here!*

The following Wednesday, I drove the forty-five minute route in traffic after work to this youth group in Hawthorne, and when I finally arrived, I fell in love. It was an unexpected love though. The kids weren't very chatty or friendly. They actually weren't welcoming at all. I was a new adult, and they were way too used to adults coming in and out of their lives more frequently than we could imagine. But I was instantly drawn to these faces. It was a love that only God could provide, because I didn't even know them yet! I immediately felt determined to prove to them that I was here to stay. I wanted to know their names, I wanted to know their stories, and I felt extremely certain that this was my new volunteer home.

I started to laugh on my way home that night. I should have known that God had shut the door on one opportunity only because he knew my efforts were needed so much more elsewhere. I had gotten entirely consumed with what I thought, how I felt, how MY ego was hurt, and practically every other selfish thought imaginable.

Commitment Phobia

I volunteered with Impacting Hearts Los Angeles, a foster youth branch of Young Life, for nearly five years. If I'm honest, the most difficult part of that time was consistency and commitment. In today's world, commitment is a tough thing to find, and it's a tough trait to possess. Relationships dissolve, there is always a new workout trend to try or a new diet to become obsessed with, everyone is constantly on the hunt for bigger and better jobs, and many times, we just don't "feel" like being consistent. Consistency is really tough with volunteering because once our Love Tank feels full, we stop.

We stop volunteering because our needs have been met, but have the needs of the community been met yet? Do not leave your post until the job is done. I am the first to admit that my life has been very inward focused, and if I don't feel like being committed to something, I usually drop it and rarely look back. But I KNEW these kids were worth the commitment. They had been dropped so many times before by other adults in their lives, I was determined to not be added to their list. It wasn't a paycheck that got me there; it was God's purpose for my life. Many days, it wasn't even my own will that could muster up the energy to drive through traffic after a long day at the office, but God's will. We are called to be God's hands and feet and eyes and ears to this world, and if we don't regularly volunteer in this world, then it's impossible for that to happen. I had to remind myself every five minutes that I was not volunteering for me, or for my own fulfillment, but for a purpose that was so much bigger than that. When you can understand the purpose of even the simplest task, you are much happier to do that task, because you realize its importance. I had to remind myself the importance of my consistency with these youth. I was showing up for these kids, just as God has shown up for me over and over and over again. God created and LOVES these kids so much, so I felt led to love them the same way: unfailingly. My prayer was that these youth saw life was not all about abandonment, but about love, compassion, and selflessness. The only way for them to realize that was through action, consistency, and patience. I couldn't just tell them I loved and cared about them. I had to show up, even when I didn't feel like it. I had to genuinely think about someone other than myself. I wanted to shock these kids with some selflessness.

As our group cheered these youth through their ups and downs and changing stages of life, we grew in our greater purpose. Individually, we leaders were stretched mentally,

physically, and spiritually further than we ever thought possible. It has become very clear to me that all volunteering
needs to come from a deeper place than "Oh, but it just feels
so good to help someone else." That is true; God gives us the
gift of satisfaction when we selflessly help someone or something beyond ourselves, as encouragement to keep going. But
what do we do when volunteering doesn't feel good, or we
don't feel like it? Many days, volunteering did not leave me
physically or mentally refreshed, but I was reminded that our
personal feelings are fleeting and change by the hour. There
were moments when we cried with our kids, when I felt their
pain, when I would visit a youth in jail, when I spoke with their
social worker and they told me their only option is *another*
foster home, or a women's shelter (if they are over eighteen);
those moments *did not feel good*. When I've been exhausted
and wondered when God was going to show up, volunteering
has not felt good. If I gave my time simply because it felt
warm and fuzzy to me, I would rarely do it. I've concluded that
I am weak, but through God's love for humanity, I am made
strong, and God's just sharing a sliver of his strength. It is not
about me, or how helping someone helps me gain some sort
of satisfaction. *We were not placed on this earth to be served,
but to serve others,* just as Jesus did. Proverbs 11:25 says,
"A generous person will prosper; whoever helps others will be
refreshed." We, as Christ-loving volunteers, will be refreshed
in a way that rejuvenates our souls, refreshes our perspec-
tives, and leaves the footprint of Christ on this world.

In these last four years, I have had to check my motives
for volunteering over a thousand times. I absolutely adored
our youth, and their tenacity genuinely lit up my week, but I
am very human, and many times after work, I did not feel like
fighting traffic to go help out. If it were up to me, I would go
home, make some dinner with my roommates, go to a spin
class, or get errands done. For a short period of time, this

honesty with myself left me feeling convicted. Was I portraying the wrong picture of this "selfless volunteer," when some days I simply wanted to go home to my bed? Was I putting out the storyline that I was some Mother-Teresa type, while deep inside I was tired and wanted to go home? But yet again, I had come to realize that this life is not about me, what people think of me, or what I feel, and it's certainly not about being comfortable! No person in all of history, religious or not, has ever left a legacy from a place of comfort. It's not about security, but about being used for God's strategic plan. Volunteering is not the photos that people see, the money that is raised to support (although that is a crucial part), or the publicity surrounding any philanthropy. It is the heart, the willingness to be used for something greater than our own benefit, and the tenacity to not give up.

Never Done Being Selfless

God has a very clever sense of humor. Not too long ago, I was raising money and finding donors to sponsor inner city foster youth for Christmas gifts. Long story short, juggling work, the craziness of the holidays, volunteering my time with another homeless outreach, attempting to keep a social life, and finding gifts and donations for seventeen kids was not easy. I bit off more than I could chew during the hectic holidays, but friends and family graciously stepped up to the plate until each of my kids finally got sponsors for their Christmas gifts. Collecting the gifts from people one by one was like herding cats, with arranging schedules, getting the presents wrapped and finished in time, etc., but by the grace of God, every youth had a gift with their name on it for Christmas. For many, this was the only gift with their name on it that they would receive for the holiday season. After the holiday party where all the gifts were given out, I drove home and took a deep breath of gratitude and thought,

Thank you, Jesus! That was so insanely stressful leading up, but the smiles on the kids' faces were so worth it. Now it's still ten days until Christmas. I am REALLY looking forward to kicking up my feet and just relaxing. I have given plenty this season, so now I am just ready to concentrate on myself, my family, and friends. I've earned it. At that very moment, God must have laughed on his heavenly throne. I didn't know it yet, but I was not done giving for the season, nor should I ever be so eager to be done giving.

The very next morning, I woke up with a text from my mentee, whom I had looked after for the last five years. Let's call her Sarah. Sarah was twenty-one years old, so she was no longer in the Impacting Hearts program, but I still mentored her and closely kept in touch. That morning, she informed me that her mother was just taken back to jail, so she was left to look after her four younger brothers (ages two, five, ten, and sixteen), who were all living in Inglewood. At twenty-one years old, Sarah suddenly had to care and provide for four young lives, in addition to trying to make ends meet on her own. And Christmas was ten days away! How was she going to pay for an entire Christmas? Was her five-year-old little brother going to wake up to an empty tree? Would the ten-year-old brother feel forgotten about or unloved?

I didn't get into fashion PR or styling for the paycheck. If I wanted to make great money, then I would have definitely chosen another path; I didn't have the money to supply Sarah and her family an entire Christmas! Additionally, I was confused with God because I felt like I had used a ton of resources and asked a ton of friends to donate with that Christmas drive we JUST did to supply those other children with gifts for Christmas. I couldn't ask friends and family AGAIN to donate, literally the day after the other event! What was I going to do? AND I WAS TIRED! I thought I was done giving for the season.

I started praying, and I heard God whisper to my heart, *"Dear one, do you not believe in my great capabilities? Do you not believe that I created the entire universe and everything in it? Do you not believe that I have generously given to you so much before? Do not grow weary in giving, because I am about to shower Sarah and her brothers with so much love through provision, and I am going to use you to do it!"* I felt like moaning, "But God! I am TIRED! Use someone else!" But nope, God was teaching me very, very valuable lessons: 1) This life is not all about me and my own personal strength (shocking). If I am tired, then he will renew my energy. And 2) we are NEVER DONE GIVING. I was foolish to kick my feet up and believe that I had "done my portion as a nice Jesus-loving girl." As long as there is need and hurt in the world, God is going to use you and me to inject our neighborhoods with hope and mercy.

I rallied my inner Beyoncé strength (I only pull out my Beyoncé strength in fierce times), and sent messages to my Monday-night church community group. Instantly, my friends jumped in and donated. Their willingness was amazing. (Whoever said that Los Angeles is full of heartless, selfish people has clearly never attended Vintage Church in Santa Monica.) I was astonished to see the love, prayers, and funds come flooding in. My dear friend, Emily, who worked in the corporate offices at a toy company, got permission to go into their company Toy Closet, where they kept samples of brand new toys. She filled up two entire boxes to donate to Sarah's brothers. Through my friends' generous donations, I was able to afford gift cards so Sarah could shop for additional presents and groceries, and we were even able to sneak in an extra gift card for her birthday (which was also in December). It was ALL God. He was ready to show off and graciously used us to do it. It was the most incredible reminder of his love, provision, and care. We don't need to have all the answers, funds, or time, but whatever you are lacking, God will make up for it. We simply need to remind ourselves, "This is not all about me."

Keep Marching Forward

At the end of the day, God sees every ounce of effort, and I can tell you right now, if you volunteer and don't feel appreciated or feel as if you aren't impacting anyone, YOU ARE! There is no doubt in my mind. You are building your treasure in heaven with every selfless effort, and God is lining up the blessings you didn't even know you wanted. If you see no immediate relief for the cause you are working for, just remember you are planting seeds. When those seeds are planted in good faith, you may never see the fruits of your labor, but God will make sure that it doesn't go to waste. Not every animal will be adopted in a day. Nor will every homeless person be given a second chance by next week. That is where faith kicks in. It's not you or what your eyes see that validates your efforts; it will be God. I am not doing this volunteer work so I can personally see the fruits of my labor. Volunteer work needs to be done simply because it needs to be done! My prayer is that we make doubt so small it fits underneath our feet while we march forward with selfless hearts. Witnessing miracles would be insanely incredible, but I only want it if that's what God has in mind. It is all about his timing, not mine. A teenager may come to know God fifteen years from now because of a conversation we had one Wednesday night. Or a friend might open an animal shelter program three years from now because of the seed you planted in them due to your diligence and commitment to volunteering at the local shelter yourself. Or your neighbors/friends/colleagues/family might start to think that volunteering must not be as scary as it seems; if we can do it, then anyone can do it! It's like dropping a pebble into a still lake. You see the immediate ripples, but then the ripples continue outward until you can't even keep track of how far they've gone. That will be you. You are the pebble. Just allow God to drop you wherever he sees fit, and watch the ripple effect of the incredible impact you make.

There is such widespread desperation in this world, but you don't need to travel to a foreign country and live in a hut to make an impact. Although God calls us each to a different adventure with him (some require a passport, and others don't), God has you right where he wants you. He simply wants you to stop pressing snooze on your alarm for life, to purposefully wake up to the world around you, use your eyeballs, and be aware of the hurt and need in your own community or city. I have been guilty 956 times of filling my life up with so many activities, appointments, and meetings, I zip through my day without realizing the opportunities right around me. We would like to think that we live in a free land, but too many of us are chained to our schedules. You can absolutely serve in your own neighborhood! Suggest carpooling if your neighbor needs a ride to work, sit with the person at school who always seems to be alone, offer to get lunch for someone in your office who is struggling, buy a sandwich for the homeless man on the corner, pay for the groceries for the person in line behind you at the grocery store who is counting their pennies, surprise that stressed single mom with a spa trip solely for her while you volunteer to watch her kids. The possibilities in our country are endless. There are thousands of organizations to get involved with, but it's not about the organization—it's about the thousands of lost souls around you who feel neglected, lost, rejected, and hopeless. I encourage you to put the microphones, megaphones, and signs down. If we spent half the time selflessly serving our communities that we spend yelling at them through a speaker, or condemning them through words on a poster, then our world would be radically changed. My prayer is that we could adjust our eyes off ourselves quickly enough to realize we have the capacity to change someone's whole world with the smallest gesture. Sometimes all it takes is a hug. I have hugged hundreds of people in my day, and I'm still very much alive and well, and I have no doubt that you'll be able to make it through too. Have you ever considered the possibility that God has you living in your exact zip code because he has a purpose for your time there? As a Christ-loving community, we would spread the love of Jesus so much more efficiently if we started genuinely loving people. Actions speak louder than words, but what are your actions saying?

So many times I thought, *I am so overwhelmed and under-qualified, but God has shown me that THAT is when the miracles happen!* And if you haven't gotten the theme by now, it was never about me (or you) anyway.

Questions:

1. What have been your motives for volunteering in the past?

2. What causes has God placed on your heart? (ex. pollution, homelessness, disease research, animals, the ocean, foster youth, people with disabilities) Have you answered that calling for the cause, or ignored it?

3. What are the things in your life stopping you from getting involved in your community?

#TruthToRemember → We were not placed on this earth to be served, but to serve others.

CHAPTER 8

Perfectly Imperfect

I have never been accused of being perfect. There is literally an avocado stain in my Bible serving as evidence of a multitasking *#Fail*—eating breakfast while trying to read in the morning. Paying for parking tickets has drained my bank account; the city of Los Angeles should have a plaque in City Hall with my name on it for all my generous "donations" to the city. I've totally blanked on my best friend's birthday (sorry, Lauren!), I've sought my personal validation in men, I've overspent repeatedly on clothing I've yet to wear (you would think I learned the first time!). My list of imperfections could go on for a very long time. I don't mean to tell you any of this to be self-deprecating, but to actually encourage you! If you are ever feeling as if your imperfections are scrolling across the jumbo screens in the middle of Times Square, then you're not alone. We are capable of loving ourselves because God first loved us, flaws and all (I see you, Beyoncé. Yes, I did wake up like this.) There is a difference between acknowledging our imperfections and being absorbed by them. Recognizing our imperfections: good. But obsessing over our imperfections: bad.

If we were all perfect, then there would be no hurt in the world, jails would be put out of business because there would be no crimes, we would treat each other flawlessly, no one would steal or cheat, we would never be grumpy (or "hangry!"), there would be no sicknesses, children everywhere would run around with full bellies, we wouldn't curse at the car in front of us that cut us off, and we wouldn't lose our patience when our spouse doesn't read our minds! We wouldn't need God, because apparently, we would have all the answers figured out and we would have perfect peace, joy, and unending love on our own. Like I said at the beginning, this not a self-help book; we cannot help ourselves, because this world is very, very flawed, largely due to the humans like you and me and our neighbors that live in it! But thank you, Jesus, this is not where the story ends. This world is blemished, but there is hope! As much as humanity is the problem, when we team up with God, we can be the answer.

Going to church does not mean you're slapping a Band-Aid on your life so society doesn't see the wound. The church is the perfect place for the wounded and hurt (which is precisely why you will see me there every week soaking up God's teachings, which I refer to as my medicine for life). Going to church doesn't mean that you're perfect. It means that you're honest enough to say, "Hey, I don't have all the answers. I can't love 24/7, 365 days a year on my own. This life is not about me. I am here to see what God has to say about this life, because I can't do it alone."

In the Bible, God's biggest game changers were usually considered the most undesirable, according to society's terms. God's most trusted history makers considered themselves far from perfect, and society's response to them only heightened their own opinion of being unusable. But God saw things differently. Since it is not about us and what we think of ourselves, we can give praise that God sees vast capabilities in us, mostly capabilities that we don't even recognize in ourselves. God doesn't see through the tiny lens that we do; he sees infinitely more. For example, God used a modest, loving man like Noah to build an ark to save all of humanity (Genesis 6–7). He used an ordinary man like Abraham to do incredible miracles and change the course of history forever with his descendants (starting in Genesis 12). He used an unassuming baby named Moses, who was rescued at a young age, to later rescue the Israelites, who had been slaves to the Egyptians (starting in Exodus 3). When God calls us and we say, "I can't," God says "You can." When we say, "I'm not experienced," God replies, "You are qualified." When we say, "I am the worst," God replies instantly, saying, "You're forgiven, and I'm not keeping score." Too many times I've said, "But God, no!" And he gently whispers, "But Kristen, go!" God makes no mistakes; no mistake in creating you, and no mistakes in entrusting you to do his work to live a purposeful life. Our lives cannot be measured by our opinions of ourselves, whether good or bad. This life is not about us!

#RealTalk. Here's a typically believed, but fabricated, "fact" about following God: once you start going to church or form a relationship with your heavenly Father, you become perfect. *Bzzz.* WRONG! I am living proof this is far from true. No matter how hard anyone tries, they will never be perfect— ever. One would be a fool to befriend God because they think it will make them perfect and righteous. The world is a deeply flawed place, so as long as we are living and breathing on the earth, we will be flawed too.

There is a story that I love in the book of Acts. Basically, there is a really, really terrible man name Saul. If Saul were alive today, he would be labeled a religious extremist: "But Saul tried to destroy the church; going from house to house, he dragged out the believers, both men and women, and threw them into jail" (Acts 8:3). He approved of the murder of a man named Stephen, "who was richly blessed by God and full of power, performed great miracles and wonders among the people" (Acts 7:8). And in Acts 9:1, his cruelty continues: "Saul kept up his violent threats of murder against the followers of the Lord." He was not a very obvious candidate to eventually commit his life to Christ, but it was not necessarily Saul who struck me in this story.

One day, when Saul was on his horse with his soldiers, he was on his way to the next town to kill more Christians. Suddenly the Lord from heaven above spoke to Saul in such a majestic, terrifying, and thunderous way, his horse was startled enough to jolt Saul from his saddle. When Saul went to stand up, he was blind. The Lord told Saul to go to a specific nearby city and stay there. In the meantime, God spoke to one of my favorite, and one of the most overlooked, characters, Ananias (pronounced Ann-a-nye-us). Ananias was a faith-filled believer in another nearby city. He was a simple man, and likely very flawed and normal. God came to Ananias in a vision and said, "Get ready and go to Straight Street, and at the house of Judas ask for a man from Tarsus named Saul. He is praying, and in a vision he has seen a man named Ananias come in and place his hands on him so that he might see again." God was about to use Ananias for this remarkable and nearly unbelievable miracle of healing and deliverance. But I love how Ananias responds: completely human and completely flawed. He says, "Lord, many people have told me about this man and about all the terrible things he has done to your people in Jerusalem. And he has come to Damascus with the authority from the chief priests to arrest all who worship you" (Acts 9:13–14).

I love how God gives Ananias strict, very clear instructions and Ananias responds basically with, "Are you *crazy*? God, I'm not sure if you are aware, but my friend has alerted me that this man has inflicted tremendous harm and fear upon Christians, and he is finally blind, so hopefully he'll stop his terror. Yet you want me to not only put myself in danger by visiting him, but you want me to help you heal him?!?" Ananias reacted perfectly imperfect, and undoubtedly how I would react. I would have definitely questioned God and said "Ciao for now."

Actually, correct that, I have been in similar situations where God *was* telling me something and I react perfectly imperfect. I have doubted God many, many, many times. I think I actually have looked at God and literally said, "See ya later!" Looking back, God has given me very clear instructions, but I felt so inadequate, and I didn't want to fail or be embarrassed, so I became too stubborn to react. Or I responded with "But God, I am so beyond faulty, how could I ever be used to help anyone?" Or "God you are crazy, I could never do that." Maybe it's just me, but I've spent too many days allowing my own feelings of inadequacy to overtake me, so I deemed myself "unusable," possibly right when God was going to do something awesome.

Thank God that he didn't call on me for this mission, because Ananias listened and did as he was told. I believe his one action to obey God despite his humanness changed the course of the Bible and history. The story continues with "So Ananias went, entered the house where Saul was, and placed his hands on him. 'Brother Saul,' he said, 'the Lord has sent me—Jesus himself, who appeared to you on the road as you were coming here. He sent me so that you might see again and be filled with the Holy Spirit.' At once, something like scales fell from Saul's eyes, and he was able to see again. He stood up and was baptized" (Acts 9:17–18).

I imagine how bad Ananias's hands were shaking as he entered that killer's house. I imagine that he was thinking about his own safety, his own life, and his own faults. But something powerful happened when Ananias took his eyes off himself, listened to the Lord, and placed his hands on a man who had brutally torn apart families. Not only was Saul healed from being blind, but he was immediately BAPTIZED!

Saul was so moved by what had just happened that he finally went from selfish to surrendered.

Soon after that, Saul (this fear-inflicting man) was so transformed in his heart and head, he changed his name. He decided to be known as Paul, and went on to be one of the biggest, most notorious followers of Christ. None of this would have ever happened if Ananias concentrated on his own imperfections, or measured himself to the world's standards of who is useful and who is not. He never would have had the courage to listen to God and obey him. My heart longs to have ears like Ananias to hear when God is calling us. My prayer is that we allow our faith to be bigger than our fears, just as Ananias exemplified, and my hope is that we would take the physical action to honor God's instructions when he brings us our task. Being used by God has nothing to do with perfectionism and everything to do with faith. In Matthew 17:20, Jesus says, "I assure you that if you have faith as big as a mustard seed, you can say to this hill, 'Go from here to there!' And it will go. You can do anything!"

The weight of perfectionism was one of the hardest hurdles to opening up to the world about my relationship with Christ. I knew that through God's love for me, I was made perfect in his eyes through Christ, but I had a fear that I would portray myself as faultless. I didn't want to come off as phony or fake, but as authentic and genuine in my journey with God. I was so scared of alienating people with any sense of perfectionism, as I had witnessed so many other Christians do before. I was criticizing myself so harshly before anyone else even had the chance. I was secretly so ashamed of things in my past that I figured it would probably be best to keep my mouth shut. Without fully realizing it, I had become so anxious about how to live, I began to hide my faith, feeling that was the safer route. I wasn't necessarily introducing anyone to Christ, but I wasn't turning anyone away, either. I was just kind of *there*, standing on the sidelines while everyone was playing in the game. What an uneventful life I started to lead! I had this awesome gift of love, acceptance, peace, and joy, but I was too focused on my imperfections to truly let that light shine. But as I've mentioned before, God loves us too much to leave us wasting time in confusion. After spending many years walking with God, arguing with him, questioning him, loving him and apologizing to him, I realized that my faith had grown so strong and sincere, it just naturally started seeping out. When I FINALLY lifted my eyes off the perfectionism debate, I shifted my eyes off myself, and I found so much peace to my walk with God. I finally surrendered and just said, 'God, you do the talking for me. You speak to people's hearts around me, and if you want me to assist in any way, then let me know.' And suddenly, just with the simple submission of my anxious heart, the internal battle within me was settled.

Filtered to Perfection

The world we live in these days is so interesting when it comes to perfectionism. Not only are there incredible editing tools with professional magazines to trim celebrities' hips, thighs, stomachs, and even faces, but there are so many tools on our home computers and cell phones. There are apps to alter our bodies, whiten teeth, and smooth over skin, and an Illustrator program that can practically make my dog look like a Victoria Secret model. There are bloggers who are "everyday women just like me and you" that make their lives look insanely flawless with the click of a post.

First of all, as someone who works in the fashion industry, I can tell you that these celebs have makeup teams, hair teams, and fashion teams to make sure every inch of them looks perfect (and many of those team members are dear friends of mine, and they do a wonderful job!). It's not that these celebrities are bad people, or their teams are bad people; they are all just doing their job like you and me. But my point is that you need to understand the truth: no one is perfect; not even the beautiful faces you see grace the red carpets or pose in the magazine spreads. These people have help! They have whole teams! Everyone wakes up with bad breath, we ALL have days when we say "we have nothing to wear," we all have "fat" days, and we all have breakouts. If you never have had any of these, then I can guarantee that you will. There are many days when we feel like we MUST live behind a filter, we must nip and tuck any imperfections, and we have to appear flawless. If you take one thing from this entire book, please at least take this: we absolutely cannot compare our "behind the scenes" to someone else's "high-light reel." Too many times, we see someone else on social media with the "perfect family," or "perfect hair," or "perfect skin," and we deem it #Goals. I am all for encouraging others via social media, but you cannot make your goals what someone else's filter has done.

Now that we've established that insecure days are perfectly normal; the real discussion becomes this: what to do when these days of doubt and self-loathing sneak in—because they will. The enemy would love to amplify all your insecurities until you cave. But my dear friend, listen to me closely: Don't you dare do that! Don't you dare. You are so beautifully and wonderfully made (Psalm 139:14). When my imperfections drench my mind with lies, I remind myself of a few simple truths to fight back: 1) The more you love and honor God in a fierce manner, the more you will love and honor yourself, because we were created in his image. 2) These crippling lies about your imperfections are trying to keep you down for a reason. The enemy is using your insecurities to keep you from moving forward into your purpose. The enemy doesn't actually care about the size of your waist, but he knows you do, so he will manipulate lies until you are concentrated on all the wrong things and stop concentrating on the right things, like Jesus and your purpose.

An Audience of One

As I have mentioned before, I grew up dancing, practicing, living, and breathing ballet, jazz, lyrical, hip-hop, etc. I *loved* dancing and I was determined to make it my career. For my first fourteen years, I had trained meticulously in ballet. I loved pointe (where ballerinas dance on their toes), and I wanted nothing more than to be a prima ballerina. In the ballet world, flat chests, flat booties, no curves, and long limbs were idolized. Thanks to how God built me, I certainly didn't have any curves, but I also wasn't the thinnest in the class. After years of striving for the "perfect ballerina body," it just never happened (I liked food too much . . . sue me). I was thin, but not thin *enough*. But as one goal slowly faded away, I found that I also really enjoyed contemporary, lyrical, hip-hop, and jazz dance. When I was seventeen years old, I auditioned for a dance agent in Los Angeles and made the cut. Instantly, I was thrown into massive auditions for big, big musicians and commercials. (Hello, Rihanna "Pon De Replay," anyone?) Suddenly, my flat-chested, curveless body was less than desirable, as I was competing with these beautiful, fierce, talented dancers who had curves for days. Suddenly, the body type I had strived for my whole life was not what anyone wanted in the commercial world. I hardly ever got booked for a single job. I was so worn down, I couldn't do it anymore. I was trying to be someone I wasn't. I needed to just be Kristen: the girl that would never be prima ballerina or a backup dancer on tour. Suddenly, I became like Goldilocks. I sat in a chair, it was too small; I sat in another chair and it was too big. I ate a small bowl of porridge, it was too hot; tried another bowl of porridge, but that was too cold. No matter how hard I tried, I just didn't seem to fit. Every audience has a different idea of what is "perfect"; it just depends on who your judges are. I was letting spectators form my opinion of what perfection looked like. I needed God's vision of how perfectly he made me. As much as that realization stung my ego at first, it set me free.

You were created to be just your size and shape. Who is to decide what is desirable and what is not? Is it a guy at a bar, an editor at a magazine, your colleague at work? Here's a newsflash: You are desirable and perfect to the one who made you. When you live for an audience of one, and concentrate on your heavenly Father, the critics slowly get quieter and quieter. The truth is that there is only one critic to point out your imperfections: Satan. This enemy knows that once you've figured out that you are pure excellence with every ounce of your being, you have potential to shine, and he definitely doesn't want that. This enemy wants to keep you drowning in a sea of inadequacies. He is SO scared of you realizing your true potential that he will do nearly everything to keep you down. So shine, girl, be perfectly imperfect, and give God your glory, because when you step out of bed in the morning, you want the enemy to say, "Crap! She's up!"

Questions:

1. Are there any areas in which you tend to be a perfectionist? If so, what are they?

2. List six things you love about yourself: three physical traits and three emotional, intellectual, or personality traits.

3. Right now, place one verse or reminder of how perfect you are in Jesus' eyes somewhere that you will see every day (ex: the mirror in the bathroom, the refrigerator door, on your computer or the screen saver on your phone).

#TruthToRemember ➔ Perfectionism is so last season. Shine and be the perfectly imperfect woman you were created to be.

CHAPTER 9

Where's the Mute Button?

Our anatomy is no mistake; God gave us two ears, two eyes, and ONE mouth for a reason. We are meant to *listen* and *watch* twice as much as we speak. I challenge you right here and right now: let's become a generation that *watches* for how God is working and *listens* to how he wants to use us, more than interjecting our own thoughts. What an incredible revival that could be. In so many instances, I think, *I just feel like I'm not being heard.* But when I take a step back and look at things from a larger perspective, it occurs to me that I haven't been very good at listening to others, either. A reoccurring behavior, commonly known as "selfishness," wiggles its way into my ear drums and makes me deaf to those around me. If we are going to be the change in this world, that selfless metamorphosis can begin with something as minor as listening to someone else.

After close observation, I have found that we often listen to respond, but we don't necessarily listen to listen. If I am honest, I am sometimes listening for the purpose of conjuring a response, and not really soaking in what someone is telling me. What if when the pastor was speaking, our friend was crying, or our family needed us, we actually LISTENED, soaked up what they were saying, paused to let God take the lead with our words, and *then* spoke truth that is not about us, but points lovingly back to our Creator? Proverbs 11:2 states, "Pride leads to disgrace, but with humility comes wisdom." I have spent too many years being subtly disgraceful; I want wisdom.

I know that God is leading us to be a generation that longs to listen and read about the miracles of Jesus, rather than just spitting out our prayers to him. God sent Jesus to earth to pick up the check for all of our sins so we can enjoy an eternity with our gracious Creator, but as an added bonus, we get to recount Jesus' thirty-three years on earth as an example of how God would like us to live. We should be fixing our eyes on Jesus' life, while listening to the truth, but we have perfected the art of interposing our opinions so hastily and quickly. We are called to be wise, and not foolish, and the quickest way to gain wisdom is to open our ears, eyes, and hearts to those examples.

One of my favorite stories from the Bible is in the book of Matthew, when Jesus' disciples were on a boat and the waves surrounding them were crashing uncontrollably. They cried out for help (much like I do when I am in a disastrous situation), and Jesus showed up. But just like Jesus shows up in my life in unexpected ways, he did the same for his disciples; he came walking toward them on the water!

> When they saw him, they thought he was a ghost. They were terrified and screaming. At once, Jesus said to them, "Don't worry! I am Jesus. Don't be afraid." Peter replied, "Lord, if it really is you, tell me to come to you on the water." "Come on!" Jesus replied. Peter got out of the boat and started walking on the water towards him. But when Peter took his eyes off Jesus for a minute, and saw how strong the waves were, he was afraid and started to sink. "Save me Lord!" Peter shouted. At once, Jesus reached out his hand. He helped Peter up to safety and said, "You surely do not have much faith. Why do you doubt?" (Matthew 14:26–31)

How many times have I been Peter? I clearly witness a miracle happen, but I have the audacity to open my mouth and continue to test Jesus. How many times has Jesus clearly spoken to me to keep my eyes on him, yet I choose to look at the disasters around me and talk myself into doubt, until I start to sink in my own despair?

Many times we underestimate the power of our words before we speak them. When we are so homed in on ourselves, it is tough to have loving words for others, because we are too consumed by loving ourselves. I am only an expert on this topic because I have perfected the art of speaking out of turn, saying something offensive, and offering unsolicited advice. Many people have referred to this as "word vomit": I project my opinion or my "help" without even having the capability to stop it. The only thing that helps me swallow my words is lifting my eyes to Jesus. It gives us an incredible capacity to not speak on behalf of oneself, but speak words of love, truth, and honor to others on behalf of our heavenly Father. You have such an ability to give hope or take it away, to shine the light of an all-loving God or demonstrate that his love is conditional, all through your words. No one is ever profoundly changed by any opinion spoken about them, but they *have* been radically changed by the love spoken over them. Proverbs 12:18 says, "The words of the reckless pierce like swords, but the tongue of the wise brings healing." My goal is to be a *healer*, not a *hurter*.

When Words Burn

Going through my adolescence, I didn't always have a clear idea of who Jesus and God were, and I let the church dictate that for me. I had felt the love of God sporadically throughout my young life, but during my very impressionable teenage stage, I allowed my church peers to dictate the person I was becoming in my walk with God. During my early teens, my curious nature got the best of me. I became acquainted with rebellion, and shortly following, the news that I had experimented with marijuana and frequently drank alcohol hit the church circuit. Seeing that my family was really active in our local church, this didn't go over well. I don't blame anyone for that; I was in the wrong. At that time, I knew I had made mistakes; but what left the imprint on my heart wasn't my actions; it was my church's reactions. I truly had no business experimenting with that stuff, but in a place that preached "God is love," I was so confused to see these godly followers treating me as an outcast. The last thing I felt was love; I was only left with judgmental stares and whispers behind my back. Before I knew it, the prayer chain turned into a gossip chain. I never knew whispers could be so loud. People's willingness to talk about my path to destruction was masked with concern. "Please pray for Kristen Perino; she is headed down the path of destruction. Please, God, be with her." I was searching for a mute button. I literally wanted to silence the church.

Then my dear mother had to take the heat for my mistakes. Some of her peers questioned her mothering skills, and they preferred to seek advice from "parents who were doing it right," with the passive-aggressive indication that she was obviously "parenting me wrong." Being the spicy, protective Italian that I am, this did not go over well with me. Nobody messes with my momma. Sheep will go to space before I ever let someone attack my momma's character. These churchgoers' words left me with an impression that their only concern was to critique and condemn, while disguising it as care. I wanted them to stop talking about me, and stop talking about my mom's parenting skills. Any time someone would offer to pray for me, I interpreted it as "I feel sorry for you," or "there is something wrong with you, so I'll pray that God will have mercy and fix you." I knew I needed God's mercy, but I did not want anyone's pity, whether their motives were sincere or not. I happily declined offers for prayer, with the idea that I didn't NEED their prayer. I didn't even want their prayer. I felt as though they were throwing stones from their glass houses. I absolutely believe that it takes a village to raise a child, but that village should consist of God-loving adults who call members of the younger generation by their identity and not by their sin. That means knowing when to use that mute button and simply love.

If any of you have felt burned by the church, I apologize. My heart hurts for the pain that unnecessary words may have caused you. I'm sorry that some individuals cannot locate their mute buttons. Careless words can cut like a sword, and that is not how God intended it. As a human race, we often don't understand the impact our words can leave on people (good or bad). As Christians in the church, we tend to create these boxes only ourselves can see, and when someone steps out of that invisible box we created, we get upset. It's not about our box; it's about God's box!

It took me a couple years to get over that condemnatory pain of my youth, but it taught me a lesson that I will never forget: loving actions speak so much louder than words. I respect my mother and father tremendously for *simply loving me* during that difficult time as a teenager. It wasn't what they said to me that made the difference, but how they treated me. Of course, I still got punished when it was due (and I still absolutely believe in discipline), but I genuinely did not want to disappoint my mother and father, because they showed me such incredible grace and mercy. Looking back, it was just a fraction of the grace and mercy that God has continuously shown me, which is a greater gift than I could ever express.

As a Christ-loving church, wouldn't it be awesome if no one wanted to mute us? What if we lived in such a way that people were curious to hear us speak? What if we lived in such a humble way, the neighbors *asked for our opinions*, because they were so interested and intrigued by our actions?

A wise friend once told me, "Never call someone out in their sin unless you are committed to their restoration." Wow. What truth! I would never want to publicly air someone's "dirty laundry," and then just leave them there in the cold, but if I'm honest, how many times have I done that? One too many. It's time that we invested in relationships so we *earn the right to be heard*. Sometimes I need to use the mute button on myself. How many times have I offered an uninvited opinion or advice? Going to church (whatever denomination or religion) doesn't entitle us to play police officer. But when we speak out of love, like Jesus did, we *can* call fellow Christians out for living in their sin instead of living up to their identities. When we can become a generation to lift each other up with our words, and confirm each other's identities in Christ, then any sin in the conversation is an afterthought. We can believe the best in one another and rise by lifting others. And sometimes, before you truly help lift someone up, you must get down to where they are at, in order to give them a good grip so they can use your stability to rise again.

I have noticed that whenever I open my mouth to judge someone, rather than listen to what is really going on, 70% of the time, I am pointing out the same sin in someone else that I carry. I have such sharpened eyes and ears for that particular sin because I am in that battle too! Who am I to judge and throw stones? In John 8:7, Jesus approaches a crowd who was condemning a young woman for a sin she had committed, but he says, "whoever is without sin among you, let them throw the first stone at her." I love how clever Jesus is. He bluntly says, "That's fine, if you think you are 1,000% perfect, then go right ahead, throw the stone at your sinful neighbor." He knew that each person had as much immorality as the next. The judgmental crowd became instantly convicted because they got called out!

Can I be honest with you? (We are in Chapter 9; I would hope I could be by now!) I still battle with scenarios like this daily. Isn't it so easy to cast judgment? It almost comes naturally with social media, magazines, the internet, etc. Right when I start to think that it's all about me—what I see, what I hear, and the conclusions I've drawn amongst my internal jury of one—I start to gather my pile of stones to throw at others. Then Jesus comes up to me and says, "Go right ahead, but just know that you have the exact same pain, sin, and hurt in your heart as she does." After getting such genuine clarity from our heavenly Father, I embarrassedly put my stones down and try to tiptoe away.

Please do not get dramatic (like I would) and think that you have to sew your lips together and never speak again with the fear of offending someone. I beg you to keep in mind that there *are* times to pump the volume button, and other times to hit the mute button. My prayer is that you *have clarity to know which button to press in certain circumstances.* When I can take a deep breath in a heated situation, get my eyes off myself, remind myself (yet again) that it's not all about me, but about God, then I can usually decipher whether to speak or to listen.

As you attempt to keep your mouth closed and your eyes and ears wide open, God may very well be giving you the answers that you are looking for, but they are not the answers you want. So many times, God has laid before me what he wants or what I am called to do, but I refused to acknowledge him. I've thought to myself, maybe if I just look away and pretend like I don't speak English, then he will change his mind. (Yes, I am very mature and rational.) Too many times God gives me my answer, but I don't like it, so I seek out my own answers. But when I shed my selfish I-know-what's-best layer,

I can understand what God is doing loud and clear. You may not be hearing God's response clearly, or seeing what you would like to believe, but he is there, showing up and trying to teach you something incredible in this season of your life. He will never leave you without answers, but the answer may be in a much different form than you're looking for. God longs to give you perfect 20/20 vision for what he is doing in your life, but if you are not open to it, he will not perform the spiritual Lasik without your consent. If you feel like you are losing your hearing for God's voice, he not only wants to renew your hearing, but make it loud and clear.

So, as my dad used to say on long road trips, "Let's play the quiet game."

Questions:

1. Reflect on one time specifically when you felt that you should have simply listened, rather than spoken up. How did you feel afterward, and what did you do?

2. How has it felt when someone around you gave "advice" that you didn't ask for, or otherwise sounded judgmental?

3. Who in your life is a great listener, or seems to consistently speak life into you? What traits do they seem to have in their daily life that you would like to adopt?

#TruthToRemember → God gave us two ears and only one mouth for reason.

CHAPTER 10

The Surrendering Struggle

I often envision myself standing before God with a small rock in my hand. It's gripped so tightly my knuckles are nearly white, as it is something I cherish so much; I wouldn't dare let it slip away. I can hear God say, *"Surrender your rock to me."* And I reply, "But God, no, I don't want to! If I give you this, then what else do I have? I will have nothing. This rock is special to me." God says, *"But Kristen, I have something so much greater for you than that rock. Something you can't even imagine. You just have to trust me. But you cannot hold onto your rock in one hand and my gift to you in the other. My gift requires you to hold it with both hands because it is that great. So if you want my gifts, you must surrender what you have."* I have a recurring inability to trust God, and I constantly get trapped in the power struggle because I start to get mind-warped that this entire time on earth is all about me. Because I am naturally disobedient, stubborn, and genuinely think that I know what is best, it is no surprise that I continue to grip hard onto my cherished rock, but I can feel my hand getting tired and sweaty from the pressure of my tightly clasped hand. God patiently waits for me to figure it out, until I *finally* surrender my precious rock to God. Yet while my hands are still open and empty from surrendering my little rock that seemed so precious to me, he hands me a massive, beautiful, magnificent diamond. And he was right; I do need two hands to hold its great beauty. And before you can spell Mississippi, I've already forgotten about my "precious" rock.

As Christ followers, let's not be so afraid to lose what we have. We are reminded that all great things come from God (James 1:17), so they are a gift, which should be shared, treasured, celebrated, and enjoyed. I can tell you that God has honored me with so many more amazing gifts than the ones that I was scared to lose.

A couple years ago, my dad got a job on the East Coast. My parents made the move across country from Southern California to Charlotte, North Carolina. With that move came the selling of my childhood home, which my family had lived in for twenty-two years. This house was nothing extravagant, but it was a fantastic place to grow up, and the walls held most of our family memories (my tiny eight-year-old hand print is still imprinted in the cement out front by the light pole). It was one of my many "rocks" throughout life that I gripped tightly, never wanting to let go. I was so sad to lose this home, and I thought, *God, why are you taking this away? There's no way you'll ever be able to replace this home. And you're moving my parents so far away. What will I do without them?* Well, I was half-right. God couldn't replace that home, nor did he want to replace those memories. Instead, he wanted to bless my parents with an even bigger home for my family to create new memories! And that is exactly what he did! When it came to missing my parents, I found that I talked to them more than I do now that we live in the same state! My mom and I would talk multiple times a day, and I would fly out to visit every couple months. If God hadn't provided that job for my dad, and that gorgeous home for my parents, I never would have gotten the opportunity to get to know the South, and fall in love with it the way that I have. Because my parents moved to the South, that lead to friendships, which led to invitations to missions trips in Haiti, and then later sparked Mom's fire to fight human trafficking within the United States. If I held on to my childhood home, our family never would have experienced the growth it has today.

Whether you feel as though your cherished plane seat is being taken away or you're forced to part ways with a beloved home, remember: whatever your heart desires, God is longing for you to submit to him, simply so that he can bless you even more. There is a much bigger plan. "I alone know the plans I have for you, plans to bring you prosperity and not disaster, plans to bring about the future you hope for" (Jeremiah 29:11). Surrendering can be a struggle, until we completely understand that God is not just tolerating us; he is pursuing us. He has a much bigger plan.

It is important to remember that God does not want to deprive you of the true desires of your heart. He placed those desires there when he created you, so he will give them to you when he knows you are ready. God is a good God, but he will give you things in his timing and way, not your own. In the Old Testament, in the book of Isaiah, when people were back in Jerusalem, they craved reassurance that God was going to honor his promises to them and the nation. God assured them, "When the *right time* comes, I will make this happen quickly. I am the LORD!" (Isaiah 60:22, emphasis added.) Whatever circumstances you are waiting in right now, know that God did not create you, give you desires, and then simply forget about you! He gives you the same reassurance he gave Israel.

Sometimes, the waiting is particularly painful, as for those who desire motherhood. God would never create you with a hunger to become a mother just to deprive you of children. Still, it may not look how you intended it. The road may seem long and even cruel at times. If you can't conceive on your own, it's not that God is punishing to you, but maybe he is gently whispering, *"My darling, I have the most amazing, beautiful, intelligent child for you to adopt, and you will love them more than you ever thought possible. You are going to provide for them a life they never imagined."*

Or maybe you have a growing desire for a specific job, but it's just not happening. God sees you and says, *"My precious one, I know the job you desire, but I have an even better one in a city that you will love even more than your original plan. If you could just surrender your plan to me, then I promise you that you won't be disappointed with what I have in store for you. It may not look like what you imagined. But my plan is so great that you cannot imagine it."* Philippians 1:6 says, "And so I am sure that God, who began this good work in you, will carry it on until it is finished on the Day of Christ Jesus."

Be Seen with the Party Crowd

Over the years, I've heard a rumor circulate that if people decide to follow Jesus, they will have to give up all the things special to them, with nothing in return. The theory goes that they will have to sacrifice all their money, not do anything fun for the rest of time *(#lame)*, accept some crummy job as a "sacrifice," move to an unreasonable city "where the Lord is calling them," never have a sip of alcohol, live life silently miserable, be consistently well-behaved, and so on. What a sad lie! Yes, we are called to surrender ourselves and sacrifice certain things, but *the gain is so much greater than the expense.* We are meant to have more fun and more celebrations than general humanity because we have SO MUCH to celebrate! We have everlasting peace, love, and joy that aren't phony or fake, but will keep us going through the darkest of times. That everlasting peace, love, and joy came in the form of Jesus Christ when he rose from the tomb two thousand years ago. To me, that is the real jackpot; grace has won for eternity. Hello??? Why wouldn't I celebrate? If I won the lottery, I would celebrate. If I got a promotion, I would celebrate. If I pass a test, then I celebrate. (I especially celebrated when

I passed Algebra. *#MiraclesDoHappen*) Life with God doesn't evaporate the problems, pain, or heartache, but we rejoice because we have sincere grace and hope to get through it all. A relationship with God is every celebration, promotion, and joyous moment rolled into one. Forgiveness, purpose, hope, peace beyond all understanding, and love have been drenched over my life; why wouldn't I celebrate?

But *superficial understanding leads to superficial celebration*. For example, when I go to a sports bar to catch some football games with friends, I don't truly understand the intricate details of the game. I am familiar with sports (I did grow up with two older brothers!), but football is nothing I have a deep understanding of. When a team makes an incredible move and the bar erupts into roaring cheers, it's difficult for me to genuinely celebrate. I have a rush of confused excitement; my arms fly up, I high-five strangers, and I clap overhead. I really have no idea what the heck is going on, but I know it must be good for my team. Even though I might be wearing the team's jersey or colors and look like I fit in, my heart and mind are not there. I am having a good time, but I would be having a better time if I valued and understood the ins-and-outs of what just happened. If you don't recognize what you are celebrating, then the loud cheers and high fives are empty. You see everyone else embracing each other in happiness, but no matter how much you long to be a part of that, the lack of understanding leads to shallow appreciation.

For many years, I did not truly understand the goodness and selflessness of God because I was stuck in a selfish pattern of living, which led me to a lot of shallow celebrating. I dressed the part. I observed from the crowd, cheering with everyone when something great happened, but never really understood the full scope of why I was cheering. It was difficult for me to value something when I didn't deeply understand how it worked. But as soon as I surrendered my selfishness, I grasped how much God loves me, and how he already won the game two thousand years ago with a VIP rise from the grave; and that is something that is worth celebrating! And when I started celebrating the freedom in a life lived for God, it was much easier for me to rejoice with the people around me. For example, when someone gets baptized, we may dance with joy and party until the bonfire burns out. If a friend's failing marriage is restored through faith in God, then may we surround them with love and "hallelujahs" at the victory just won.

Once the flood gates with a relationship with God opens your horizons, grab your party hat, put on your favorite celebratory outfit, and *let the world see that Christians are here to celebrate, not condemn.*

Plan on God's Plan

I love to dream and plan. I dream it, and then I "real-life" it. Dreaming and planning are not bad things, but we have to leave room for God's dreams and plans for us. Are our dreams selfishly small, based off of what our own capabilities are? Or are our dreams as big as our God? God's dreams for us will move mountains, change hearts, and leave people fulfilled. This is not about us, but the dreams that were woven into our hearts by God. Those are the dreams that are SO much more powerful and life-changing. Jesus says in John 15:16, "You did not choose me, but I chose you and appointed you to go and bear much fruit, the kind of fruit that endures." God chose you because you have a magnificent destiny to fulfill, and an enduring legacy to cultivate. The Creator of the universe placed hopes, dreams, goals, and ambitions on your life long before you took your first breath. But we must forfeit our selfishness at the feet of the cross and selflessly allow God to perform his great works in us to fully comprehend God's plan.

As we move forward to selflessly plan on God's plan, we also must plan on being attacked by the enemy of heaven, who will do everything in his power to distract you from God's plan, lurking around maliciously while taking great joy in deceiving you. "Be alert, be on the watch! Your enemy, the devil, roams around like a roaring lion, looking for someone to devour" (1 Peter 5:8). When we surrender to God's plan, we are able to boldly pick up weapons bestowed on us from heaven. Just because we surrender to God, doesn't mean that we lay all arms down. No! Quite the contrary actually. In Ephesians 6:16–17, Paul says, "At all times, carry faith as a shield; for with it you will be able to put out all the burning arrows shot by the Evil One. And accept salvation as a helmet, and the word of God as the sword which the Spirit gives you." The moment that we bow at the throne of our heavenly Father, the enemy attaches a target to our back. This scheming enemy plants insane lies in your head and heart, which start to grow when you water them with belief. He looks at you as a chess piece in the game of the world, and once he takes you out of the game, he is one step closer to attacking your King. But let me whisper to you how this game ends: our King has already won, no matter how many "pieces" the enemy collects. Do you want to be a part of the winning team or captured by the losing team? "But thanks be to God who gives us the victory through our Lord Jesus Christ!" (1 Corinthians 15:57)

Even though you can't physically see or touch your heavenly Father (trust me, I would LOVE it if God could text me or send me an email to remind me of his promises, or even just give me a hug on those hard days), that doesn't mean the Creator of the universe can't bless you with your deepest desires or bestow upon you a life worth living. Many have compared God's love to the wind: you can't physically see the wind, but you can see the effects that wind has on things, and you can feel it yourself, therefore you believe in your heart that wind is truly what it is. God IS there, he is performing miracles all around you, making things move in your favor (Romans 8:28), and he is capable of fulfilling all desires. This is best experienced if we would surrender by realizing that life is not about us, our comfort, our understanding, our reasoning, what we see and what we don't. "For our life is a matter of faith, not of sight" (2 Corinthians 5:7).

Change of Focus

It can be difficult to follow Christ because it requires a change in focus from ourselves to a loving God, who is actually longing to take care of us and love us more than we ever could imagine. I don't know about you, but I find it very easy to focus on myself—on my opinions, my job, my dating. But focusing on God is almost like a trust exercise where you fall blindly into someone else's hands in the plank position, just praying you'll be caught by something that can bear the weight of your insecurities. Sometimes we start to think, *Wait, if I take the focus off myself, then who will look out for me? I have to handle everything. I have to be in control. If I put my trust in God to lead my life, then who will take care of me?!?* The answer is in the question itself: if you focus on God, trust him to lovingly lead your life, and stop worrying about yourself, then God WILL take care of you. That is not a maybe, not sometimes, not when he has nothing better to do. He will take care of you ALL the time. As Jesus says, "Look at the birds; they do not sow seeds, gather at a harvest and put it in barns; yet your father in heaven takes care of them! Aren't you worth much more than birds?" (Matthew 6:26) In fact, he has been taking care of you and watching out for you since your first cry, whether you change your focus or not. Yesterday, he loved you. Today, he loves you. Tomorrow, he will love you. Nothing will change (see Hebrews 13:8).

Living life surrendered is still not a walk in the park for me, but that's just it: it's not about me. I am still very human, I make mistakes by the minute, and God is well aware of this. But at least I've finally learned the importance of focusing on God. It's a lot like in dance: One of the earliest lessons you learn in dance class is that you must "spot" while you are turning. This means to focus on something directly in front of you and keep your eyes coming back to it each time your body rotates. This helps you maintain your balance. Each time your head whips around with your body, you quickly identify the exact same spot to focus on, and keep your eyes returning there rotation after rotation. If you don't spot, then you will not be successful at turning, and you will get completely nauseated because you'll be so dizzy. That focus is your success, and no real dancer would ever try to turn without setting their focus first. A similar principle applies to us as Christ followers. How can we expect to live a genuine, fruitful, joyous life without setting our focus first? In dance class, I learned that you cannot focus on yourself (because you cannot see your own eyeballs). You must focus on something outside your body, something in the near distance to keep you balanced. The same applies for life: you cannot balance if your focus is on yourself. You must keep your eyes on God in the near distance to keep from getting dizzy in this journey of life. The spotting and focusing technique is so basic and imperative to a dancer's success, they learn how to focus within their first weeks of training. Sadly, many Christians missed this basic step in their first weeks of life training. It should be one of the first things we take into account when surrendering ourselves. In order to keep balanced, we must shift our focus from ourselves to God; otherwise, our walk with God will be far from successful.

Shifting your focus from yourself to God requires the humility to realize that we do not have it all figured out; we cannot balance on our own, and when we cannot balance, then we cannot move how we are supposed to. God did not create you to live a selfish, ignorant life. He created you to live with your eyes wide open, absorb what is happening in the neighbor-hoods around you (whether that is good or bad), be alert, and to constantly be stirred. We, as humans, do not have all the answers. When we only consult ourselves and what we can observe, and don't think about the bigger picture of what God may have in store, we draw narrow, judgmental conclusions on our own. When we see a woman on the street in a skimpy outfit hustling to get a "client" to make some money, we are too self-consumed with our safety zone to realize that this woman is being sex-trafficked and does not want to be there. When we see a mother in front of the grocery store with her hungry kids, we are too focused on our busy schedules and do not even spend one minute finding out this woman's story or figuring out how we can help. When we get so focused on ourselves, we miss out on the impact that God has marked for our lives. We must learn to spot on something greater out-side ourselves to truly understand what living life is all about.

Here is an idea for your first exercise to lift your eyes upward and outward: try walking down the sidewalk without pulling your cell phone out. I know, it sounds stupid, but go with me. I thought this was a ridiculously silly challenge, until I found that I couldn't complete a walk down the sidewalk by myself without naturally pulling out my phone to check mes-sages, respond to a text, check social media, make calls, etc. One day, I was making one of my multiple walks to Starbucks from my office to get some "work fuel." As I was breezing down the street alone, by habit, I pulled out my cell phone. I instantly became so entranced with whatever I was typing that I did not notice my surroundings. In my deep hypnosis typing away on my cell, I walked straight into a bus stop. My body slammed into the bus stop poster wall like a train unable to slow down, resulting in a shattered ego and a shocked body. Bus Stop: 1, Kristen: 0. I felt like even God was giggling from heaven. I just ran into a bus stop! Who does that? Oh, right, someone completely consumed with themselves and what they are doing, as opposed to simple life happening just inches away. After the shock of the unexpected collision subsided, I realized that there was a homeless man on the bench inside the bus stop area. My unknown homeless observer even laughed at me! I walked into that thing so hard that he probably thought his "home" was under attack. After my face recovered from its fire-engine-red color, I processed what had just happened, beyond my stunned body and hurt ego. I realized that there was a homeless man right in front of me, and I nearly walked right by him without even glancing up to notice another human in need. Because of my self-absorption and my inability to take a moment of peace and have eyes for anything that God wanted me to do, I missed an opportunity to buy this guy a meal, ask him his name, and let him know he matters. On the flip side, I have no doubt that this guy saw me as every other woman in Los Angeles—walking too fast, being too busy, trying to be too important, not paying attention to what's around her, because nothing else mattered except for what she was doing on her phone. I didn't stand out as different, and I certainly didn't stand out as a Christ follower. Sometimes God will allow us to walk into bus stops so we can be stopped in our tracks and learn our lesson!

Humble Beginnings

You can be surrendered to God and so strong through his strength. I had a really tough time realizing this. I had a notion that all Christians had to be smiling consistently, always speak under a certain volume, never shock anyone with enthusiasm, and for the love, never, ever be honest about our trials, failures, or fears. Well, if these notions were true, then WHY did God create me with a speaking volume that rivals a blow horn, the constant enthusiasm of a child at Disneyland, and unhindered honesty that sometimes makes people uncomfortable or gets me into trouble? I had perfected the art of oversharing, but meanwhile, every "good Christian" around me seemed to have perfected the art of not sharing at all; did I miss something? Did God not want me to fit in with other Christians? Did he want me to feel like a daisy in a room full of roses? I began to feel like a zebra in a pony show, so in an attempt to fit in, I started to observe and emulate the Christians around me. I was *trying* to be humble, so I constantly spoke in a whisper (because that's what I thought humble people did). I was trying to not speak up and stand on the outskirts of a conversation, with the intention of trying to come across as unpretentious. I longed to be humble, but I felt this attitude slip quickly into self-deprecation and confusion. Before I knew it, I had silenced the woman that God had created. I silenced my own joy, enthusiasm, honesty, and friendliness. I longed to be genuine and open. I craved some additional clarity, so in my desperate attempt to figure out my issue, I researched synonyms of the word "humble" to get a better understanding. I was intrigued to discover that words like "shy," "meek," and "unsure" popped up. Oh, no! I have never been identified as shy. As an Italian, I am naturally the furthest thing from meek you can find; and I have always somehow been able to muster up confidence within myself. Holy guacamole, have I not been humble this whole time? I am none of these "humble" synonyms. Did God not create me to be humble? Where do I belong?

After much more research, guidance from a trusted few, and lots of prayer, I found that you *can* be completely humble, yet still outgoing, friendly, and assured in who you are. You can be entirely confident in the love Jesus has for you and the person he created you to be. Once you realize that you can be humble AND influential, you are one step closer to becoming the change that this world so desperately needs. I finally understood that I am not supposed to fit a mold that the world created; I am meant to have a personal relationship with God! God created me with my not-so-subtle volume so I could give a voice to the voiceless and bring awareness to causes near and far. My (sometimes inappropriate) personal honesty and oversharing was meant to put others at ease. They'd know I wasn't judgmental of whatever trials they were facing, because the chances were that I'd already shared about my own trials and fears. My cheerleader enthusiasm was meant to encourage others to "go, fight, win" when the battle seemed too hard. Every characteristic God gave me has a purpose, and the same is true for you! I may view some of my characteristics as "imperfect," but God sees them as important to do the work here on earth that needs to be done. He created me to shine, just like he created you to shine! I came to the realization that it wasn't about what *I* thought a Christian should look like; it was about focusing on God and striving to love people as much as he loves people. It was never about me trying to fit the worldly standards of "acting humble," or identifying with the synonyms of "humble" that I had researched, but about acquiring a humble heart that is focused on God and God alone. It is not about proving your personal modest supremacy (which is a bizarre oxymoron, but people still attempt it every day), but allowing God's strength to work through you. Being humble is putting others before yourself, thinking about others' needs and how you can help. If you've ever offered your assistance to a friend, or helped the hostess who had you over for dinner, then you've been humble. If you've ever offered your support to colleagues who are struggling, or classmates who are hurting, then you've been humble. If you've purchased a bagel quietly for the homeless person on the street, then you've been humble.

There is no attention drawn to these loving acts of kindness, as they are performed under the radar. They are not done for the gratitude or applause of those watching, because you put someone else's need over your own. While obtaining a humble attitude, you are not meant to roll over and become helpless, useless, or self-deprecating. Quite the contrary, actually: You are one step closer to becoming more happy, helpful, and hopeful!

Not up for Negotiation

Frequently, when I put my faith in God and start to live "selflessly," I begin to think that everything is going to go my way, according to my plan. It's as if God and I made a deal: I promise to follow him as long as he does what I want. And when he doesn't perform the miracle I wanted, or deliver when I feel that he should have, then I believe that God has left me high and dry, and I begin to start second-guessing this entire relationship. Dear friends, don't follow my selfish, foolish behavior! God is carving out his perfect plan for us. Who am I to think that I know what's best for my future, or for my heart? I didn't create me, so how would I know what is best? The creator of a machine will know what the machine needs to run properly, and how to charge it to keep it going. The machine cannot tell the inventor what it needs! There is no negotiating with God about being selfless; there can be no ulterior motives. Sacrifice all you want with your version of "selflessness," but all God wants is a relationship with you, and for you to let him lead your life. What we may look at as an unpleasant sacrifice, God sees as protection. Isn't that why we are going through this book together right now? We have tried things on our own, and that was not a good plan. You would never allow a child to run with scissors; that is not a smart plan. The chances of the child getting hurt are 50/50, but that is a risk too big to take, and a potential pain too much for a child to endure. That is how God sees his children: many times we are running with our treasured scissors, entirely unaware of the potential disaster, but God calls us to give up the dangerous item. We might see that as a great sacrifice because we don't entirely understand, but he has a scope of understanding larger than we will ever know.

The core reason why a surrendered life is extraordinary is because it is the life that Jesus led, and I would like to mirror that as much as possible. What a remarkable, adventurous, exciting, and mysterious journey that would be. It was a difficult life, but nothing was too difficult for his heavenly Father to take care of. Jesus lived a life of unconditional love and compassion. He did not judge by outward appearance but was concerned with the heart. "For God did not send his Son into the world to be its judge, but to be its savior" (John 3:17). He called the social outcasts his friends, and he had such faith in his heavenly Father that he led a completely selfless life, even until his dying day. Because of his noble faith, there are remarkable events that have been shared through generations, and incredible miracles that occurred during his thirty-three years on earth which have created a ripple effect for thousands of years. THAT is a life I want to live. I would love to live a life that leaves a fierce, unapologetic legacy of love, truth, and honesty. I know God created me to live in complete love and joy that radiates deep in my soul, which is only possible because God was so selfless to sacrifice his only son (John 3:16). It's not some made-up theory that says, "If you *try* to live more sacrificially, then you might have a happier life." Through the Bible, we have proof of a life lived selflessly painted out for us. Philippians 2:8 says, "He was humble and walked the path of obedience." Because Jesus was so selfless and laser-focused on God's will, we also receive the same great honor and challenge to a life that leads to meaning, generosity, and sincere joy. But to have that, we must lay our earthly, selfish desires at his feet and say, *This life is not all about me.* "Don't do anything from selfish ambition or from a cheap desire to boast, but be humble towards one another. . . . And look out for one another's interests, not just for your own" (Philippians 2:3–4).

There is no way that I will ever come close to being in the same arena as Jesus, but that is still the goal. I will realistically fall short of my goal because I am entirely flawed and human, but I am capable of striving for more, and I know that God wants to bless me and challenge me with more. For example, if I wanted to live my life as a champion gymnast, I would closely follow someone who made an impact, like Olympian gold-medalist Gabby Douglas. I may never actually get to her Olympic level, but studying her moves, understanding her daily diet, replicating her training patterns, and mirroring her demeanor will likely make me a much better athlete. Even if I never make it to the "Olympic" level in striving to be more like Christ, I know that any effort, training, or lessons learned along the way will only improve my heart.

I encourage you to shift your focus to the bigger plan that God has for your life and prepare your heart for an exciting exfoliation from the inside out. Let's let go of the "precious rocks" that we are so tightly gripping and lay them at the cross. I pray we continuously shift our focus from inward to outward. May this steady concentration of focusing keep us balanced—and dancing! May we be a generation that plans on God's plan, and not our own. Let's come together to wave the white flag on the filtering frenzy and change our lives in a way that is "filter free." I know that God has called me to live from *#selfie* to selfless, and I have a feeling he's called you to it as well.

Questions:

1. What are the "little rocks" in your life that you are hesitant to hand over to God?

2. What is your idea of a "humble person"? Have your ideas changed at all as you've read this chapter?

3. Have you ever viewed your walk with Jesus as celebratory? What are some ways that you could celebrate Jesus in your everyday life?

#TruthToRemember → Let's change our daily focus from inward to upward.

Final Remarks:
Get Dressed to Bless

Most days, I genuinely enjoy getting dressed in the morning. I rarely ever do my hair or makeup, because my wardrobe has me entirely occupied. As I am coordinating my look for the day, I always think, "Where am I going, what meetings do I have, or what friends will I get to hang out with? Is today a day off where I can dress 'Sporty Spice' in my yoga leggings and Nikes, or do I have an important meeting that requires a blazer ensemble? Did I shave my legs, or are jeans necessary to cover up my laziness?" (#*Truth*) Colossians 3:12 says, "You are the people of God; he loved you and chose you for his own. So then, you must clothe yourselves with compassion, kindness, humility, gentleness, and patience." Notice the word *clothe*. Most of the population gets dressed every morning, whether they enjoy the process or not. Getting dressed before you leave the house is not only the law in most places, but part of an expected routine. It's something that we would never leave the house without completing, nor should we! The Bible cleverly states *clothe* because clothing ourselves with those qualities is something we should be doing every single day before we even step out of the house. Clothing ourselves with compassion should be as fluid as putting on a necklace. Clothing ourselves with humility should be as normal as putting on our shoes. But this wardrobe is only accessible with a selfless state of mind. It is very difficult to get dressed with kindness if I'm still wearing yesterday's

selfishness. We are supposed to "get dressed" in these qualities every single day.

Sometimes, it feels as though it's laundry day, and I am
fresh out of kindness, selflessness, patience, and humility.
I've got nothing to wear. I can maybe scramble for a pair of
mismatched gentleness and compassion socks, but that's
about as good as it's going to get. Other days, it feels like my
wardrobe is full of selflessness to slip on in the morning to
take me through my day, wherever it may lead. Dear one, do
not get discouraged whenever you face those "laundry days."
They happen. These tough days do not mean that you are failing at being selfless; they just remind us that we are human
and we need God's selfless love to recharge us, before we
can go out into the world to recharge others.

These selfless gifts of compassion, kindness, humility,
gentleness, and patience were given to us, so we are to freely
give them to others. They are not ours to keep and stash
away for ourselves. We get dressed in these gifts to bless
others. We are also supposed to selflessly give kindness to
someone who so desperately needs it, just as we are called
to give a sweater or scarf to a person who is cold.

You are nearly to the final period of this book, and after
you close it completely, my prayer is that you get dressed in
selflessness every single day. I pray that people no longer
compliment your scarf around your neck, because they are
too busy admiring the kindness that oozes from your actions. I
pray that people no longer lust after your new shoes, because
they are too busy looking at your lifestyle of selflessness. My
prayer is that people would see you wearing selflessness,
they would ask where you got it, and they would go get some
for themselves.

As you move forward in your own daily routine, take a
solid look at where you can shake things up in your own life.
It's all about baby steps and listening for God's guidance, so

keep your eyes and ears alert for what he might be stirring to get your attention. Maybe you're being called to take the leap to being a little more selfless in your relationships. Or, quite possibly, God is calling you out of your comfort zone to act out selflessness through volunteer work. Or potentially to dive into the selfless waters by reevaluating how you approach your social media. Whether we are at church, work, or Starbucks, life is happening all around us. There are so many ways to get involved and be the change in the cities we live in. I pray that our actions speak louder than our posts, and our selflessness speaks louder than our words.

Notes

Chapter 4: New CEO—God

[1] Pastor Ger Jones. "The Other Six Days: Why Are We Here?" Vintage Church. Santa Monica, CA. April 3, 2016.

Chapter 6: Anger Is So Last Season

[2] Pastor Rick Warren. Saddleback Church. Fall 2014.

M000014225

Woman of Valor

woman
of valor

Lihi Lapid

gefen
publishing house בית הוצאה לאור
JERUSALEM ◆ NEW YORK   Est. 1981

Copyright © Lihi Lapid
Jerusalem 2013/5773

All rights reserved. No part of this publication may be translated, reproduced,
stored in a retrieval system or transmitted, in any form or by any means,
electronic, mechanical, photocopying, recording or otherwise, without express
written permission from the publishers.

Cover Design: Benjie Herskowitz, Etc. Studios
Typesetting: Irit Nachum

ISBN: 9781792678080

1 3 5 7 9 8 6 4 2

Gefen Publishing House Ltd.
6 Hatzvi Street
Jerusalem 94386, Israel
972-2-538-0247
orders@gefenpublishing.com

Gefen Books
11 Edison Place
Springfield, NJ 07081
516-593-1234
orders@gefenpublishing.com

www.gefenpublishing.com

Printed in Israel

Library of Congress Cataloging-in-Publication Data

Lapid, Lihie.
[Eshet Chayil. English]
Woman of valor / Lihi Lapid.
pages cm
Originally published by Kineret : Zemorah-Bitan, in Hebrew as Eshet Chayil.
Includes bibliographical references and index.
ISBN 978-965-229-640-5 (alk. paper)
I. Title.
PJ5055.29.A646513E84 2013
892.4'37—dc23

1

It is not good that the man should be alone...

(Genesis 2:18)

I sat at night, in my empty house, and after so many years of longing for a moment of quiet for myself, I realized that I hated this silence. Suddenly I knew that what I'd thought I wanted wasn't what I really wanted. I understood that I was so preoccupied with sorrow and anger that I wasn't looking at all the good things that I *did* have. I had erased them. In this moment of clarity I suddenly understood a number of things.

I have to stop wasting and sacrificing my life on the altar of small details. I have to separate between what is important and what isn't. To let go. Because you can't control everything anyway. I won't be able to save my daughter, even if I devote all my time to her – my entire life, all my energies, all of myself. Because sometimes you just can't save someone. I have to stop being angry about what was, agonizing over the past and worrying about the future, because whatever will be, will be. I have to remember that the here and now is also important, and I have to enjoy it. Because *now* will never come again.

This moment can be good. And this one good moment plus another one is what happiness is made of. Because happiness is something that suddenly emerges, illuminating the sky for one second, for one moment, and then it passes. It's so easy to miss them, those tiny moments of happiness. For too many years, I had let them pass without even noticing them. Without even stopping to rejoice in them.

And for the first time I thought about what I wanted. Not what I wanted from other people – not what I wanted others to do, to be, to give me – but what I wanted from myself. And I wanted so many things. Too many things. I knew it wouldn't be easy, that I would have to change myself. But considering the fact that I hadn't smiled for so long, that years had passed since I had last laughed, and that I had pretty much ruined my life, I didn't really have anything to lose.

Dear Lihi,

I'm 32 years old and single. Educated, employed, and making an honest living; attractive, healthy, thank God, and happy with my life. God in heaven and my heart know how much I yearn and long, after so many frustrating dates, to meet *the one*. How I long to stand, deliriously happy, with my love, my partner, and vow eternal love; how I long to start a glorious family of my own, to hold my firstborn in my arms and weep with elation. Yet, unfortunately, my private pain has become public knowledge to all those concerned. "Don't you want to get married already?" "How come you haven't gotten married yet?" they hurl at me in accusatory tones. "Why do you reject everyone?" They label me, without having any idea whether I actually do the rejecting, or perhaps I'm the one being rejected. One kind soul even berated me for

the aging of my ova. I cried for two days. I've
had enough! They should just stop.
Sharon

I thought of the first time we met. The sun was rising and the city behind us emitted the first sounds of morning. We rose from the reclining deck chairs on the empty beach, and he asked me what he had to do in order to see me again. I found a piece of paper, wrote my phone number on it, gave it to him, and said that I'd be very pleased if he called. He laughed and told me to remember that I was the one who made the first move.

The few friends I told about him, who had only my best interests at heart, immediately summoned expressions of concern and hastily explained to me that there was no future here, and that at my age – not even twenty – it was foolish to get into a relationship with a man who was divorced and had a child. But I wasn't thinking that far into the future. He was interesting, different, and he made me laugh. It was enough for me to fall in love. Two and a half years after that sunrise, he went away for several days, and I missed him so much that the minute he showed up with his suitcases, I ran to him and asked him if he wanted to marry me.

Hi, Lihi,

Many thanks for that moisturizer you recommended.
Several friends of mine and I bought the product
and our skins are glowing and looking better
than ever. Now all we need is to hear your
recommendations as to the type of men we should
marry, so if there's any preference whatsoever,
do tell.
Rina

He agreed to marry me. My mother told me that getting married so young was a mistake, but I was twenty-two and a half, and felt ready and mature enough to start real life. I loved him and wanted a commitment. I wanted to commit to him and him to me. To do the right thing. For him to be my husband and me to be his wife. I was prepared to move on to the next stage.

I never had any fantasies concerning event planning, and the wedding itself wasn't important to me at all. So we decided on a small ceremony in a restaurant. I hadn't worn a dress since third grade, and my hair had been short since fifth grade; I never wore makeup, and I wasn't about to make an issue now about what to wear. One day, I went out and bought a white dress. As far as I was concerned, this was where the preparations for the big day ended.

Two days before the wedding, his parents brought me, as a gift, a small, delicate gold watch. That same day, my mother appeared with a gift of her own: a massive silver necklace. His parents and mine expected me to wear their gifts at the wedding. Even a girl like me, clueless and lacking any passion whatsoever concerning anything to do with fashion, could see that these two pieces couldn't be worn together in any way.

On the day of my wedding, in the afternoon, we went, my man and I, down the steps of our rented apartment and into our car. It was all so ordinary and so routine, except for one thing: I was dressed up in a long dress made of a rich and wonderful cream-colored material, and for the first time in my life, I looked like a woman.

I got married wearing the large silver necklace that my parents gave me and the small gold watch that his parents gave me. Even though they didn't go together.

I am 25 years old, and perhaps, according to your standards, I'm still young. However, as an Orthodox woman, whose girlfriends were all married at the ages of 19 or 20 and already have children, I'm no longer considered young. The only "merchandise" left at this age is people on the fringes, or as we call them, the riffraff. When I heard that a good friend was pregnant for the third time, I thought that all was lost for me. But I decided that I wouldn't compromise, even if I was still alone.

Suddenly, one month ago, he appeared. He was there, all the time, right under my nose, and I had no idea. It's been a month already and I'm walking around with a smile smeared all over my face, understanding that I haven't missed a thing, and that it was worth waiting.

Just when I thought that it wouldn't happen to me and the pressure from home and from every direction had reached a peak, this angel appeared. The strangest thing about this entire story is that he's not religious, and we're slowly learning to compromise. He'll honor what's important to me and in return, I'll honor him. So, that's it. Now it's my turn. Now it's my turn to love.

Rachel

The princess is dancing at her wedding ball, her long white dress flying with every movement she makes, wrapping her in an aura of purity. She's as beautiful as a princess in a fairy tale, just like she dreamed she would be. She's floating on a cloud of happiness that dulls the pain of the blisters caused by her new shoes, and she's spinning around, celebrating the moment, the pinnacle, the peak, the most important evening of her life, the end of this process, of the questions, the wonder, the hesitancy about this decision that was so difficult to make. The decision to entwine her life, forever and ever, with someone else's life. Through thick and thin. For better or for worse. Of all the people in the world. It took her so long to find him. And him to find her.

She stops for a minute, catches her breath and searches for him among the celebrators, and she sees him somewhere, at the edge of the large ballroom – the prince, swaying drunkenly. *My sweet*, she thinks, *doesn't really know how to drink, which is good*, she says to herself, *and he laughs too much, which is nice, and here are his charming friends surrounding him*, friends who will accompany them forever and ever, and no, she won't ask what happened at the bachelor party because she knows that he loves her. And he knows that she loves him.

The princess is so happy – everyone keeps telling her that she's so beautiful and glowing – she forgets everything that happened before this evening, all the arguments between his parents and hers, that fight they had, he and she, when they were torn between former loyalties to the families from which each of them came and their new commitment to each other, and the indecision between the purple napkins that she wanted and the pink ones that his mother wanted. Another waiter passes by, crossing the room with a tray laden with dirty dishes, and for a second, she lands with a crash from her cloud, petrified. For a moment it seems to her as though she's no more than an actress in some end-of-the-year school play, hiding the fact that she's not who everyone thinks she is, and that she actually still feels like a little girl, that she's afraid, that he's not really a man but just a young prince who has just started his life, and that there's no chance that the wedding gifts they'll receive will cover the expenses for this evening, which have unintentionally swelled to monstrous proportions. She doesn't really understand how it happened. They had promised themselves a small, modest event, and now she's wearing a dress that costs more than all the clothes she has ever bought in her life.

She inhales deeply, observing all the aunts and uncles eating, and all the strangers scrutinizing her. Her parents are approaching, their chests puffed out with pride. They hug her, and the photographer captures them with his flash, the bride and her parents, and she hastily summons a smile. Today she's the star of the evening. Someone pulls her onto the dance floor, and again she's spinning on a cloud somewhere. *Mazal tov*, congratulations. From the other side of the room the prince smiles at her, and she smiles back at him. She loves him so much, and she knows that he loves her deeply, and that they're going to be happy together. They're a wonderful couple.

2

And she became his wife; and he loved her…

(Genesis 24:67)

One day, I received a phone call from the newspaper where I worked as a photographer. They asked me if I wanted to fly to Rwanda the next day. Members of the Hutu tribe had perpetrated a horrendous massacre against members of the Tutsi tribe. Ever since I had started taking pictures, somewhere around the age of sixteen, this had been my dream: to be a real press photographer sent to the battlefield. I didn't hesitate for a minute. I said yes and started packing. The next morning, together with the soldiers, I boarded a military plane that contained an entire hospital in its belly.

It was easy to discern between them, between the Hutu and the Tutsi. The Tutsi were tall and thin, and the Hutu were short and husky. Thousands of lost, orphaned children, naked and famished, wandered shell-shocked among the tall and short tribe members. The old people died from hunger on the side of the road, between rows of bodies wrapped in wool blankets, secured with ropes. I tried to hide behind the camera, struggling to maintain sanity in the presence of all the inconceivable pain and sorrow, death, helplessness, and doom.

At one point, through the fog I had wrapped around myself, I heard the crying of a little boy. I approached him. He was so small, no more than two years old. He sat on a rock and cried. We asked the people in the area whose boy he was. Without looking at us, they said that they didn't know. "How long has he been here?" we asked. "Two days," they answered. "Did you give him anything to drink, to eat?" we asked, and I had to stop myself from screaming at these people, who had lost everything they had, including their compassion. No, they hadn't given him anything, because they didn't know him.

We took him to the camp that was a gathering point for the orphaned children; I told the woman in charge that I wanted to take him with me. I even called home and told my man that I was bringing a child. For several seconds, silence descended on the other side of the line. Then, he told me that he'd stand by my side no matter what I decided. But they wouldn't let me. "Perhaps his mother will return," said the people in charge of the orphans' camp, while they weighed him on cattle scales.

Like everyone who was there, I returned from Rwanda a different person. Things that had excited me before lost their significance. Photography, which up until that day had seemed to me the most significant and most essential thing in the world, and for more than a decade was what actually defined me, suddenly became to me nothing more than work. The enthusiasm that had burned within me dimmed. It was no longer exciting. I had already taken a bite out of the career apple. I had flirted with the snake of success; I had even had a solo show in a museum. It's true that I hadn't touched all the heights that I had meant to reach, but I felt satisfied with what I'd achieved. Now, I wanted something else. Something that would truly fill me, that would be important and real. Maybe my age had started affecting me. I knew what my next assignment was.

I always knew that I was one of those girls who took her time. I started studying for my degree only at the age of 30, and now, I'm facing a wedding, and I'm terrified! I'm still a student and at my "old" age, I still don't have a career, and I have no idea if I'll ever have one, because I really want kids, and it goes without saying that I can't really wait, which means that there's already no chance of going out and finding a career, because childrearing requires time, and I want to give it time, and treat it seriously, but everything looms so big and threatening.

Suddenly, I have to consider someone else's wishes, and if, until now, I worked as a bartender in dark pubs and clubs, now I'll have to find another job, because my man doesn't really like the fact that his girlfriend is working in shady places. It's understandable. And it's not.

Now, I also have to consider my man's tight-knit, united family. And the thoughts: Will I succeed; will I fail; will I be a good wife, a good friend, a good mother? What will happen? What's the method? How does it work? And where, in this entire mess, do our private, personal dreams enter? Where do they disappear? Suddenly, I have a feeling that when you get married, something stops and you enter a routine of commitment and obligation. Children, mortgage, and husband: we have to try to please them all. Isn't that true? Oh, I'm so confused...tell me, is it natural? Are there others like me? Am I alone?

Nava

The prince and princess's love story isn't so thrilling that a fairy tale was written about them. They weren't forced to cross mountains and rivers in order to be together, nor did they have to slay dragons or witches, and an evil queen didn't even interfere with their love. Some stories are more romantic: Romeo and Juliet, Julia Roberts and Richard Gere. Some stories are also less romantic: online matchmaking sites, dates set up by an aunt. Even though their love story isn't unique, and poems haven't been written about it, they certainly aren't just another couple. They are two charming young people, full of potential. Each of them separately and both of them together. Two young people who have done all the right things, and who now face the beginning of life with all the odds in their favor.

Two days after the wedding, they get up and go to work. The prince is slightly older than the princess. That's how it usually is, with regular mortals as well as with royalty. The prince earns slightly more, because he has a bit more seniority at his workplace than she does at hers. They don't make an issue out of it. The prince never makes her feel as though he is more important because he earns more. Neither does she feel as though she is less important because of that. Money isn't an issue for them anyway; they don't need much of it. They have each other, and they are full of expectations for the great future. They know that they will have to work hard, and they don't have a problem with that, because they are two diligent people.

They start devoting themselves to building their shared future. They know that they can do it. They also know that they can always count on each other. For the prince and the princess are, above all, true friends for life. It's obvious that they'll help each other, come hell or high water, and even while cleaning their apartment, the rent for which, incidentally, eats up half of their combined salary.

Time goes by. He's worked hard and he's been promoted. She's also succeeding pretty well. Slowly, things are starting to come together. They even buy a new refrigerator. Just thirty-six monthly payments. Occasionally, the prince brings her flowers on Friday, and she pampers him one day by cooking a dish that he loves, a recipe from his mother. One day she decides to invite some friends for a real dinner. For three days she is under an enormous amount of pressure but in the end it is wonderful and everyone compliments her.

After some time, they start feeling that itch. They feel it's time to move forward to the next stage. They also start to hear the ticking. The ticking of the clock. The princess hears it before the prince, and it bothers her a bit more, but the prince also realizes that the time has come. It's the next logical step. The love is there, the friendship is there, and there's even a little savings plan that will one day be a big savings plan, and now they have to make all this potential into reality. They start talking about a child. After all, there's one goal to this entire business, which is to bring into the world tiny princesses and princes who will later wander the world with noses or eyes just like theirs. Preferably the prince's eyes and the princess's nose. And if not, no big deal. Nowadays, plastic surgery is an option.

3

*Be fruitful, and multiply,
and replenish the earth...*

(Genesis 1:28)

The man I married was a father before he met me. His fatherhood
was one of the most significant things about who he was, and
I loved and admired him for it. As time went on, I was further
exposed to the force of this love, this pure love, the love of
a parent for his child, and I tried to be part of that love, to be
Daddy's good wife. Now, I wanted to feel it as well. To feel this
thing, this love I had heard so much about and seen close up. My
return from Rwanda, which precipitated my disillusionment with
photography, left me with a feeling that something was missing,
and I felt that this was what could fill the emptiness, the gaping
void within me.

And from that moment, nothing else interested me. Only that.
Doing the most important thing: bringing a child into the world
and being a mother. To touch those endless skies, that peak, to
feel that enormous experience. I'd still have time to climb up the
ladder of success later on; I'd still have time to try to scratch the
earth and leave my mark. All of these things could wait. Okay, I
told myself, I'm doing it. That's it. I'm at the age to jump through
the hoop, even if it's a bit scary –terrifying, actually – but I have to

13

take a deep breath and do it. There's no point in waiting anymore. I have to do it and get it over with. Just like a bungee jump. You close your eyes and leap.

Another routine checkup at the gynecologist. I was three months pregnant. It was also my third pregnancy. The first two had ended in failure. Nothing special; they just fell into the statistics that no one ever told me about. I fell apart those first two times, certain that I was infertile, that I'd never hold a child of my own in my arms. And now, once again, that look on the dear doctor's face, his smile faltering. I stopped breathing. When he said, "Listen," I knew that it wasn't going to be good news, and I tried not to cry, cursing myself for having come alone. I'd come by myself because I didn't want to be a burden and felt uncomfortable calling my man each time. I could do everything independently and I didn't need anyone to hold my hand. I was strong. I was self-sufficient.

But I did need someone to hold my hand. Desperately. And like the moron that I was, I hadn't even told him that I had a checkup, and I'd just stopped in at the doctor on my way somewhere else. The good doctor saw that I was on the verge of tears, and he said that everything was okay, just some bleeding that was bothering him, and that he wanted me to lie down. I was so overjoyed that I wanted to hug him. Nevertheless, tears coursed down my face, and I promised to rest. Then he said that I had to rest a lot. So I asked for how long, and he said several weeks.

Dear Lihi,

Many times, when you write about your children, I cry. I'm not a depressive type - quite the opposite. I'm usually happy. The thing is that

I've been trying to get pregnant for the last two years, with no success, and I'm not alone in this. We all know what menstrual pains are, but we don't know how painful our menstruation is when we don't want it to arrive. Only someone in a situation similar to mine can understand. I am writing to you and hoping that you'll print these words for the sake of all those kind souls, the majority of them women, who know you for one year, five years, and sometimes only five minutes and ask: "Don't you want kids? Why? Because of the money?"

People find so many ways to nose their way into our wombs and twist the knife just a little bit more. I want them to know that it doesn't really demonstrate friendliness or interest. Whether we've decided that we don't want children, or that we have no way to sustain a child, or we're having fertility issues, it's simply nobody's business. Stop with this nosiness. Please stop. You're hurting us terribly.

Shoshana

The prince and the princess announce to everyone, with great festivity and excitement, that they're pregnant. She and he are pregnant. Both. And they're not afraid. Yes, they already know about morning sickness; they've heard in detail about all the symptoms. So many aunts and other elderly women have tried to scare them, telling them that the princess should rest a bit, slow down. Sometimes, even young mothers holding wipes in one hand join the congregation of alarmists and tell them that they have no idea what is yet ahead of them: the vomiting, the nauseating sickness, the distorted body, the swollen feet – and don't forget to put your feet up to prevent varicose veins – but all that doesn't scare them. They grasp each other's hands and smile at everyone, well aware that it won't happen to them, because they're together and they'll support each other, and nowadays things are different, and she isn't spoiled, even though she is a princess. Besides, pregnancy isn't a sickness.

The princess, who before her pregnancy had wandered the globe and hung out in remote locations, who studied, worked, moved mountains, and headed projects, isn't alarmed. She isn't so easily alarmed. She's strong. She's read; she's heard; she knows that it's up to her what kind of attitude she'll have. She knows that she's going to approach this with love and joy, entirely willing and prepared, and that's how she'll get through it. She's not going to become one of those fat women who walk like a duck. Not her. She's going to have a lovely pregnancy, like young women have nowadays, and she'll continue everything as usual. She's going to continue dancing, and rejoicing, and will float lightly and proudly with her belly protruding, so that everyone will look at her and burst with envy. Because the princess knows she is embarking on the biggest journey of them all. She is going to complete the perfect picture of her life.

■ ■ ■

I lay in my bed; a week passed, and then another. From a girl zooming around independently on a motor scooter, with a job, a studio, an assistant who came in every day after surfing the waves – and if the waves were good he wouldn't come in at all, and I couldn't get mad at him – I had turned into a breeding tank that had to ponder every movement, to lie down as much as possible, and do as little as possible. I remained horizontal for another week, and another week, staring at the television, becoming addicted to daily installments of the life story of Antonella, an orphaned housekeeper who's in love with the son of the landlord. I became stupid, and saw how all the things once important to me were growing further and further away from me, fading, and I didn't care at all. Because I wanted a child. That was the only thing on my mind, the only thing I cared about. I wanted a child. I wanted it more than anything; I wanted it like someone who couldn't have it wants it. Madly.

So I lay in bed for six months, as women do when they're going through a high-risk pregnancy. I lay in bed and gained fifty pounds and three chins in front of my soap opera. It really was the most wonderful thing that had ever happened to me. And no, it wasn't a sickness. Of course, there were always those who said it was terribly sexy. Right, sexy, no doubt about that. I was a sexy, stupid hippo, who lay in bed and was supposed to glow with joy and feel as though I was doing the most wonderful and important thing in the world.

> I'm in my early thirties, and I know that it's not going to be like it is in the commercials. Yeah, yeah, children are wonderful. However, I was many things before them and I know all those things are going to have to wait their turn on the sidelines. When I wake up in the middle of the night, vomiting, with heartburn, and I have to pee and eat, we both remember the sentence "Pregnancy isn't a sickness" and laugh tiredly. I am completely exhausted and it's only the first trimester of the pregnancy. Anyway, we've gone

```
through massive bonding processes so we can feel
as though all this is right, and wonderful, and
instinctive.
    You said that kids can be born ugly, and I
wanted to thank you for saying it because no one
is willing to admit this fact. I was told that
"when it's yours, you won't see things that way."
I doubt it. Not a lot of people say it as it is.
And although it may not be comforting, it still
helps me feel less lonely. Thank you.
    Shira
```

The prince and the princess go together to childbirth education class, and when they sit there, he hugs her and strokes her belly. They hear all the explanations and decide to do it naturally. They want the birth to be as natural and genuine as possible and the experience to be perfect. The course instructor says that it depends on them only. On their willpower. The strong princess knows that she wants it natural; they both want it, and besides, she knows that the prince will be there with her. He'll help her. He won't wait outside like his father did. He'll be there with her, breathe with her, hold her hand, massage her back. They will arrive at the delivery room prepared and ready for the greatest experience of all. He knows what to do. He even sat for one whole evening and chose what music he'd play for her in the delivery room – all the songs that she loves best.

Occasionally, during the night, the princess wakes up in alarm. She's afraid of the birth. She recalls all sorts of scary stories, and she's concerned. She, who until this pregnancy didn't even know that her body has other uses apart from finding it a flattering item to wear, dieting it, or finding its G-spot, is now encased in a body with a life of its own. A life that has nothing to do with her. Her breasts grow to enormous dimensions, tears erupt from her suddenly without control, and this feeling of nausea – which she was told would pass in a minute – did pass, but then other things replaced it: she has heartburn, and her pretty legs have swollen up, and pimples have covered her entire face, and her hair has thinned, and then there are her nerves, which are completely frayed.

She wakes the prince, and he strokes her – her sweet prince – and soothes her. "You're wonderful," he says. "You were never more beautiful," he whispers, and he'll be there with her during the birth, he'll protect her, and she has nothing to worry about because everything will be just wonderful. And she calms down.

4

*As a woman with child, that draweth near
the time of her delivery, is in pain,
and crieth out in her pangs...*

(Isaiah 26:17)

The big moment finally arrives. The prince and the princess go together to give birth. The princess doesn't understand why it's so complicated, why it's so painful, why it isn't proceeding smoothly and calmly like they were told in the course, why all the breathing isn't helping. Okay, it's true that she *is* trying to push a watermelon out of a relatively small hole in her body, but the instructor said that it wouldn't be hard if she'd just make the effort... Suddenly, everyone surrounding her panics and calls the doctor even though she begs them not to, just like she was told in the course where she was told not to give in. The doctor insists that the baby is stuck and that there's no other choice.

She doesn't understand why this isn't working out like she wanted it to. What's the big deal? So many women have done it before – billions of women – and nowadays it's easier, we know more. Once, women gave birth without all the anesthesia and the medication and the paraphernalia that we have today. She's already blurry from all this pain, and the voices around her are beginning to fade away. All she hears is the monitor beeping and the thumping of a tiny heart, which sounds like horses galloping, a gallop growing slower and slower, and she understands that the little heart of the little creature within her is slowing down and suddenly she recalls that once women died during childbirth. Many women and babies died.

But what does that have to do with what's happening now? She tries not to think about it and reminds herself of what the course instructor said, about her being responsible, and that it has everything to do with what she wants, with her inner strength. The instructor told them about women giving birth in the hot tub, at home, and the baby slipped out of them in fifteen minutes, and while they're giving birth, they're also dancing the samba, and if only she had the guts, she'd give birth to the baby at home, easy as pie, but she's a pathetic coward – that's how she feels about insisting on going to the hospital, about panicking at the last minute, during the last wave of pain. She's forgotten all her promises, and her decisions, and even though the prince tries to remind her that they decided on natural childbirth, without epidural, in the end she's taken to the operating room and has a C-section.

■ ■ ■

I pushed and pushed and there, the midwife said, the head is crowning, just a little more, a bit more; my man held my hand and I pushed a bit more, even though I no longer had the strength, and suddenly he was out. That was it. I did it. And it actually wasn't that awful; as a matter of fact, it was even wonderful. I was so grateful for all the drugs that they shoved at me and I couldn't believe that I'd really done it. I was in seventh heaven. And they put my baby on me.

Even though my purse was jammed with his ultrasound pictures, I was so surprised. Surprised that until several minutes ago, I really did have a child inside that enormous belly. A real child. I mean, almost a real child. He was much smaller, dirtier, shrunken, and bluer than I thought he'd be, but now he was lying on me, this tiny boy, and he was the most amazing thing in the world. And he had everything, knock on wood, and everything was in its rightful place. He was the sweetest baby to ever leave his mother's belly. A magical boy.

I fell in love with him like I never imagined that I could. I never imagined that this love would sweep me away, shake me, capture me, take me from myself, and put me in another place.

I was happy. And proud.

Then they took him to wash him and said that they'd return him in a minute, and they moved me to the recovery room. I lay there alone, my entire body still trembling from the effort, and all I wanted was for them to bring him back to me, so I could look at him for another minute, at that tiny wonder, and I couldn't even talk. I thought about how happy I was. And suddenly I realized that I was also terribly afraid. Actually, I was terrified.

Nevertheless, I told everyone that I was happy.

Because that's what you're supposed to say.

So I smiled at everyone, even though I was frightened. Here's this little creature who emerged from me just today, and in no time I'll be sent home with him, still bleeding and bruised, to take care of him. To tend to him and all his needs. To understand him. "Nurse, can you please explain to me again how to put my nipple in his mouth?" Why hadn't I been told that breast-feeding is so complicated and painful? Why couldn't he hold on to the nipple? Without the diaper he looked so small and fragile, and beyond the problem of this little mouth that just couldn't get a hold of my nipple, I was in a heavy fog.

From the faint voices that reached me, I understood that everyone around me had started organizing things in preparation for the brit. They were sending out invitations and they asked me if I wanted meat or dairy, and I was so tired that I didn't care. Everything is fine by me, I said, and I tried to smile but I was in so much pain and my hospital gown had the entire whatchamacallit open in the back, and I had stitches and the doctor said he made a special effort when he sewed them and that they came out very nice, and even a nurse and a medical student who just happened to be passing by in the corridor were impressed and said that the stitches were really nice, and I immediately tried to close my legs but it burned so badly; will someone please cover me up, dammit; thanks for the *mazal tov*, and no, no need to visit; you shouldn't have come; thanks for the lovely flowers; and after every pee I had to wash, and my mother was asking me what color tablecloths I wanted for the dinner after the circumcision ceremony and I didn't want any circumcision ceremony.

I didn't want anything. I just wanted everyone to get out of my face for one minute, to take away their chocolates and smiles, and questions about how did it go, and how much does he weigh, and who does he look like, Mommy or Daddy. Because I was choking and I was terrified. I loved him so much; I just needed everyone to give me one minute by myself.

And I didn't have one minute.

Dear Lihi,

Congratulations. My friend just gave birth for the third time. Laden with sweets and gifts,

I walked into her room in the maternity ward, full of expectations and excitement. Yet, when I opened the door, I found a terrified woman staring at a screaming baby asking, "What do I do with it?" ("It" being the baby.) I wasn't sure what to do, but I didn't want to raise the tension level in the room so I recalled that this was a stage in which babies were in one of three possible states: sleeping, eating, and diaper changing. Since sleep wasn't relevant, I suggested we check the eating or diaper-changing options.

Imagine this, two adult women, experienced mothers, standing helpless before six pounds, nine ounces of screaming sweetness. A situation that did not bring to mind, in any way, a commercial for baby formulas. The new mother did not look like the flat-bellied and meticulously made-up model who was shedding a tear of happiness as she breast-fed for the first time, and I didn't portray the supportive friend, reaching serenely for the baby.

Mothers are supposed to feel total and immediate love for their children. There is an expectation that the mythic bonding will occur immediately, and every mother will feel a profound love for her baby and will be guided by this special feeling while tending to her newborn. But in all actuality, many women need time to form a relationship with their babies.

Yael

The princess and prince leave the hospital with their little heir, and now they're home. The princess is terribly tired, but she doesn't care; she's happy. She waited for this for so long, to be with him already, to get to know him, and now she has the time just for that. Just for him. Now she's on maternity leave; she doesn't have to work, and all she has to do is take care of the baby. No big deal. She's done things much more complicated, and she can certainly take care of this tiny thing, who needs only to eat, sleep, and have his diaper changed every three or four hours, like a simple cycle, with a daily bath. All he needs is right here in her breasts, so there's no problem.

It's true that sometimes he cries and she doesn't understand why, or what he wants, and sometimes he really screams, and her stitches hurt her so, and she no longer knows if he's hungry or tired, and when was the last time she fed him, and suddenly she has too much milk and it's painful, and her nipples are bruised and bleeding and she doesn't remember from which breast she last nursed him, because she lives in these short cycles, sleeps for thirty minutes and then gets up. She's completely disoriented and can't control these thoughts that are running back and forth through her head, and sometimes she almost cries, but tries not to, because she knows that it's only her raging hormones, because she's so happy; she's so content. This is what she wanted more than anything else in the world, and she's really trying to get used to living without sleep, to recover from the stitches, and her body is exhausted.

Every hour feels like a week. Guests arrive to congratulate her and they want to see the little wonder, and there she is, sitting in front of them and smiling with her lacerated nipples, with a painful abundance of milk, and she doesn't understand why it's so hard for her. Because she was looking forward to this. To the real thing. To this pleasure. And she feels as though it's wrong that she isn't only happy and delighted. She takes a deep breath, and even though she's exhausted, and her body isn't behaving and feeling like she expected it to, she knows that she's happy. That she's touching the real thing.

It's just a little tiring.

And a little difficult.

Before the birth, the princess asked the Queen Mother, her prince's mother, how they managed things in the past. The queen told her that after she gave birth, she lay in bed for six weeks. It was customary. And her mother and the king's mother were with her and they did everything. Food. Diaper changing. Housework. The princess thought to herself that back then, things were different. Today it's impossible. She can't even think of having the queen suddenly move in with them for several weeks. And it goes without saying that the prince would never agree to have her mother move in with them. Both the queen and her mother offer to drop by and help, but the princess just smiles, thanks them prettily, and says, "It's okay, I'm okay, we're okay, we'll manage." She and the prince.

The princess thinks about how very young the queen was when she gave birth, and she just wasn't ready. She, the princess, is so ready; she's more than prepared, and besides, she knows the king. He's from a different generation. There's no doubt that the king didn't help the queen. Her prince isn't like those old-fashioned men. He's the new man – the man in touch with himself, who has waited for this moment, for this baby, to take care of him and be with him, just as much as she waited for it, and he even takes some time off to help her.

She's sure that the king didn't take any time off.

> I wanted to tell you that on Tuesday, I gave
> birth to my child, and that all around me, there
> are these "kind" people who impart advice and
> forget that every person has their own way of
> doing things, and perhaps because of all the
> hormones raging within me, I'm reading and crying
> and sympathizing so. I just wanted you to know.
>
> Rebecca

The prince wakes up in the morning, after three days, kisses the baby, tells the princess that he'll miss them, and goes to work. Now, more than ever, he feels that he's shouldering a heavy responsibility, that he has a real role: to provide. That's his role now. He's the man, and he's in charge of his family, in charge of bringing bread to the table, because from now on, it's serious, it's real, and it's no longer just the two of them. Now there's a child. An heir. There are a lot of expenses, and the layette itself, with the changing table and the crib and the best stroller that money can buy, finished all their savings. He knows that there are going to be many more expenses.

He feels this burden settling on his shoulders, the burden of honestly providing for his family. He wants to be able to give the heir the best there is, to open all the doors when the time comes, and in order to do that, he has to aspire to move up. He knows that in order to achieve that, he'll have to work longer hours, and work harder, and give all he has to give, but he doesn't care. He isn't doing it for himself, but for their future. His family's future. And he must succeed. He already knows that it isn't easy to succeed in this modern world, so he has to put his heart and soul into his work if he wants to lead the race; he has to try to be the best; to impress, to invest, to concentrate, to stand out, because he's building their future.

And after three days, when he goes to work, he feels different. He can actually feel the load on his shoulders; he feels the weight of the assignment.

And that sums up the difference between the old-fashioned man and the modern one: three days.

■ ■ ■

I stayed alone at home with my baby. Before I gave birth, I was told that with the birth of the baby, my maternal instincts would awaken, and they'd guide me, so that I'd know what to do, so that I'd understand him immediately and know what he needed. But he was born and I didn't discover a sixth sense in me. I didn't turn into someone else; I didn't know more than I'd known before. I was the same person. The same girl, just with a little baby whom she loved terribly, and who needed her terribly, who cried and whose mother didn't always know what he wanted. And I was very, very tired.

So I hid it. I hid the fact that I didn't really feel this endless joy, because I was afraid that people would misunderstand me. Suddenly, all those horror stories about women who didn't want to touch their babies came back to me – crazy women who did such terrifying things to their children – and I knew that I wasn't like that. And I kept quiet, because I was afraid that people would think that I was suffering from postpartum depression. But I knew that I wasn't. I loved my child; I loved this tiny creature like I had never loved anything in this world before, with an intensity that I had never known before. He was everything to me; he filled everything; he was as pure and lovely as a dream. I wasn't depressed. I was just exhausted, spent, confused, and frightened like I'd never been in my life.

Today, I know that there's a name for this feeling. A sweet name for that tiny depression that is caused by a combination of hormones and stress and this completely new thing that we're facing, that rocks us in recurring waves between terrible sadness and enormous joy, and in the end spits us on the shore, leaving us empty and a bit bleary. Or, in short, depressed. It's called "baby blues." I didn't know back then that I had the blues. I only knew that I was scared to death that I wouldn't know how to be a mother, that I wouldn't be a good mother, that I'd make mistakes. I was overwhelmed by the thought that I was just a simple girl who doesn't understand a thing and now has to be someone she doesn't know how to be: a mother.

I tried to remind myself that I was on maternity leave. A wonderful maternity leave. But I didn't feel like I was on a vacation in Thailand; I felt as though I was in prison.

> I'm sitting here and reading, with an eight-day-old baby in my arms (yes, today was the brit with the help of God and David, the mohel), and what surprises me, each time anew, is how my most personal and intimate worries and difficulties are basically everyone's business. My little worries are those of every mother, wife, and woman. As special as I am, I'm just like everyone else. There is something comforting and at the same time diminishing in this recognition.
>
> Daphna

The princess is at home all day with the heir. They have many magical moments together, and she doesn't stop inhaling him, breathing into her that pure and perfect scent. She looks at his tiny hands in wonderment and a friend tells her that she has to cut his nails, but she's afraid to because everything about him is so tiny; she'll ask the prince to cut his nails because he's already scratched himself. The hours pass by and even though she napped for something like half an hour when he slept, she's tired again, and it's already afternoon, and she's simply exhausted, and he's crying again, and she's feeding him again, but it doesn't help. She holds him and presses his belly, like she was told to do; she summons up all her energies, and all her patience, and rocks and swings and looks at the clock.

Evening is approaching and she feels like taking a shower, but she can't leave the heir, so she waits for the prince to arrive already. To take him for a minute. And another fifteen minutes pass. He was supposed to be home by now. And finally, the door opens, and he's standing there, the prince; and instead of throwing everything from his hands, snatching the child away from her, covering him with a million kisses, telling her that she's the bravest princess of all Snow Whites, covering her also with a million kisses, listening to everything she went through today, all the wonderful things as well as the number of times that she cleaned up poop, how and where the heir spit up on her, instead of all that, all the prince wants to do is to sit quietly for one minute and eat something. Because he had a tough day at work.

He wants to talk to her about his day, and she wants to listen and support, like she once did, but she waited so eagerly for him to come home, to get excited by this tiny creature who screamed all day and if not that, to at least hold him for a bit so that she'll be able to take a shower, and perhaps eat something, and talk to someone. After the prince eats a little something that he warmed up in the microwave, he relieves her of the heir, and she goes to take a shower, and later, when he holds the heir in his arms, she sits down and eats a little something. Alone.

5

And the woman took the child, and nursed it.

(Exodus 2:9)

It was obvious to the prince and princess that they would breast-feed their baby. They read a pile of books, and they know how important it is for their child, for his connection with his mother, for his soul and health. So they breast-feed.

The prince tries to help as much as he can. He even gets up at night, when the heir cries, but as long as she's breast-feeding, the prince can't do much more than bring the heir to her. To her breast, to the only thing that calms his crying. The prince changes his diaper and thinks about how his father definitely never did this, and he is in seventh heaven. He also burps him. And even though he says all the right things, and does all the things that his father didn't do, he begins to feel a bit unnecessary. He suspects that he isn't really helping her, and can't really relieve her. He can't calm down the baby, because this is something that only she can do. Because she's the only one breast-feeding. Because the heir wants and needs only her breasts, and that's the only thing that calms him and puts him to sleep.

Three weeks ago I gave birth to my third son after
a short and difficult pregnancy. I gave birth in

32

my 27th week to a lovely creature weighing two pounds, seven ounces. He was quickly moved to the premature babies' ward in the hospital and I was released from the hospital after two days, sent home to my older children, to a whirlwind of taking care of my house and husband, numerous trips to the preemie ward, intensive milk expression, and sad nights without the baby. I experienced little moments of joy that grew with every fraction of an ounce that my baby gained. Never in my life did I imagine that half an ounce would make me so happy and jubilant for the entire day, and mostly grateful - grateful that he's okay, that he's breathing, that he's mine.

This experience taught me an important lesson in gratitude. Nothing should be taken for granted or considered obvious. Giving birth to a big, healthy boy at the end of a pregnancy is something that many people do not take for granted. The preemie ward in the hospital is teeming with babies, and the nurses there work so hard, with such devotion and professionalism, standing on their feet for hours, going from child to child and from parent to parent. It's not something that one can take for granted. It deserves much more recognition.

Shirley

And then he choked. Just like that, suddenly, while he was feeding, he drew his head back from my nipple, tried to breathe and couldn't. And in his little face, I saw his big, blue eyes growing wider and wider, and then even wider, and his mouth opening in a desperate attempt to find some oxygen, to breathe, and he wasn't uttering a sound, not a sound, and this silence screamed in my soul, tore me to pieces, and I turned him upside down, and he still didn't breathe, and I stopped breathing too, and pounded on his back, and ran to the faucet, and then I ran in circles inside the apartment, pounding on his back again and again. It seemed to me as though an eternity had passed and amidst this horror and the earsplitting silence, I remembered the upstairs neighbor, a serious young woman with a little girl. Maybe she'd know what to do, because she probably took a first-aid course or something like that, and his blue eyes bulged even more, his mouth wide open, trying to find residues of oxygen, and I was sure that that was it, that with the time gone by he had suffered brain damage, and in another minute I'd lose him, and I ran upstairs, to the neighbor, and on the stairs, probably from all the shaking, something opened up and suddenly he started breathing, and then crying, and I cried with him, and I fell on the floor next to the neighbor's door, crying, unable to calm down; I felt shivers running down my body, and a weakness, and I realized that I was running a fever. I took my temperature and saw that it was 102°, and I took him and went to my parents.

My husband had just traveled overseas in order to interview Julia Roberts, and I couldn't bear the thought of staying alone for another minute with this fragile little creature. I was terrified like I had never been before in my life. I loved him like I'd never loved anyone in my life. I was helpless like I had never been before in my life.

I lay in the bath, at my parents' house, for hours, because only in the hot water could I somehow tolerate the pain of my milk-bursting breasts. I was in so much pain that I couldn't even hold the baby in my arms. I phoned the doctor and hysterically asked him to help me stop this volcano raging within me. He told me to try to continue expressing milk; I told him that I'd been trying for hours, and that it was as painful as cutting into my raw flesh. He told me that there was a way to stop the milk, but it would stop it for good, and I wouldn't be able to resume breast-feeding. Considering the fact that I was burning up with a fever, that I was hurting like I'd never thought I could hurt, and that I was horrified by the thought that I had almost killed my son, the only creature that I had ever been responsible for, I found it odd to discover how difficult it was for me to stop breast-feeding. My mind was filled with all those studies conducted on breast-feeding, which are published every couple of days, about how children who are breast-fed longer are healthier, stronger, and smarter, and suddenly I realized how much power there is in being a breast-feeding mother, and how much I loved it, how I loved the power of being a source of life and having no replacement.

Even though I was in pain, even though I was wearing silicon nipples, and even though my nipples were bruised, I was the one giving him something that no one else could. I was the only one who, until now, could provide for his needs – all his needs. No one else could do anything with my wailing infant but hand him over to me, the beatific mother. Only I had this immense power. Only I contained this divine product abundant with health-giving properties, and everything he needed for his intelligence and his future. And I was going to give it all up. I was going to take it away from him. I cried into the bathwater, and my tears mixed with the milk that leaked from my breasts.

The dear doctor told me to bind cabbage leaves onto my breasts, as tightly as I could, and after several hours, it would dry up all the milk. I told him that I wanted something less stupid than cabbage. We aren't living in the Middle Ages, and I wanted a pill. He said that there is a risk that anti-lactation medications cause cancer.

I went to the refrigerator, put cabbage leaves on my breasts, and tied an elastic bandage around myself. I had never looked as stupid as I did at that moment, with the cabbage peeking out of my décolletage. And then my man called. He had just finished interviewing Julia. "What's she like?" I asked. "Amazing," he replied, and then added that she was much thinner then he thought she'd be. I took a bite out of the cabbage leaves peeking from my plunging neckline, and while I nibbled on them, I told him that he didn't have to hurry back home. Now I felt seriously shitty. Not that I could take on Julia Roberts on a regular day, but this was definitely an unfair battle.

I desperately wanted to be a good mother, a mother who gave everything she had. Yes, I had also read that there was no such thing as a perfect mother, and a woman had to make do with being a good-enough mother, but I didn't want to be a good-enough mother. Just like I didn't want to be a good-enough photographer. I didn't want to be *good enough* at anything. I wanted to be a great mother, a charming, wonderful mother, and not just an *all-right* mother. That wasn't the reason I had conceived a child. That wasn't why I had left the professional path. That wasn't why I had lain in bed for six months. That wasn't why I had gained all these extra pounds. Not to be average. I had a baby because I wanted to be wonderful. To fly high on the wings of the purest and truest love of them all, the love of a mother for her child. I did it in order to realize my femininity, to be a wonderful mother from the fairy tales.

And the cabbage stopped my milk supply.

Completely.

> I usually don't write in, but this time I must.
> When I retired from a glamorous career in
> advertising in favor of raising my children, and
> a different job, which I do from home, I did it
> willingly, motivated by my internal need as a
> mother. We understand that you didn't breast-
> feed your children and occasionally you incite
> against breast-feeding and denigrate it, but
> isn't there a limit? Don't you think you've said
> enough?
>
> Ella

"How long did you breast-feed?" How many times did I hear that question? During every visit to the pediatrician, at every child development checkup, and mostly during discussions with women. "It's a shame that you didn't breast-feed for a more extended period," they told me so many times, so many women. "It's so magical, and important, and wonderful. Nothing is healthier than breast-feeding. You could have. After all, you had milk; every woman has milk. It's the most natural thing in the world." But it wasn't natural for me. It wasn't at all like in the movies, with the pleasant background music, the entire house white and gleaming, and with the smile of the happy and tranquil mother that I was supposed to be. Instead my house looked like a garbage dump, and I looked like a piece of junk that someone had forgotten there, and that's how I felt, and it was so painful, and I never knew if he was full or not, and "I couldn't," I answered.

And I didn't want to, but I didn't say that, because you don't say that you didn't want to, but that you couldn't, and hope that someone, preferably a woman, will say that it's okay that you couldn't. But no one said that it was okay. All those women, who breast-fed for a year or two years, always told me that it was a matter of willpower, and that it's a shame, because I have no idea what I missed, and there were those who went as far as insisting on telling me what I had snatched away from him and accompanied those admonishing words with that condescending expression that only those who have seen the light can muster. So I'd tell them that he choked. "It happens," said the enlightened ones. "It's a shame that you didn't see a lactation consultant." A shame. "Yes, it really is a shame," I'd answer and lower my eyes, going back to that first time in my life when I held a human creature who wasn't breathing – the first and sole creature in the world for whom I was responsible. And I felt terrible guilt. I felt like such a failure.

And he wasn't even two months old. And until then I had been so successful.

> I'm a student and it annoys me that so many people who have never set foot on the campus, and certainly not in the Faculty of Exact Sciences, think it is their right to tell me all the time that I'm at such a wonderful period of my life. Next time you write about something that you have no idea about, try to survive one semester, or one week, in our shoes, and deal with an endless stream of assignments/tests/exams, and when you have some free time you study a bit more and when you have another spare second you have to prepare an essay and in between, you're trying to catch up on your sleep. The most wonderful period of my life?! I hope not.
>
> Danya

6

And [she] took the child, and laid it in her bosom,
and became nurse unto it.

(Ruth 4:16)

After about two months, when the princess's body recoups, and she grows used to those odd sleeping hours, and getting up at night, and breast-feeding flows along peacefully, the princess starts enjoying motherhood. Now they're two, she and the tiny heir. Connected. She's his mother. No one else in the world knows him like she does; no one else knows what he needs like she does; no one else calms him down like she does. Taking care of him fills her with joy, and their magical moments increase by the minute, filling her with a feeling of genuine worth, of fulfillment. This little creature, with a pinch from her and a pinch from the prince, and the gaze that he fixes upon her, melts her. She wanders around with the stroller, after it took her an hour and a half to fold it, put it in the car, change his clothes because he spat up for the millionth time, and change his diaper.

And now, finally, she's at a café with a friend, and everyone passing by sticks their head into the stroller, to catch a glimpse of the miracle, and says what a lovely baby, so sweet, and her face glows, and her heart blossoms with happiness, and then he starts crying, and she pulls out her breast in the middle of the street as if it's the most natural and majestic thing in the world, and her single girlfriend thinks that it's the most wonderful thing, and marvels at how amazing she is, and how does she know that that's what he needs, and how does she do it, and the princess is in seventh heaven. She knows that she's touching the truth of life. She's a mother.

And just then, just when everything begins to flow peacefully, when she starts enjoying herself, and singing to him, and teaching him things, and he starts showing interest and smiling, and she buys him black-and-white pictures, and toys that will develop her Baby Mozart, the prince and the princess have to decide what to do next.

The princess's maternity leave is almost over. The heir will be three months old in no time at all. And the princess, even though she's exhausted, and she's hauling around an extra twenty pounds, knows that there's nothing more important than what she's doing: being a mother. It's a lot more important than any job or any vacation abroad, or anything else she ever did. *Everything else can wait*, she says to herself; she'll have enough time to live the rat race when he grows up a bit. She can't even think about leaving him now. Nothing is more important than her bond with him, this bond that will serve as the foundation for his self-confidence, that will serve as the foundation for his entire emotional world. So they sit down to talk about it. To decide.

She, in her rags, cradling her heir against her bosom, and across from her, the prince, who just came home from work and kicked off his shoes one minute ago, and they look at their baby, and he looks so tiny and helpless, and each of them thinks about all those psychological studies that state how important this period is in defining the rest of the heir's life. Especially his emotional life. Every mistake that they make now, they fear, may scratch his gentle soul and leave it bruised and bleeding forever. And they'll be to blame. Because it all begins at home.

> I know that my boys are still small, and everyone says that there's still so much time, but I just can't understand how I'm expected to raise them, and spoil and love them, and then, at the age of 18, they'll be whisked away to the army. I know that this is because we, as Jews, have no other country, but I'm a mother trying to protect my children and prevent traumas, and it's hard for me to deal with this. I feel that I have to do something. I just don't know what.
>
> Jordana

The prince and princess know that if the princess returns to work, they are left with two options: a nanny or a day care center. They look at the tiny heir and can't imagine him amongst other children, not receiving all the attention and the warmth and love he needs; they can't think of him crying without being held immediately in a pair of loving arms. They agree that he is definitely too small for day care. They are left with the nanny option. They calculate the cost of a nanny, and realize that whether it would be part-time or full-time, the nanny would earn almost as much as the princess while working similar hours. Now, they ask themselves, is it worth it for the little bit of money that would be left after paying the nanny that their heir – who until three months ago wasn't even here and is now the most important thing in their world, his welfare being paramount – should be forced to pass through a stranger's hands, and who knows what they'd inflict on him, what kind of scars and damages, and all this for a handful of pennies?

The princess, who has anyway taken a break from the rat race and is immersed in the pleasure of being a mother, can't think of parting with the heir for an entire day. Besides, she is still breast-feeding. If she leaves him for an entire day, she'll have to stop breast-feeding him. It seems like a terrible injustice to inflict upon him. True, she could express milk. That's what the prince and the princess say, and then they look at him again, at their tiny, fragile heir, and they know. They know that the best and the right thing to do now is to leave him with his mother a bit more. Nothing is more important than being with him, than giving him her love, than being close to him and him being close to her. He needs her so much right now, and she wants to be there for him. To give him the security, strength, warmth, and love that he so needs now, this perfect, wonderful creature. And she wants to stay with him and help him be wonderful and perfect. And he needs her for that, because she is the only one investing and loving and giving him everything he needs, in just the amount that he needs.

She looks at him and he is so small and so new and so hers that she can't think of leaving him now, of being away from him for so many hours, not knowing what might be happening to him at any given moment. That's not why she conceived him. Not so she could cast him away into a stranger's hands, and certainly not for the few pennies left over at the end of the month.

Hi. A friend gave me an idea a long time ago, while I was deliberating about the same topic: calculate the domestic income of both the husband and the wife. When you measure the cost of child care against your combined income instead of just against the mother's income, going out to work

```
seems more logical and worthwhile. At least for
your spirit.
    P.S. My son will soon be going to a public
kindergarten, so we won't have to pay for the
private preschool anymore, and if I cut down
my job to part-time, it's more worthwhile than
signing him up for afternoon child care.
    Or maybe I'll listen to my own advice…
Amelia
```

Eight months had passed since that afternoon in which the kind doctor ordered me to get into bed and quietly expand. My son was already almost three months old, and I could leave him for a couple of hours with a babysitter or a grandmother, and after so many months of lying at home, of suffocation, and later the months of panic and life revolving around him, of changing diapers, bathing, mumbling babyish endearments, breast-feeding and then bottle feeding, of rocking, and walking around with a stroller, I felt that I had to just get out for a minute. I wanted to do something. Something else. Something that wasn't related to caretaking.

Although I had already closed my studio, because I couldn't pay rent for a place that stood empty, I knew I could still take pictures. Working out of my house was considered less prestigious and required lugging my equipment, but I felt lucky to have a job that would let me go away for only two or three hours. I knew nothing bad would happen to my son as a result of several hours without me. Perhaps it would even be better for him, because I'd go out a bit, breathe some fresh air, and return home a nicer person.

I had always been a freelancer and had worked for several places, but the bulk of my work was taking pictures for one newspaper. I liked being a freelancer. I was paid according to the amount of work I handed in, and I didn't mind the hard work. When I started phoning everyone in order to announce my return to work, I didn't expect to be greeted like the messiah, but I didn't expect the answers that I received. "Congratulations, how's motherhood? How is he? Oh, work…well, sorry, but we didn't have a choice, so we found someone to replace you, and we feel a bit uncomfortable with the situation, but why don't you call next week and we'll see." And after a week they told me, "Maybe next week."

I understood them, all those people who wouldn't wait: the advertising firms, the theater. But I had a harder time understanding my editors at the paper, with whom I'd worked for more than six years. So I was insulted and hurt, but I decided to persist, and phone, and set up meetings, because they had known me for so long, and they liked my work. So it would take a little time to work my way back into their rotation – so what? Everything would be okay. I'd make the effort and squeeze back in, bit by bit.

The process was painstakingly slow. After all the meetings, the phone calls, and the smiles, I managed to get from the paper one or two shots a week. It wasn't even a quarter of what I had done for them before. One month passed, and then two, and during that period, in which I was busy trying to learn to be a mother and to squeeze myself back into the job market, I started having second thoughts.

Anyway, I was already immersed in this world of diapers and getting up at night. And anyway, I was only working part-time and I earned pennies that barely covered the cost of a nanny who was even more part-time than myself, and I barely left the house, all the more so in the evenings, and I didn't take trips anywhere. The only thing I wore was rags because it was stupid to buy clothes before I regained my figure, and it's not as if my biological clock had actually stopped. If the children were born close together it would be easier later on, so it was foolish to postpone another pregnancy, because it had taken me so long with the first one, and because I had a sweet fantasy about two children who'd be friends. Being the practical girl that I was, and because I also thought that it would be right and sensible, I thought to myself that there was no point in waiting. I did want another child. It was just so logical.

You wrote about the endless struggle trying to acquire a figure that will comply with our times. It doesn't matter if you're before, after, or in the midst of childbearing; I feel as though it's never enough, that I have to do more. And there are those kind souls who are quick to "encourage" you and tell you, "You look so great – you've already lost most of the weight" (almost one year since I gave birth). Well, thank you, really, and pardon me that this is my third child and that I had a healthy pregnancy, and pardon me for choosing to breast-feed and continuing to eat a nutritious and healthy diet even several months after.

And there are those who insist on telling you, "Oh, you look tired." I ran into one of those at the synagogue during the recent holiday. "Thank you," I replied, "and I'm also grouchy." "Oh? Why?" she asked. "I just am," I answered, "no special reason." And I smiled impassively.

So I say okay, the holidays are behind us, we're facing a new year, a new beginning. I am asking everyone's forgiveness and am forgiving everyone. I'm trying to be calm, pleasant, positive, and loving. I woke up on Sunday morning and went for a walk with my baby daughter, full of joy and happiness, thankful for the good things that I have in life, my family, my daughters, my husband (he's actually okay), grateful for the shining sun, the grass still sparkling from yesterday's rain and dew, and my sweet little doll, smiling from her stroller at the neighbor, who stopped me with a big smile and said, "How's it going? Did you maybe put on a few pounds during the holidays?"

Yael

7

A joyful mother of children. Praise ye the LORD.

(Psalms 113:9)

The princess decides not to go back to work, and to extend her maternity leave and stay with the heir at home for another few months. Since she's a serious and accomplished woman, she decides that if her role now is to be a mother, she'll excel in it. She'll dive headfirst into this huge ocean with all her soul and with lots of love and joy. She's fascinated with motherhood. It fills her up and becomes her sole interest. She enjoys examining it, wallowing in it, touching the foundations and heavens of this experience she'd heard so much about. The experience of being a mother. *The* mother. She searches for enrichment classes for her tiny heir and runs between Gymboree and swimming, reads him stories, and walks around with a big smile because she knows that she's doing the most important thing in the world.

Nothing is as important as what she's doing. Not even what the prince is doing, even though he has a slightly ramshackle kingdom to run. And she doesn't budge from the heir. She feels she's the only one who can understand him and fulfill all his needs in a way that is supremely accurate and correct. She tries several times, just for a moment, at noon, to put him in his room, the room that she decorated so prettily. She tries to put him in his own bed, but he cries so much that she feels as though her heart is breaking from knowing that he's lying all alone in his room, scared and lonely. She knows how much he needs to feel her next to him. She read in all the books about childrearing that if he doesn't feel her close to him, he could suffer later on in life – maybe for his entire life – from the trauma and fear of abandonment, so she just lets it go. For now she's not moving him out of their room, out of their bed.

She doesn't even want to leave him for several hours in the evening, just to go out. But since she *is* a princess, she has obligations and occasionally has to accompany the prince to formal affairs. So she wears a sour expression, just so he can see how miserable this makes her, and goes out only after giving the babysitter incredibly detailed instructions. The first two times they go out, she finds herself seated next to men. She, who was always involved, and opinionated, and considered herself someone who filled an important role in the kingdom's management, discovers that all the political arguments and all the babble about work and money no longer interest her. She tries talking with these men, next to whom she's seated, about the momentous experiences of her present life with her child, about the lovely progress that he's making, and what a charming boy he is, and the carrot that he has just started eating, and about how this is the real thing – this is true happiness and fulfillment.

As she speaks, she sees how their eyes start glazing over, and at the first possible opportunity, they turn their backs on her and start a conversation with whoever is sitting on the other side. *They can't understand*, she says to herself, *and it's their loss*. She knows the truth. She knows that what she's doing is more important than CEOing some company, or climbing the ladder of success and influence that goes nowhere. She pities them. She pities them for all they are missing, for not being able to understand, not being able to relate to these depths of emotion and excitement.

After these initial experiences, the princess insists on sitting next to women whenever they go out, especially those who have already experienced motherhood. During her deeply engrossing discussions with them, she finds herself talking about the new feelings that are overwhelming her. She swaps experiences with them, examines their opinions, learns from them, and little by little begins to find things that she can teach them as well.

During one of these dinners, she suddenly bursts into raucous laughter. Everyone turns to stare at her, and her mortified prince asks that she share her joke with them. She's silent for a moment, and then tells them something, but not what originally made her laugh. She knows that it won't amuse the prince if she tells everyone what really happened to her – how, just that day, in the afternoon, she couldn't bear it anymore, and she peed behind the bushes in the park. So she just makes something up, and no one laughs.

> Do you really think that bringing children into this world and putting them in a day care, or whatever it is, until five p.m. and working full-time is a way of life? Is this how we're supposed to function as mothers? To spend two hours with our children before they go to bed? When will you understand that this isn't the right way? That the reason that the entire younger generation looks like it looks is because they don't have a parent figure to look up to at home, and they have nannies raising them?!

Look how we were raised. Most of us grew up
with a mother at home and we turned out to be
a fine generation. Instead of learning from it,
mothers today do just the opposite, and the
results aren't encouraging. I chose to be a proud
and happy homemaker to four little children. If
you want a career, don't bring children into this
world. Because giving birth to them just so that
someone else will take care of them isn't the
right thing to do. Children have to be given a
warm home with at least one parent who is there
for them.

I find it important to mention that I'm not a
homemaker our of financial privilege. My husband
is a hired worker with only an average salary,
and we still manage splendidly, because we know
how to manage our house. We don't live a life of
luxury or indulgence. Yet we have everything we
need, thank God. And we aren't Orthodox. We chose
this way of life out of ideology. Believe me,
there are better ways than sticking a child in
day care for so many hours. We can forego riches
and careers for the sake of our children. Because
family is what counts, not material things.

Elinor

When my child turned four months old and several days, when
I had just started getting along with him and with myself, and
discovering the joy and pleasure of our togetherness, and it seemed
as though I was starting to get the dimensions of my butt under
control, I found myself hanging angels in the bathroom. Since the
world of kitsch had never been my favorite domain, and angels

never were my favorite decoration, I flew to the nearest pharmacy to buy a pregnancy test and discovered that it wasn't by chance that I had been decorating the bathroom in ethereal themes.

I was so happy. I'd have another baby and get it over with. My life had come to a halt anyway, and my work was just trudging along as it was, so now I'd have two children, and that's it – I'd be done with it and be able to continue onwards.

A week passed, and then several more, and my son was passing developmental milestones, extending his arms so I'd pick him up, and then crawling. We reorganized the entire house, putting everything up high so nothing would endanger him. Now I had to keep him busy – not only feed him and rock him, but play with him and go for walks with him. And with every passing day, with every passing minute during which I had to keep him occupied, I began realizing and internalizing that raising a child wasn't exactly the "okay-we-reproduced-it's-behind-us-let's-move-on" sort of thing that I'd thought it would be. And I started realizing that I was barely managing with one, and that I wasn't even sure that I was doing it well enough. And I started feeling scared.

I was scared that I wouldn't manage with two, that I wouldn't have the necessary strength for it, that I'd rob him of the attention he deserved and needed, that I wouldn't have the required patience, that I wouldn't know how to divide myself between the two of them; and I became terribly frightened. But that didn't stop my belly from growing. It just got bigger and bigger, growing with my fears and with the realization that I was living a role that I still didn't understand, a life that I still didn't feel was mine, a job description that I didn't really know how to fill.

Hey, I wanted to scream, *I'm just a girl*. The same girl who just recently galloped around town on her scooter fancy-free, who took pictures in all sorts of dangerous places, who danced almost every night until dawn, who was destined for greatness, who wanted to conquer the world. And there I was, in the public park, running, with my enormous belly, after my son, who was crawling through the filthy sand, realizing that soon enough I'd be a mother of two. I couldn't believe that this was happening to me, and I couldn't imagine how I'd manage. Even my weight gain came to a halt. During my first pregnancy, I had gained fifty pounds. During my second, I gained only twenty-five. Because who had time to eat?

> You wrote, sadly, about the shorts that you decided you'd no longer wear. I thought so as well. And it became intolerable. I developed ugly lines of bitterness, an awful despair, and such an obsession toward my body and the mirror that I craved for old age to redeem me from my fixation on my inconsolable, unsatisfied, starved, and treacherous body. As a former photographer, you know how destructive it is to let an external glance – male, female, or your own – destroy your body image.
>
> I come from this awful, painful, desperate misery, and I have no husband or children to comfort me because I wasted my twenties on my body image, on the worship of beauty, and on the things women put themselves through – diets and eating disorders and everything that causes me to cringe when I look back at those years. What a shame. You at least have a home, and a job, and all sorts of gifts, and a lot of luck. You have a place to contain your pain, and that's much

```
more important than shorts that will contain your
thighs. Don't be sad.
Sarah
```

I was terrified of what the future held in store, and I felt more and more lost.

One day, one of my friends – who was single like all my friends at the time – called me. She talked enthusiastically about her new date and began a detailed report about what he said, what she said, and how he reacted, and how she giggled, and how he laughed, and what he did later on. When she stopped for a minute, I asked her if she ever felt like she doesn't have any time for herself.

She said that maybe I wasn't managing my time correctly; I should be more organized.

And I told her that wasn't what I meant. I meant that *feeling*. Did she ever feel that way also, as though she didn't have any air, that she was constantly giving and giving, and that she didn't have any more energy to run around; that she was fading away and nobody saw it, and nobody really appreciated her? Because that's how I felt – that I couldn't breathe.

And she was silent for a minute, and then said no. She had never felt that way.

I had never felt that way either, in my previous life. So out of control that I couldn't even shout, "Time out!" *Stop for a minute. I'll be back tomorrow. Just for today, let me put a blanket over my head and disappear. Only for one day. One day just to sleep. One day not to be. Not to take care of someone. Not to worry about someone. Not to be responsible. Not to look at the clock. To be with myself for just one moment.*

And she asked me if I thought she should call.

"Who?" I asked.
"The guy from yesterday."
"I don't know," I said.
And I felt so alone.

∎ ∎ ∎

The prince loves the heir with all his heart. He's willing to sacrifice his life for him. When he returns from work in the evening, after eating, showering, and changing into casual clothes, he takes the heir from the princess's arms, holds him, and makes funny faces at him. He enjoys the heir's sweet smiles and the way he looks at him, and joy fills his heart. Then he lifts him up high, spins him around, and tosses him up in the air, even though it alarms the princess terribly and she shouts at him to be careful. He's impressed by the heir's bravery, how he isn't frightened, and he only smiles. Yes, that's his wonderful and brave heir. And then, after some time, the heir starts crying, because he's hungry.

The prince returns him to the princess, and watches with wonderment how she nurses him, and how gentle she is with him, and how she understands him, and knows him, and he is so overjoyed by this magnificent bond between her and the baby. Knowing that the princess is a good mother generates within him a feeling of confidence – a feeling that he chose right. And he just loves her more because of it. And he appreciates her. It's true that the bond between the princess and the heir has shoved him aside, but he knew that this would happen. He was prepared for it; he knew that it was a natural and right move and considers it a small price to pay compared to the enormous gain from the knowledge that the heir is in such good, loving hands.

The months pass, and the prince, who has to confront daily difficulties outside of the palace, at his work, fighting for their livelihood in the harsh world, wants to go on a vacation. He wants several days of peace and quiet with the princess, just the two of them. Maybe they'll manage to talk quietly, because it's been impossible to complete more than two sentences for some time now, and he wants to pamper her some; maybe she'll even order a massage, and rest. He wants her to sleep peacefully for just one night, without getting up for the heir, because he sees the black circles under her eyes, and maybe if she'll rest a bit, then she won't say "not tonight" because she's really tired, and they haven't done it in ages. But it isn't only that. He misses her. He misses their togetherness.

So one evening he suggests that they go on a short romantic vacation.

And she stares at him. She can't believe he's offering something like this. She's in shock. How can she, she tells him furiously: she's still breast-feeding! She can't leave the heir now! He can't even sleep without feeling her close to him. And he needs her so badly at this stage and she doesn't understand how he even thought of it. How could he have conceived this crazy, illogical, detached idea?

And the prince knows she's right, and that he hadn't really thought it through.

And he asks for her forgiveness.

8

Thou that dwellest in the gardens,
the companions hearken to thy voice...

(Song of Songs 8:13)

My man felt me fading away, and he arranged a vacation for us. A romantic vacation – just the two of us. I was happy to get away, and happy for the chance to be with him. So we went. And I didn't leave the room. I slept. And slept. And my man took joy in me and I in him. And we were both delighted by the quiet. By being together. And then I called to ask how the baby was faring. Apparently, he was running a bit of a fever and I heard him crying in the background. I couldn't breathe. I couldn't stand it any longer, and I wanted to go home, I wanted to go back, and my heart was torn, and I knew that until I held him, until I hugged him, until I was with him, I wouldn't be able to relax. I realized that the time hadn't come yet. That I couldn't go away yet. That I couldn't break away. And we went back.

And I returned to him, to our walks with the stroller.

One day, when I arrived at the park, to collapse on one of the benches, one hand rocking the stroller and the other one placed under the humongous breasts that were mine, but not really mine, and on my belly, the belly that for the past two years had become the window sill from which I gazed at the world, I heard fragments of conversation between the other mothers who shepherded their young ones within the restricted spaces of the fenced sandbox, the concrete paths and the minute patches of grass planted like oases in the middle of the asphalt expanses teeming with buses.

"Sweetie, don't touch the cat," said one mother. "Cola is bad," said another. "And so are antibiotics, and there's this excellent new stroller, and a wonderful ointment for diaper rash, and go take a pee, I'll keep an eye on him, and take a wipe with you." And one mother yelled at her friend, "What are you talking about? After the carrot you mash a sweet potato; that's the best thing to do." "And when do you start with the chicken?" asked someone else. I didn't know either when it was finally allowed to feed chicken to a baby. I edged closer. The next day I approached them and said hello, and they immediately responded cheerfully, and asked where I lived, and how old my baby was, and how many weeks pregnant I was, and by the next day, I was already one of them. I left the house with a purpose. No more wandering. No more walking around the city lonely and abandoned. I went to meet the group. The group of mothers in the park.

> It just kills me that sometimes I'm just dying to go out or sit with a friend and I don't. There are days when I simply cry with the pain. It may sound stupid to you (it sometimes sounds stupid to me), but I'm sick of eating my heart out and feeling lonely and stuck at home all the time with only myself as company.
> Gabriella

Within this group, I could release all the contradictory feelings that bubbled and burned within me. Here, I could go into the most precise details, and I was allowed to say that things were difficult for me. And from then on, every day when I didn't work, I went to meet them in the mornings. And on days that I managed to get some work for a few pathetic hours, I ran to them during the afternoons. To our fenced territory. The territory in which everyone was like me: overweight, with dark circles under their eyes, wearing only comfortable clothes. The only place in which I was right, and I felt right.

At that place, sandwiched between one busy street and another, hidden from the eye, I found consolation. And I found another thing. I discovered that I was part of something that I hadn't even known I yearned for, that I didn't even think I was interested in, that I was sure had disappeared from the world with equality and ambition: the world of feminine wisdom. A world with a magnificent past that was just waiting there. Waiting for a day when I'd need it, and now that I needed it, it extended its arms to me so that I'd come and snuggle up within it, find consolation and warmth in its loving and understanding embrace. In their embrace. I was allowed to feel things that up until then, I was sure I was forbidden to feel. And I could talk about it. And complain. Complain and they would understand me; complain and receive a big hug; complain and discover that everyone felt the same way, and that it's okay.

I joined the Public Park Union for Complaints, and it was a great pleasure. And mostly, we complained about them. About the men. About how they didn't understand, how they didn't share our entire world with us. How they didn't help like we expected them to, and didn't understand us, and didn't understand what they were missing. And so, we sat in a circle, just like generation after generation before us sat at the tent's entrance, throwing wood into the fire, guarding it so it would continue burning. And we sat within the boundaries of our territory, throwing our pain and frustration into the sandbox that reeked of cat urine, discussing and harping on our problems, our difficulties, and first and foremost, our complaints toward our men. These complaints burned brighter than the rest. The more we complained, the stronger was the fire. As it grew higher and higher and we became addicted to it, I was mesmerized. Inebriated.

I had a place. I was part of a group that was the continuation of a historical chain whose roots were planted way back in the beginning of time, its knowledge passed down from generation to generation, providing an anchor and the support of wisdom and comprehension for many generations of women. I was part of that same chain that my grandmothers before me had been part of, and their grandmothers before them, while they sat together in their kitchens, in the menstruation tent, near the stream while doing their laundry, pouring their hearts out, giving each other their wisdom and experience, empowering each other, sharing advice. And I no longer felt alone. I had wise guides who were glad to explain to me, teach me, and help me pave the way to real life. To building a family.

And I was happy to learn from them, especially from those who had clearly been running their own lives from the age of twelve, as well as the lives of those around them. And they'd been doing it with an iron fist, and they knew all the paths, the straight as well as the winding, to get what they wanted; they knew how to manipulate, and how to organize their lives like they wanted them to be. They knew the secret and they were willing to share it with me, and I swallowed every detail that they fed me. They had answers to all my questions. They knew what my baby had to eat, and when, and they knew the best doctor in the neighborhood, and the occupational therapy expert; they knew what to do for swollen legs and stretch marks, what to say to a husband and how to give an ultimatum.

Because for every dilemma that someone flung out into space, someone else always had advice. From her own personal experience. And after a time, I felt as though I understood more, and that I also had something to give and teach and bestow. I discovered that after peeling away the scooter and the cameras, I could touch something that I hadn't realized I had within me, that had been in hiding all my life and was suddenly exposed. I was part of a group that taught me something that I had never known before. They taught me how to be a woman.

I heard so much brilliant advice. I gave so much valuable advice back. *Tell him, notify him, resign, keep quiet, yell, put your foot down, let me give you a tip about blow jobs, I know what kind of exercise you really, really need, you must go to my doctor, he's the best, and buy my bra, it's the most comfortable, and never, under any circumstances, let your kids eat in front of the television, I don't allow mine, you're making a mistake, you're too weak, you're too tough, why didn't you ask me, it's such a shame that you didn't ask me, if only you'd asked me, I would have organized your entire life.*

I loved them, my supportive circle of women from the park. I worshipped them. I didn't really care about their credentials. It didn't matter to me that I received advice on relationships from someone who had just gotten a divorce, advice on work from someone who didn't work, advice on preschools from someone who didn't send her children to preschool, advice on diets from someone who weighed more than myself. And I listened to them. I became a different person thanks to the training that I received in the park. I learned how to manipulate, how to say only half of what I wanted to say, how to maintain a sour silence, how to say something poisonous under the guise of amicability. I was mastering the art of being a woman. I even grew my hair.

I didn't care that their asses didn't look like Jennifer Lopez's, that they didn't know my man. Now that I knew how to be a woman, and what I had to do, I was set on my goal, and I had a plan. Now I was clear on how I wanted to live, how I wanted my family to be and to function. Equipped with support, advice, and information that I gathered around the sandbox, I believed that if I tried hard enough, in a short while, toward the birth of my baby girl, I'd make my life look like a perfect picture. I was prepared and ready to charge toward my goal. I had all the required material. I had a father, a mother, a little boy, and soon I would add a baby girl. Now, all I had to do was place everyone exactly how I dreamed I'd position them, and they'd look just like I dreamed they would, smile at the camera, and say cheese.

Every time my mother comes to visit, everything that's obvious and that usually weighs down on me comes out in the open in the most dramatic and grave manner. "The back of the baby's head is flat. It's so alarming" (he's four months old and ever since he turned two weeks old I've been running with him to physiotherapy); "Oh, God, look at those mosquito bites that your child has on her" (I just installed a hundred-dollar screen door); "Allow me to just say that you have to make the effort to dress up and look pretty for your husband inside your house" (I don't want to! I'll go around with my hair in a ponytail because every time I pick up the baby he tears my hair out. And I'll wear my pajamas because it's more comfortable this way. Anyway, my husband thinks that I'm pretty just as I am, and if Billy Bob Thornton cheated on Angelina Jolie, then it doesn't really leave much hope for us lesser mortals).

This week she just went on and on and I listened and justified myself, until finally, I felt that if I didn't shut her up, I'd go out of my mind. And I told her (or in all honesty, I screamed at her) that I've had enough, and if I'm not asking for her opinion, that I don't need her to give it to me voluntarily, and that she has to stop making me feel as though I'm inadequate like only she knows how to. When I was done, she stormed out of the house and slammed the door behind her.

I just stood there. I felt like an awful person who speaks atrociously to her mother who went through all the trouble of raising her (which is probably why my daughter will someday talk to me in the exact same way; it will be my punishment), and maybe I'm actually crazy and I'm in urgent need of hospitalization. Then, I read what you wrote and you reassured me that I'm only normal. Today, I'm going to introduce my mother to you.

Talia

9

She findeth no rest...

(Lamentations 1:3)

Before the baby was born, I started searching for a good preschool for my son. I checked and examined the technique of wiping runny noses in half a million places that were recommended to me by the park women, and I found the most wonderful place in the world. It also cost more than the others, which proved to me its excellent quality. For a two-month acclimatization period, I came with my son once every two days for one hour, then one hour with me and two without, then every day for half a day. And when he could finally stay there all by himself, and leave me one wonderful solitary moment for myself, the preschool teacher announced that she had received a fantastic offer to manage a boutique and in one week she was closing the preschool. She was very excited about her new challenge. She wasn't very interested in the fact that the week she was closing was the exact week I was due to give birth. Thoroughly frightened, I started searching for another place and shoved my child into the first one I found that was willing to accept him.

And then, my man received a job offer that he simply couldn't refuse. A promotion that would greatly improve our financial situation, but included crazy working hours. He was worried about me because he was a wonderful and involved husband, and he saw that I wasn't at the height of my glamour. We sat together and decided that this was a once-in-a-lifetime offer and he had to give it a go. Give it a few months. And I encouraged him because I wanted to be what I had promised him to be: his friend, his partner. So I told him that everything would be all right, that he didn't have to worry because I was strong and I could manage, and I had gone through harder things and we had promised to help each other achieve our dreams, ride wildly on that roller coaster called life, and not be afraid. I was determined to be a wonderful wife and he was terribly busy, so I'd make more of an effort. It was a fantastic offer, and it would help all of us, the entire family. It was for the family.

I gave birth. I was the mother of a newborn baby girl and a thirteen-month-old boy. And I thought that if only I tried hard enough, I'd succeed. Because I'd been told, my entire life, that it depended only on me.

■ ■ ■

The princess knows it's time to send the heir to preschool. He's already two years old. Two years during which she has been with him almost every minute. Only recently she has managed to teach him to fall asleep without nursing, but he still can't fall asleep without her stroking him, without her singing him his regular songs, and every time she goes out in the evening, rare as that is, her departure is accompanied by his heart-wrenching sobs. She knows how sensitive he is, how much he needs her, but she also knows that he already needs the company of other children. So she signs him up for preschool. After the first days, during which both of them cry terribly, they adjust, she and the heir, to the separation. It's a relatively short separation, because the program is over by one o'clock and she doesn't sign him up for afternoon care. She decides that half a day is enough for him because he needs the quiet, he needs his home, and a full day away is still too much for him. And for her. Maybe next year she'll leave him until four.

Now the princess has several free hours during the morning. She starts taking care of things that have been neglected for so long. Especially the palace. She invests all her energy in it, all her free time. She wants to resume her hostess duties, and she, who can't go to sleep if there's a dirty cup in the sink, certainly can't entertain guests if the palace isn't shining. Little by little, the princess restores the palace's former shiny façade. She organizes, polishes, and embarks on a series of small renovations and paint jobs. When she entertains guests, she does everything alone. She cooks, bakes, and decorates the room with candles because it's important to her that everything be perfect.

She also signs up for exercise classes. She compares prices of gym subscriptions, just as she shops around with everything that she buys, because she's trying to save money. She's modest, even though she's a princess, because that's how she was raised, to content herself with little. To give and not to take. To do the best she can. To be gentle. Not to push. She's not like that. She's not like those women who'll do anything to get what they want, who are inconsiderate of others. No. She's a good woman. Whenever she's needed, she's there for everyone. For the heir, for the prince, for her friends. She never puts herself on top of her list of priorities. First and foremost, she thinks about the welfare of others. And she doesn't just waste money. For herself, she buys only the essentials. She's the type who doesn't need a lot. On the other hand, she pampers others gladly. She'll buy a friend a present that she'd never buy for herself. She cooks her son his favorite food and cooks the prince his favorite food. She eats the leftovers, and it doesn't bother her one bit.

She knows that the kingdom's financial situation isn't very good now, and the mortgage on the palace is burdensome, and the preschool tuition is heavy, but it really is an excellent place, and she's not willing to compromise on that. Anyway, the prince agreed with her that it's extremely important that the preschool be excellent, private, and small, so she's doing everything she can to scrimp and save. She asks her friends about sales, she paints the children's room all by herself, she travels out of town to search for bargains, and she manages to redecorate the palace with pennies.

At the end of the month, when the prince goes over their bills, his expression conveys to her that he's worried about all the expenses, and sometimes he asks if a certain something was necessary, and she's terribly insulted. He doesn't understand just how much she's been economizing; he doesn't understand what an effort she puts into saving, and how little she buys for herself.

Only very rarely, when she's in a really bad mood, does she suddenly find herself splurging on a pair of shoes, because she can't help herself, because all her friends have such beautiful clothes and shoes and she wants some as well. And anyway, she deserves it. She, who gives everyone everything, who relinquished all her dreams in order to be a good mother, and a good woman, and all she does all day is make sure that everyone has everything, and that the palace is polished, she also deserves some pampering once in a while. And she doesn't say anything to the prince about the shoes. When they go out, she wears them and he doesn't even notice, and she's glad that he doesn't notice. She doesn't feel like giving him a report about why she bought them and how much she paid. She starts thinking about going back to work, but they want more kids, so there's really no point in waiting anymore. And the princess doesn't renew her gym subscription because they're pregnant again.

> From the early hours of the morning, I wait for noon to roll around so that they'll go to sleep, and when they wake up, I am already planning ahead for the evening bath. I bathe them at 7:45 in the evening, there's a story immediately after that, and then straight to bed. I need this time for myself, this quiet. My husband calls me a robot.
>
> Every morning I say, "Grow up, already; get married and leave home," and they're still tiny (two and a half years old and eight months). Everyone keeps telling me to enjoy it while they're still small, because it just gets harder as they grow up. But for now, it's hard enough for me to get up at six o'clock in the morning to the sounds of the baby crying, and his brother harassing me and calling out, "Mommy, he's crying!"
>
> Kayla

When my baby girl was two months old, I took her to the doctor to weigh her, check her reflexes, and measure her head. "Everything's just fine," said the wonderful doctor, and then, without any preliminary warning, I collapsed into the chair and burst into tears, and through those tears I mumbled that I'm not managing. She ordered me to get a sitter today and go have a coffee by myself. On the way back home, I stopped by my son's preschool and peeked through a hole in the gate. A neighbor who was passing by saw me peeking and tutted while casting a pitying glance at my baby napping in her stroller. Shaking her head decisively, the neighbor expressed her firm opinion that I shouldn't sign the baby up for this preschool.

"Why?" I asked.

"You don't know how much they cry," she said. "Sometimes it tears my heart out and I think that they're simply left to fend for themselves." And even though I knew it wasn't true, and even though I had already cried plenty that day, I cried again. At that moment I decided to move my son to a big, established place. I wanted a staff; I wanted an inspector who would observe everything. I no longer wanted a small, personal, special, intimate place. I wanted somewhere secure. I went to a big day care center and settled down in their office until they signed him up for the next year. And I also signed up my new baby. I would have to wait six months for that moment to come. At the time, it seemed as though that day would never arrive. The mere thought that one day I'd get up in the morning and leave both of them somewhere for several hours, without having to take care of them, worry about them, run after them, and feel like a terrible mother, seemed to me like a sweet fantasy that was entirely out of reach. Through this veil of exhaustion and guilt, going to work suddenly seemed to me like a vacation. And I was desperate to return to work.

> Last year I gave birth to a lovely baby girl (my
> second). I stayed at home with her for five months.
> Bit by bit, I felt depression overwhelming me. I
> felt that if I didn't leave the house with makeup
> and without someone hanging around my neck, I'd

collapse. I envied my husband for having the
privilege of going to work, meeting people, and
having a genuine, civilized conversation that
wasn't about "what she did today." I had thought
that it would improve with the second child, and
that you no longer have this itch to get out of
the house and go to work, but I realized that
staying at home wasn't for me.
Ilana

Experience had taught me how hard it is to work your way back into the job market. As I knew how problematic it is to disappear from the eyes of your employers for too long, after my baby girl was born, well before my three months of maternity leave were over, I started calling the newspaper I worked for. Even though this time I had been away for a much shorter period (since this time I had not been on bed rest and had worked throughout the pregnancy), I once again discovered that many things could change in such a short time. Once again, some of the editors had been replaced; new photographers had arrived on scene and were the rising stars of the moment. They were young, and willing to do anything, at every hour and at half the price, just to get themselves started. Again I found myself fighting. I, who just two years ago had been swamped with work and could pick and choose the jobs I wanted, who had a dusty catalog lying at home of my one-woman exhibition, who thought I had reached the promised land, found myself scrabbling for some crumbs like a new photographer. After several weeks, I managed to get one or two assignments a week from the newspaper.

A few months passed and I wasn't getting more assignments. In fact, I was getting fewer. But I insisted on being on constant standby, waiting for them to call. I tried putting together several hours of sleep, between his teething and her waking up to eat every few hours. I made sure I had a standby babysitter whom I could alert when the moment arrived and I was urgently summoned, and I didn't miss even one phone call, because maybe that would be the call that would send me to work. My salary was per photo. During those months, I earned less than half of what I paid my babysitter to be on call for me.

Already after the first baby I had had no success returning to work for the advertising agency and the rest of the places I had done occasional work with before, because they really didn't have any obligation to me. But the newspaper had been my home. I'd worked there for eight years. I didn't want to throw away everything I had achieved and give up on everything I had built, even if all that was left of my successful career was some pathetic leftovers. I decided to grit my teeth and continue trying to juggle all the balls in the air, all the while hoping that they wouldn't fall and shatter. *Two little babies and one part-time job*, I cheered myself on: that was the whole story. I reminded myself that I had already taken pictures in warzones, I had been beaten up in demonstrations, and I would manage.

Then, that phone call came through. On the other side of the line, the producer, a twenty-something-year-old, laid it out for me. The editor wanted me to travel two and a half hours that afternoon to Be'er Sheva – in the south of Israel – to take pictures of a family.

"But today's Friday," I said.

A silence descended on the line. We both recalled our last two conversations. After almost three weeks during which I hadn't received any work, I had phoned to ask what was going on, and if

I could speak to the editor. He had told me that she was busy and that he'd leave her a message. Two days later, when I still hadn't gotten any response and I'd been sitting by the phone like a junkie, I called again. Once again, she couldn't talk to me but she had left him instructions on what to say to me. He tried to avoid saying it. I asked him to tell me. He tried to weasel out of it again. I told him that I knew it wasn't coming from him, and he should just say it already, because my dignity could only go so low. So he said that she said that either I go out on any assignment I'm given, or I won't work there anymore. Because she won't work with prima donnas.

And I knew that my dignity had just reached rock bottom.

And I didn't go to Be'er Sheva that Friday afternoon.

And no one called me from the place where I had worked for eight years to say goodbye. They still haven't.

We are the same age. Give or take two years. I'm sitting and writing even though it's late, and the children are sticking close to me in the living room (my husband is doing army reserve duty), because it's now or never. We have two little children. I would have another ten (it all depends, of course, on our financial situation), because apart from the fun of a big family gathering around the table, in childrearing I'm the one with the authority.

All our lives we have to meet the standards that society and our parents outlined for us. We have to finish high school, go to the army, study in university, get married, have kids, and find a good job. I passed through all of the above with relative success - even my mother approved - until I got to the work part. I am 32 years old and I can't make up my mind about what I want to do when I grow up. All the things I want to do are considered impractical, and I am, after all, a practical and conventional girl. Furthermore, my situation is pretty golden right now (not exactly 24-karat, but it's shiny nonetheless), and who wants to give up a good thing?

Anyway, my second, wonderful child came along (a shame that you can't give birth to the second one first) and here I am, at home for an entire year, having the time of my life, and what's more important is that I don't have to prove anything to anyone. People ask me what I do and I say, "Me, well, I'm at home with my son." "Oh, that's great, good for you." And that's that. No competition, no colleagues, no annoying bosses, no getting stuck hysterically in traffic at four in the afternoon. The house is always clean, there's food in the fridge, there's no guilty conscience. And everyone's happy – and that, miracle of miracles, includes my husband.

When I told my mother that on the day I decide that I've had enough of being home with the kids I'll be really sad, because then I'll no longer be doing the one job that is uniquely mine, without competition from others, she laughed and said, "Stop talking nonsense." What she meant, of course, was *wait till your children reach their teens.*

My husband says that it's my decision to make, and on this point I'm glad that I'm not a feminist, because the burden of bringing a salary home falls on him and it suits me just fine.

That's it. I did it. I'll send this letter quickly without rereading it because after a proofreading, all my inner truths will be erased and only the clichés will remain.

Miriam

10

Give me, I pray thee, a little water of thy pitcher to drink...

(Genesis 24:43)

In the evening, after my shower, I approached the mirror. Only three years had passed since that young woman with short hair and fire in her eyes had looked back at me. I let go of the towel in order to put cream on my bruised and bleeding nipples, and looked at my breasts lying there like deflated helium balloons forgotten under the sofa, at my stomach with its flabby rolls leaning on each other, at the lank hair that hadn't seen a hairdresser for months. And then there was my brain, which hadn't read a book for more than a year and a half. Now the thirty-year-old woman who was me looked back at me from the mirror with those same eyes, but there wasn't any excitement in them. Just an endless ocean of exhaustion and lethargy.

After weeks in which I had wandered the streets or sat in public parks rocking the twin stroller, which contained my son and my baby girl, regardless of the heat or the cold or the dark, trying to find a moment in which neither of them needed me to feed them, diaper them, give them something to drink, clean, soothe, burp, pick up, all I wanted was to go to my parents on Friday, eat something, and have someone hold and hug *me* for a change – have someone, for one minute, take care of me.

But my editor wouldn't work with a prima donna.

And I knew she was right. I couldn't deliver the goods. She wasn't running a charity organization. She was running a business, and she wanted to employ people who would be available at every given moment, who could jump to her every alert, who were grateful for every call. Yet I was still angry. I was angry that I had been fired. I was angry that I wasn't earning money. I was angry about how I looked. And what made me the angriest was that I felt as though I had been cheated. I was angry for having been told that it was all up to me, that nowadays, raising kids and working isn't a problem, which caused me to believe that times have changed, that there is no difference between men and women, that you can do everything if you just want it enough. And I wanted, I desperately wanted, and I made the effort, and I worked my ass off, but I didn't make it.

And I still didn't know that things were going to get much worse.

> This time you led me to the sofa in my parents' living room. I'm trying to take a nap and they're asking the grandchildren to be quiet because Mommy's sleeping. I told my husband that I'm also a little girl, who sometimes needs to be taken care of. You're writing about yourself, and actually, you're writing about me, and I'm crying. We could've been friends.
> Ora

The prince and the princess have an heiress, a little sister to the heir. At night, the princess gets up to nurse the heiress, and in the morning, she tries to take advantage of the hours during which the heir is in preschool to do some shopping and tidy the palace; and there are so many errands to run. In the afternoon she takes the heir to his afternoon activities with the baby, and then they return home for dinner, bath, and bedtime. She no longer reads the heir two stories at bedtime. She barely has the energy for one.

And around the time that she's utterly exhausted, the prince comes home. He arrives at home after dealing, all day long, with dragons that threatened him, that endangered his status, his promotion, that tried to overtake him and leave him far behind; and he's been fighting them. He fights with all his might, trying to prove himself, staying one more hour, two more hours, trying to be the best, to receive a raise. And he doesn't do this for himself; he's doing it for his family. For his princess and heirs, for the mortgage on the palace, for their future, so he can give them everything they need. And when he arrives home, to the princess for whom he fought, for whom he built the palace, he desperately wants to tell her about his victories and wants her to be proud of him. And there are bad days too, days when he fails, days when it seems as though nothing is working. Then, the only thing he wants is to come home already, meet his princess, lay his head in her embrace, and hear a kind word of solace from her, from his friend. From his love.

When he opens the door, he discovers a depleted princess.

The princess doesn't have the patience to hug or express appreciation. She wants him to be the one who's impressed, who appreciates, and she can't understand why he doesn't make the effort to come home earlier, why he doesn't think about her sometimes. Why he doesn't think about how difficult things are for her, and why he doesn't try to come home before darkness descends. One day, when she tells him that the heir has his end-of-the-year school party, he says that he doesn't know if he'll be able to make it, and she gets terribly upset. *He doesn't know how to distinguish between what's important and what isn't,* she says to herself. *His priorities always were confused.* Yes, she knew that before. Back when she fell in love with him she knew that she'd have to teach him a thing or two, but she thought it would be a piece of cake. She believed that after the wedding, she'd be able to do it without any problem. She'd teach him. But he didn't learn.

He isn't sensitive enough. He doesn't court her sufficiently or doesn't court when and how she prefers. He works too much but he isn't getting the promotions that she expected him to, or supporting her like she expected him to. He doesn't function like the caring and sharing father he promised to be, and he doesn't cook, or he does but leaves the kitchen filthy. And he's too tough with the heir, or too soft with him, and he barely spends time with the heiress. And he doesn't talk to her about his feelings, and he's not exactly interested in hers, or he is but not genuinely, or he loses patience in the middle, and she doesn't understand why he insists on putting his heart and soul into work, and why he doesn't try to spend more time with them. With her and the children.

In the end, he comes to the end-of-the-year party but she sees that he isn't as excited as she expected him to be and she's terribly disappointed with him. And he doesn't tell her what a mess he left behind at work and that he got into a lot of trouble because he insisted, on that particular day, on leaving early.

The day that my own personal serenity arrives
will be the day that I'll stop the devil's dance,
the exhaustion, and the race for survival. It

will be a kind of day when I'll wake up in the morning and my body won't ache because I'll allow someone to take care of me. It will be a day when I'll walk into the neighborhood supermarket and for once I'll be able to buy whatever I feel like buying. Yes, it will also be the day when I'll collect all the bills hanging on the refrigerator door and pay them, all at once.

On this day, I'll go out with my daughter for a morning of fun (cafes, shopping sprees in the mall), and fantasize about a weekend in a rural bed-and-breakfast with a good friend. I may even go as far as daring to order a plane ticket to some magical destination in one of the neighboring islands in the Middle East (because New Zealand shall remain a fantasy).

And I'd also like to decide that on this day, I'll resign from all my extra part-time jobs and focus only on one. Decide something and do it! On this day, I'll get a house cleaner, even if it's just a one-time thing. And what I'd like most of all, on the day that serenity comes, is to give more to those who don't even dare to dream of the day when serenity comes.

A single mother

My baby girl wasn't easy. *That's just how some kids are*, I said to myself. That's what everyone said to me. She still woke up many times every night. I got up with her, and the days and nights turned into an inseparable jumble of getting up and lying down. During the morning, I was with her, and in the afternoon, I was with both of them, trying to scrape the remains of my patience from the bottom of my barrel of resources. When she turned nine months old, when I no longer remembered how to sleep a full night, or what a pub looks like inside, when I no longer had any idea who I was or what I had ever wanted in life, the day arrived when I left her at the day care center and went to have a coffee. Alone. Without rocking the stroller, sticking a pacifier in anyone's mouth, pulling out a breast, mixing milk, changing diapers. An hour went by. And then another. I watched all the people walking down the street, those in a hurry and those not. Those who have time. And suddenly I felt odd having nothing to do. With my hands. With myself.

The next day, I told my man that I wanted to go away for one day. That I wanted to celebrate. Go to a hotel, sleep, pamper myself. Spend twenty-four hours in complete silence. The next day, I brought the children to day care and went to the train station. I could have driven, but I chose to travel by train. Maybe so I could feel far away. I sat on the train, and during the hour-long train ride, I filled the notepad that I had bought at the station. When the ride ended, I had chapter headings for a novel. A novel about four women, together in a room, who have all just given birth. I still had to write it, this novel, but I had a beginning. And I had the foundation. And from the moment I arrived at the hotel, all I did was sleep. I slept peacefully, as I hadn't slept for what seemed to me like forever.

Many times, I just want to stop everything, and everyone can go to hell for all I care. And I'll just do whatever I want to do. These moments in which we shake off responsibilities toward the various people in our lives and do something

```
spontaneous are few and far between, but when
you decide to do it, it certainly feels great. I
apologize if it's a bit odd for me to come here
and pour out my emotions or involve you in the
life of an 18-year-old girl whom you don't even
know personally.
    Lila
```

After I returned, I sat down in front of my husband's computer, and with one finger, letter by letter, I started typing. After some time, he upgraded his computer; I took the old one, went into the laundry room, disassembled my home-based darkroom and packed everything in boxes. All the negatives engraved with precious moments on which I had toiled day after day during all my years of work were stuffed into several more boxes. Dozens of thousands of tiny rectangles that were once exposed to the light were now returning to darkness. After sealing them with thick packing tape, I wrote dates on them with a magic marker. A decade and a half of invested effort, of passion and ambition, of my own personal art, of what defined me and what I had thought of as my path in life ever since I had conscious memory, now closed in several boxes. And I moved them to my parents' storage room.

Between the washing machine and the dryer, I arranged for myself a little corner where I could write, and I promised to write every day, but my baby still wasn't sleeping through the night, and I was awake with her for hours on end. In the morning, I tried to catch up on a few hours of sleep and then run some errands, because there were always errands to run. There was shopping, and we were out of diapers, and she was sick and then he was running a fever, and at three o'clock I already had to run to bring them from the day care. She wanted to go to the park; he wanted to watch television. She ate only cheese puffs; he ate only chips. She was skinny and had to be fed; he was a bit chubby and I had to keep an eye on him so he wouldn't gobble up all the cookies. She wanted someone to push her while she sat on the swing; he wanted to jump from the highest slide straight down to the asphalt. And they both had a costume party, and there were costumes to prepare, baths to run, lice to comb out, play dates with other children because we must develop their sociability, and then, after the nightly War of Baths, one must summon up all of one's patience to complacently tell a bedtime story, with a very calm voice. And I did want to tell a story.

And I wanted to write. And every moment that I wasn't sitting in front of the computer, I dreamed of getting there, and continuing to develop my story, my characters, the women who had become my friends, who were trying to make my voice heard, and yet another day went by during which I didn't have the time to get to it. Another day went by during which there were so many things that were so much more important and urgent, and I knew that if I didn't make the time and place for it, then it wouldn't happen. I understood that I had to get some help to free myself for writing, but it seemed a bit over the top. Because it wasn't really a job. It was an experiment. It was a dream. It was something that would probably amount to nothing in the end. It wasn't a job. Because a job is something that someone pays you for.

My entire self-conception as an adult was as someone who worked, who earned, and who supported herself. I never lived on anyone else's tab. I never had to thank anyone for my food or my clothes. Now, I was someone searching for herself, who invented occupational therapy for herself, who tried to take it seriously, and knew that the chances were that she was doing something that she'd later throw in the garbage, something that wouldn't lead her anywhere. And I didn't dare indulge myself and take a nanny for several hours just so I could write, because I wouldn't allow myself to spend money on this ridiculous attempt to achieve a groundless and illogical dream, which would never really come true.

My man was wonderful, and he supported me, and he wanted me to hire someone to help me as much as possible, just so I'd be happy, but I felt stupid. I felt ridiculous. Especially next to him, because he became more and more successful, earned money, became someone and something, while I turned into something that I never thought I'd be. A housewife, a caretaker, someone lost and confused, searching for her way. Someone so remote from the person I had meant to be and was expected by myself and others to become.

Hi, Lihi.

Do you know how it is when you crave a change in life, when you find that you haven't achieved what you wanted to be when you were young? Do you know that feeling when you have everything, but deep inside you feel confused about everything? That's where I am. In ten more days, I'll be 34, and I haven't done anything with my life, except of course, create the amazing family that I've managed to raise, for which I'm grateful with every passing day. Really, I am.

But professionally speaking, I am an office manager for a CEO and I want to move on, but there's nowhere to go and no way to climb up. I don't have an academic degree. So for now, I'm sitting in the office, serving him his espresso exactly like he likes it. And I have to smile and show that everything's just great because we have to be nice, quick, thorough, sharp, and understanding. We earn a thousand dollars a month, work from eight to four, and return home happily to do our Bible homework on the Book of Joshua, which we studied for the entire term (fourth grade).

I need a change at work; I need real action; I need active assignments that will give me the energy to get up in the morning. Do you have any ideas?

Well, there you have it. I wrote and unburdened myself to a person who doesn't know me, but also doesn't silence me, and I'm sure even understands me. Thanks for listening.

Gila

11

What is thy request? it shall be even given thee to the half of the kingdom.

(Esther 5:3)

The princess is with the heiress in the morning, and runs around in the afternoon with the two heirs from one activity to another, and invites other children over to play with them. They arrive with their mothers, and they sit, a circle of mothers of toddlers and preschoolers, at each other's houses, or on the bench outside the enrichment classes, and discuss child-development issues, share information, learn from each other while wordlessly scrutinizing each other and comparing the children.

One day the princess arrives to collect the heir from preschool and the teacher calls her aside. For the past week, the heir has refused to help tidy up the blocks at cleanup time, and that certainly isn't normal behavior. They're both extremely concerned by the matter. In the afternoon, the princess arrives at the occupational therapy clinic and tells the therapist that all the other children at preschool pick up the blocks and only the heir refuses to do so. Adamantly refuses. The therapist is silent. She's also extremely concerned by this information. "And is he willing to tidy other things?" she asks, trying to extract further details concerning this worrisome deviation. "Yes," the princess says in heartbreaking concern. "The truth is that this is very strange," says the therapist, and after a minute suggests giving him a present every time he tidies up the blocks at preschool. The princess heaves a sigh of relief. There's a solution. The heir is saved. She'll bribe him, and he'll behave normally.

It's her role now, the princess's, to ensure that everything continues normally with him. She knows how important it is that the heir do all the right things on time. She's responsible for his development, for molding him into who he'll grow up to be. Every compliment he receives is in fact a compliment that she receives. If he's nice and polite, it's thanks to her. If he's friendly, it's thanks to her, because she's such a wonderful mother. But if he screams and stamps his feet, or God forbid, won't pick up the blocks, it's because of her. It's her fault. She's the one who screwed up. She's read all the psychology books about child development, and she knows that she's responsible. She knows that if she doesn't teach him how to pick up the blocks on time, it could affect his entire life. She can't understand how, after all her investment, despite all the attention she gives him, this has happened.

At a certain age, he's supposed to draw a man without legs, and at a certain age he's supposed to draw a man with arms, and if a drop of black seeps into a child's drawing, well, that's that. He's a goner. She's a goner. Perhaps it has something to do with the fact that she put him in preschool too early, or too late, or because yesterday she didn't have the patience to read him a story for the third time and she told him to go to sleep already and even yelled at him that she was too tired. Or maybe because two weeks ago, when they played at home with his blocks, she picked them up for him. Because it was easier than getting into a struggle with him over the entire issue. And she knows that it is entirely unacceptable. And she decides to make more of an effort, and be more patient, because you can't turn back time, and time is so important and so significant, and she swears that she'll summon all her strength and be wonderful, because she believes that only if she is wonderful will her children be wonderful as well. Like the neighbor's children. Or even more wonderful than them. Now she's a woman raising children. It's not her happiness that's at issue here. She mustn't choose what's good for her, what makes her happier, because they're the ones who matter now. Only them.

I'm 32 years old, married, with three daughters. I was also one of those girls in class who weren't popular and weren't unpopular. I was the kind of girl who hoped that the boy I had a crush on would notice me, and I hoped that everyone would discover who I really am, and that I'm great, and I always tried to please others. Apparently, I still do. I always think that everyone is better than me, that I'm not as smart as my friend, that I haven't achieved enough for my age (is there really such a thing???).

It's unbelievable how we carry these stupid things from the past. I've achieved so much in my life. I was an officer in the army. I graduated from university successfully. I got married and have three daughters, a supportive husband, a good job, and I also look much better than I did when I was sixteen. Yet nevertheless, I'm still trying to do the right thing, and I'm still in an inferior position (if only in my thoughts), and

I'm still hoping to discover at our class reunion
that the most popular girl in class turned out to
be ugly.

How does one make it this far? I'm already an
adult! Perhaps parents should be told to praise
their children; tell them that they're beautiful
and smart and that we love them unconditionally,
and maybe then, they'll think the best of
themselves. On the other hand, maybe they'll
become spoiled rotten. Who knows?

Nili

The princess knows that every moment in which she loosens her
grip or gives up or falls or screws up will come back to her later
in agonizing lashes of regret. Because children remember. They
remember mistakes that remain like scratches that scar their
young souls. And she has to be careful to avoid that. She mustn't
screw up or say the wrong thing – those things that parents do
or say, and then the children carry them for years. Just like she'll
never forget how her mother told her that it's a good thing she
didn't get the solo dance in the ballet class because the soloist really
was better than her. And that's what she's afraid of. She's afraid
of becoming one of those scarring mothers, those bad mothers,
inattentive, who think only about themselves, who raise children
with problems and complexes that haunt them for life, who later
on go to therapy for years to complain about them, about those
mothers who didn't give them what they needed, exactly what
they needed, and didn't notice that they were having a hard time,
and didn't help them, and now, here they are, miserable because
of them. And because of this fear, the princess tries to make sure
that everything is as perfect as can be.

She insists on adhering to the rules. No eating in the living room; no eating in front of the television; no playing with food with your hands; no candy; toys must be returned to their proper places; no budging from the set schedule, especially before bedtime; teeth must be brushed thoroughly three times a day. And she won't neglect those things, and she'll take care of all the details. She fills their afternoons with enrichment activities because, as it is, she's in agony over all those hours during which the heir was at preschool without her to watch over him.

And when the prince once again raises the issue of their vacation, she hedges and postpones, and postpones again, because the heir really needs her now. This is exactly the stage in which he needs to feel that they believe in him, just now when he's developing rebelliousness – for example, the blocks – and neither can she leave the heiress, whom she still breast-feeds, and perhaps it's his reaction to the birth of his sister and that's what's hurting him so, and that's why he's behaving like this, and is refusing to tidy up the blocks. And even though she feels that she needs a vacation and some space, because her nerves are shot, she doesn't dare leave them, either of them, because she swore to herself to be a wonderful mother, and she won't hurt them, and she certainly won't put her needs before theirs.

But late at night, when she's alone, the princess knows the truth. He's sweet, the heir – the heir whom she tied to her chest and walked around with proudly as though she was the first mother in the world, as though she had managed to do the unbelievable, as though he's the most wonderful answer to all of mankind's ills. Yet, she also knows that he's not exactly Leonardo da Vinci, even though she bought and played for him the entire Baby Mozart series. She knows that the little heir is smart, but he also has some problems. He isn't very popular, and he also has some difficulties, and the teacher says that she has to work harder with him because in a short time he's starting the first grade, and even though he's so charming (they both agree on that), he needs more help, and perhaps he has an auditory or attention problem – many children do, but these things should be checked out, otherwise he'll have a very hard time in the first grade, because it's a serious school and it's important that he arrive prepared. The princess starts running around in order to bring him to that line, that correct line where he has to stand with all the rest, exactly the same. And she no longer wants her heir to be a genius. She just wants him to be happy, and be like everyone else. No more, no less.

And it drives her mad that he doesn't eat enough vegetables.

Only you can understand what I went through today. On Friday, all the kids were asked to dress up as characters from the Bible. My youngest (second grade) chose a brown sack that would give her an ancient appearance, a long wooden staff, and a white beard and eyebrows (she talked about this costume all day long on Saturday and was so excited). She called it "Moses." When she returned from school I asked her how it went. She said to me, "Not good. I almost fell off the stage because the sack got tangled between my legs."

I hurt for her so badly; I wanted to protect her. Had I been there, I certainly would have helped her. The mere thought almost made me cry in front of her. Because of the disappointment, the difficulty, the need to cope (I'm sure some people will laugh at me). I didn't even tell my husband because he wouldn't have understood why

I'm making such an issue out of it. And yet, how
else will they grow up? Can we always be next to
them? Can we always reach out and give them a
helping hand? It hurts…and it doesn't get easier…
Tova

One day, when I came to pick up my little girl from preschool, the teacher called me to the side, and with a worried look in her eyes, she told me she thought there was a problem. My daughter didn't respond like the rest of the children. I told her that we'd noticed that something was wrong, and we'd set up an appointment with an ear expert. During the days that passed until the appointment, we circled her in the house, my man and I, trying to check whether she could hear us. We raised our voices suddenly, dropped things on the floor, and clapped our hands behind her back. She didn't really respond. My man tried to calm me down, I tried to calm him, and neither of us calmed down.

The ear doctor said that he couldn't tell for sure what the problem was, and recommended doing another examination, this time in a hospital.

While we waited for the next appointment, going out of our minds from worry, we started asking questions and gathering information. With every question we asked, and every answer we received, we became even more worried. We started to understand that perhaps it wasn't a hearing problem. We couldn't breathe, and late at night, before the fateful examination, my man held me close to him, as close as he could, and I held him, and we both shut our eyes but couldn't fall asleep. I lay down and prayed, and vowed, and promised God everything– everything I had, everything I could give – on condition that we'd find out that she was deaf. Because I wanted a deaf child. *Please, God, give me a deaf child*, I begged, because all the other possibilities were much more frightening.

12

He asked water, and she gave him milk;
she brought forth butter in a lordly dish.

(Judges 5:25)

The princess was destined for greatness. As she was growing up, she knew exactly what she was going to be: a real superwoman, in leggings or in a ball gown wrapping her perfect body, who would float with a smile and ever so lightly amongst her beautiful, tidy children who would receive all the quality time in the world, and never watch television out of boredom but only for developmental and educational purposes. From them, she would continue floating, without ever being late, into the board meeting where everyone would be sitting with suits and laptops that projected PowerPoint presentations on the walls, and she would knock them all off their feet from enthusiasm and admiration. Her hair would always look wonderful, tidy, and blow-dried, and in the evening she'd go out, evening after evening, clubbing and dancing, and at night would become, in the blink of an eye, a wild, sexy animal, competing with all the twenty-two-year-olds with the pouty lips, and she wouldn't have extra fat anywhere, or cellulite, or wrinkles. She'd never say that she was tired, and she certainly wouldn't say that she had a headache; beneath her suit she'd wear seductive thongs, and she'd be flexible and wild enough to achieve all the things they do in porno movies, and she'd get up early the next morning singing with a happy smile on her face, like a sweet Mary Poppins, wake up the children, prepare them for day care and school, and then continue on to work, where she'd be brilliant and efficient and would never make mistakes, never miss a day because one of the children was ill, and happily do whatever she was asked to do, and her boss would be so satisfied.

However, the princess's life is now far away from that fantasy. After everything she's done, after all her studies and work and hopes and dreams, she turned into a housewife. She says to herself that it's just for the time being, but she can't stop thinking about the fact that she's not any different from the Queen Mother.

During these moments, when she's a bit disappointed, and a bit confused, and a bit far from what she thought she'd grow up to be, she reminds herself that she's doing the most important thing anyone can do. She's a mother.

And she takes the heirs to see a play. She dresses them nicely and wears her new white pants, and she's proud of herself. Here she is, the dedicated mother providing her children with a cultural experience, and when they leave the play, the heirs will be enriched; they'll be smarter and more successful than they were before they got there. She stands in the foyer of the local cultural center, looking around her at the dozens of young mothers, who at that moment – regardless of their body measurements, of what they're wearing, and of the fact that in another hour they might go out in the evening and look wonderful – all look awful to her. Grey. Hunched. Exhausted. Every one of them is coaxing her child, or children, not to scream, not to eat another ice cream, not to ask for another candy or another present from the vendor circling the area with all kinds of lame plastic made-in-China toys that he sells at exorbitant prices; to please stop eating chips, climbing, crying, and just be content for one minute. And she knows that she looks just like them. And she's behaving just like them. And in the car on the way home, when they cry over some toy or ice cream that she didn't buy them, she discovers that her white pants are smeared with stains from one of the candies she *did* buy them, and she screams at her children.

> When my youngest (now a year and a half old) was born, my oldest child was three and a half. A mommy's girl and mommy's only. Her preschool teacher told me that because I breast-fed for so long (a year and a half) my daughter is overly attached to me. Okay, I'm also very attached to her. Now she's five, a difficult age. She's a good girl, sensitive, and somewhat spoiled. When her brother was born, she was very jealous. You're probably familiar with those waves of jealousy. And I feel like this mothering business only gets harder, because not only am I not an ideal mother, I feel like a lot of the time I really don't give my all. But, what – am I not allowed to get annoyed when she dawdles before bedtime? Okay, it's not so terrible, and she does it so sweetly, but I get really angry. Or when she chatters endlessly before bath time and giving her a quick shower takes me an hour. What exactly am I so angry about? And I do get really angry. And then later, I'm angry at myself.
>
> Shayna

And the princess is mad at herself. She's mad that she's mad at her children, when they're not to blame. After all, they're only children. They're beautiful, they're sweet, they're smart; but she has to admit that they're not perfect. She tries to understand where she went wrong, what she should have done, why she doesn't have more patience, and why she explodes at them. She tries so hard, gives and provides – why isn't she succeeding? She's disappointed with herself for taking out her anger on them – her anger at her life in which she just gives all the time and never receives anything in return, her anger at feeling that she's sacrificed so much and no one seems to notice. No one seems to appreciate it. No one calls her to the victor's podium and, in an extremely majestic ceremony with numerous participants, hangs a medal on her breasts – which no longer stand high and perky inside the push-up bra after the births and breast-feeding – and tells her that what she's done is unbelievable, really unbelievable; because after all, she *has* done so much, and she deserves many thanks for all her efforts and sleepless nights, and all her running around, and her attentiveness and attention to miniscule details, and her internal conflicts.

She really *is* a champion. She wants everyone to think she deserves a medal, but she begins to understand that no one really sees all she's done. No one even notices. Especially not the prince, who doesn't grant her the thanks that she needs and craves so desperately. And suddenly she realizes that the prince doesn't even know how difficult it is for her. He thinks it's easy for her. He thinks this is what she loves to do and wants to do more than anything. Because all the princesses in all the fairy tales have filled this role so joyously and lovingly, feeling sated and content as they give, bestow, and nurture. This is the supreme goal of the good-hearted princesses in the fairy tales: to give. She also wanted to give and bestow and nurture and that's what she told her prince.

Yet, she also wanted him to appreciate what she's sacrificing, not for herself, but for both of them, for their family.

She thinks about all the fairy tales and realizes that they all end before this stage. They end with the prince and princess riding off into the sunset, and then it's just "they lived happily ever after." Fairy tales never describe how grey, exhausting, and consuming it is after the sunset. She's mad at him, at the prince. She's mad because she's fulfilling her side of the agreement, and he isn't fulfilling his. His side of the agreement is that he's supposed to cherish her and worship her, and provide her with everything. She wants the entire package promised to her. Including the castle, the horse, and the prince washing the dishes. And he must wash them joyously, not because she asked him to, but because he wants to. She doesn't want to settle for almost, or half, or a quarter of what she dreamed of, of what she was promised. Of what he promised her.

"Tell me what you want," he tells her, "and I'll do it gladly." But she doesn't want to tell him; she doesn't want to ask. She wants him to see. To see her. And he doesn't see. So she implies. With a look, with a gesture; and she makes some comments, here and there, corrects him a bit, tells him what he should have said, done, brought, remembered, forgotten. And with all her insinuations and instructions, he still doesn't do exactly what she wants him to do. Or the way she wants him to do it. And she's mad at him.

> I'm on maternity leave, probably too extended (in a minute, he'll be off to university [he's a year and a half old]). I still haven't managed to find a job where I can come home at three o'clock. (How is it that I haven't received even one answer after all the resumes I sent? Doesn't anyone want

a mother of two?) This week, we returned from an exhausting weekend in Eilat with the two ninjas: our eight-year-old and the baby. My husband was in shock. He kept asking if the baby cries as much at home. "No," I replied, "at home he reads books and sits with his hands folded."

After three difficult days full of yelling and crying (mine as well), he still didn't understand what I wanted him to do. After all, he works so hard all day (and now I'm at home), but I was hoping that maybe he'd just say that he feels sorry for me, and thinks that I deserve (at least) a gold medal. Of course, it was a forlorn hope. After I told him what I wanted him to say, the moment had passed. It's so easy for us to understand, and so hard for them. Why is it so hard for them? Why?! After 12 years of marriage, we probably won't stop hoping, trying, and experiencing disappointment.

P.S. This letter was written under uproarious objections, while chips were being shoved down my bra, and with the kiddie channel screaming in the background, all under the patronage of the little ninja. Help.

Tammy

The prince tries very hard to make her happy, but whatever he does, it never satisfies her. It's never exactly as she'd like, and most of the time it even just annoys her. When he buys her something, she exchanges it. When he suggests they go out to a movie, she's too tired. He tries to listen more and understand more, and still nothing works. He begins to be afraid to even try. He fears that perhaps he'll never manage to give her just what she wants, the way she wants it, exactly when she wants and with the right words and facial expressions to make her happy.

The prince recalls how once upon a time, she, his princess, looked at him with adoring round doe eyes, and laughed at things he said, and was happy with everything that he bought her; and he hopes that one day, he'll be able to make her happy. Maybe then, the joyous sparkle will return to her eyes, and she'll simply be happy that she has him. He, who had dragon-high fantasies, who believed that his princess would never grow old, never gain weight, and would forever remain sweet, graceful, and full of life, no longer dares to fantasize about the simplest thing in the world: coming home from work and sharing with her that he had a difficult day, without her immediately telling him that she had it harder. He no longer dares to expect that when he opens the front door she'll be genuinely happy to see him; that they'll laugh together again, go out on a date together, that she'll really want to have sex tonight. That she'll initiate it. That maybe she'll even have several daring ideas. But she's tired, and the kids have already pestered her so, and the sink is packed with dishes that have to be put in the dishwasher, and once again, he forgot to fix the dripping faucet. He no longer hopes to return home and be welcomed by a smiling princess, or that there'll be that old twinkle of appreciation in her eye, let alone adoration. When he returns home from another day of work, all he hopes for is that just this once, today, just today, she won't be so angry with him. She won't be so disappointed in him, again.

Without even noticing, he starts searching for detours. Paths that will bypass the togetherness that is his and hers, trying to postpone the moment of their meeting, the moment when he'll come face to face with that look, or receive a scolding for something truly shocking that he did, such as failing to notice that his towel fell on the floor. Before he enters his castle in the evening, he finds himself standing by the front door for a moment. A moment in which he inhales deeply, trying to postpone the encounter between them for just another second. Postpone the moment when she'll explain to him that he's in the wrong, again.

> It's so great to know that everyone goes through the same things (even though you have two kids and I have only one, 11 months old). We've only been married for two years, but it feels to me like ten at least. I guess it's only the beginning of all the arguments and the power struggles. How do you stay married to the same person for 20-30 years and more (like our parents) - how?!? I have no idea. We'll see how long we last - if we last.
> Dahlia

The prince and the princess, who just several years ago promised to walk down the path of life together, to support, to help, to be friends and to share their dreams, suddenly discover, each on their own, that they're no longer one being. Each of them is now carrying his or her own baggage on their backs; each of them is coping with his or her difficulties alone. Each of them is walking down a different path. There's no longer *their* desires, *their* hopes, *their* needs. Their goals are so different that they can't even see the needs of the other, or how hard the other one is trying. He's coping alone. And she's coping alone. Some of their needs even turn them against each other. Him against her and her against him. And neither of them remembers when they last sat down with each other, just for the fun. Or the pleasure. Or when they laughed together. When they got a hug. When they received encouragement, support, or appreciation. There are too many struggles, complaints, and reinforced silences in their encounters. And their bed is more full of children than sex.

13

*And she sat over against him,
and lift up her voice, and wept.*

(Genesis 21:16)

The examination concluded that the little one wasn't deaf.

We sat with her on the bench outside the hospital, holding each other, trying to absorb, trying to breathe, and the tears silently streamed from my eyes. I understood that until this moment, I hadn't known the meaning of pain.

```
I'm known as a person who has ants in her pants.
I've always searched for ways to break out of the
routine. Almost every day had to hold in store
an adventure, or some form of entertainment or
meeting, so it wouldn't be boring. The years, the
children, and life have taught me (just recently)
how blessed is the routine.
Ayelet
```

My man and I decided to fight. To fight that dragon. *We're the kind of people who don't give up*, we said; *we'll do everything and save her*. We'd do everything. We'd raise hell. We divided the roles between us. He inquired and investigated the methods with which we could treat her, and wrote and called people all

101

around the world, and questioned experts about new methods of treatment, and each person said something else and no one could say exactly what we had to do. And each expert had his own way, and what he believed in, and a new study was published every day, with new promises, and we had to decide. We constantly had to make decisions, and choose who to believe, and which path to pursue. I ran with her to appointments and evaluations and tried to understand exactly what she had, and what it was going to look like, and what the future held in store for us, and what hope we had. And here as well, every expert said something else.

One day, I went to spy on her at the preschool, and she was standing at the gate and staring out. And after several hours, I went down to buy something at the supermarket, and she was still there, still staring out. It was obvious that we couldn't leave her in preschool anymore. And from the next day she didn't go there anymore. From that moment she was at home with us. We didn't have the advantage of time on our side, which was another aspect that we had to fight, because as long as she was young, there was a good chance for improvement, for progress. We ran with her to more and more assessments and consultations. And during all that time, she hardly slept at all. Barely four hours a day. And we had to keep an eye on her every second, every minute, all the time, because she could climb, and run up and down, and pull and pour and dump things out, and that was the role that I assumed. I was in charge of the house, which in an instant had become her house. A house that revolved around her only.

We had to bring in experts from abroad, and find people in the country who knew what to do. And we found teachers and brought experts to teach the teachers, and she was at home all the time. And there were treatments, and the house was always full of people and resembled a train station, and there wasn't even one moment of privacy. And all this needed funding, and my man took this upon himself. "Don't worry about it," he said, and took that burden on his shoulders, and took care of it, promising himself and me that he'd bring her the moon if that was what she needed. And I supervised all the time. Every second and every minute. Examined what exactly they were doing with her, and how, and what we hadn't done yet, and what we still hadn't tried. And we knew that we couldn't count on anyone. Only on ourselves. So we did the most important thing: we fought for her, and I knew that never before in my life had I done anything as important. And I wasn't interested in what was happening around me in the world, because the entire world had been sucked into a fog. I wasn't interested in anything. Only one thing was clear to me. I was the mother of my child. And I had to save her.

14

Two, the male and his female.

(Genesis 7:2)

The prince arrives home from another hard day at work, this time early enough, while the heirs are still awake, and he tells them a story, and then joins the princess in the living room. They sit together. The house is sparkling clean, and she's prepared a delicious meal, and they chat a bit, for the first time in a long while. He tells her what happened to him today at work, and who he saw, and what sort of problems he came across. And she's so happy, even though she isn't familiar with most of the names, and even though she doesn't have an opinion concerning most of his dilemmas; she's just happy that they're talking and sharing.

Then she tells him about her day. About something that the preschool teacher said about the heir, something that someone told her this afternoon in the park, and about the lady who stood on line at the supermarket, in the express line, with two items more than the limit. "The nerve," she says to the prince. "Wasn't it rude of her?"

And he's silent.

He maintains that silence of his. A silence that she also maintains sometimes. And these silences, which settle between their sentences, stretch and take over, marking the widening gap between them. The gap between what interests them, between what they need, what they want, what they give. A silent testimony that he isn't really interested in what is happening to her, in what she's going through, and he isn't really interested in sharing his world with her, and she isn't genuinely interested in his world. This silence has always annoyed her, but this time it's different. Maybe because she isn't tired, because she snatched a few hours of sleep in the morning, she isn't annoyed this time. This time, something else happens to her. Suddenly she sees herself.

After years during which she has examined the world only through the lens of what seems important to her – her difficulties, her efforts to make her little family perfect and their children wonderful – suddenly she sees herself as though she's looking in from the outside. She sees herself through different eyes. Suddenly she's aware of herself, sprawled on the couch. How she no longer makes sure that her chin is coquettishly extended, and how she's neglected her hair like never before, how she's wearing rags, and without even checking, she knows that she has hair on her legs.

And not only does she suddenly see herself, she also hears herself. Hears what she was talking about, what her life revolves around, how her world has narrowed down to their neighborhood, and who said what to whom, and that the highlight of her day was that rude lady in the supermarket. (Actually, there was another highlight when she found that soup pot she's been wanting at a crazy discount.) And it frightens her. She imagines a young her, a twenty-something-year-old, sitting with them right now, with all her passion, and thinks what her younger self would have to say if she were looking at her now. The princess she used to be wanted to swallow life, eat it, dance with it, climb all its heights, confront all its dangers, touch all its flames. And now, here it is, her life, sprawled like a rag on the couch, silent and small. As distant as the distance between fairy tales and real life. And she knows that the princess she once was wouldn't have let it happen. She swore that it wouldn't happen to her, that she wouldn't surrender to this game, that she'd fight the story's confines and change the end. Because she believed in happily ever after even after the story ended.

Now, it seems so far away. And she also seems so far away, from her life and from herself, from what she hoped and swore she'd be. And her heart aches because she knows that she's disappointed herself, the young princess she once was. And she knows that had her younger self been here and seen her now, she would have dismissed her as a total sell-out. Because she turned into everything she swore her entire life not to be. She's a woman crushed under the wheels of a truck bringing fresh rolls to the supermarket.

And she knows, at that exact moment, that she is no longer a princess. She has become a queen. A queen like all those fairy tale queens. A queen who's obsessed with the little details, who's mad at the entire world – a cranky, sour queen, with a face that has lines of bitterness distorting the corners of her mouth with a twist that can turn even the prettiest face into an ugly one. A queen who's angry that her glory, beauty, and youth have withered.

So she stretches a bit, sits up, straightens her posture, and runs her fingers through her hair, tousling it mischievously. But the prince has already turned on the television.

I have two children, thank God. I didn't want to have any more. Work, running about, and life in general… My husband really wanted more kids, and

I enjoyed his courtship and pleas for another
child. I enjoyed the control over my body and my
spouse. I always promised that after I finished
one more thing that I hadn't yet achieved, then
we'd have another child. At the age of 35, I was
diagnosed with cancer.

Never mind the physical and mental agony. I
knew that now I'd never have another child. I
didn't know if I should feel sorry for my husband
or for myself. I'd pay a fortune for a baby to
wake me up at night, to interrupt me in the middle
of whatever I'm trying to get done, smear the
house with chocolate, scatter the Legos around
the house, force me to drop everything at four
o'clock in order to pick him up and take him to
his afternoon activities.

Please enjoy your children, because it never
returns. And yearning for it just unsettles
you. Now, I'm 38 years old. I have a 19-year-old
daughter and a 13-year-old son, and I feel old.
And with my husband, there are many silences.

Mona

I was angry. Terribly angry. Angry with God for hurting my child,
who never hurt anyone. I was angry with the people walking
down the street. I was angry at the world that continued as
though nothing had happened, as though the sky hadn't fallen. I
was angry at the fact that not everyone stopped, not everything
came to a standstill in the face of this sin, this punishment that
this little girl, this gentle and heartbreakingly beautiful child, had
to endure. The whole time I was pregnant with her, I thought
that since her brother had inherited my blue eyes from me, she

probably wouldn't. I was positive that she wouldn't have blue eyes. But she did have blue eyes, because God really did make her beautiful. More beautiful than anyone else.

Why did He do that? Why didn't He forego the sweet nose, the blue eyes? Why the hell did He have to ruin it in the end? Why couldn't He sit for one more minute, one more second, and do what was truly important? I was terribly angry with Him. With God. And with the world. I was angry that you could send a man to the moon, and there were satellites, that someone had solved the mystery of atoms, that there's such a thing as a fax, that humanity has done so much and evolved so much and knows so much, and no one can teach my child to say "Mommy."

■ ■ ■

The princess looks at the prince, at his profile, when he's looking at the screen that flickers and paints him in cold, artificial colors, and she sees that the years have left their mark on him. She sees his receding hairline. His little paunch. And suddenly he looks like an adult. A man. And she remembers her prince from long ago. She remembers how handsome she thought he was, and how he excited her, and how she loved to lean her head in the hollow between his shoulder and neck, where she felt safe, and where she felt loved, and how just one single look, and one single smile, made her feel like nothing bad could happen to her. And she misses him. She misses who she used to be, and who they used to be, and their togetherness. She feels like extending her hand and inviting him to run away together. She has this wild impulse to ask him to leave everything, take the kids with them, and travel, travel without a plan, to the big world that lies outside. Without a thing, they don't need a thing, only a backpack: Africa,

South America, forget everything. No more carpooling, no more cleaning, no more cooking, just lounging together on a distant beach, far away in the Far East, barefoot.

But she doesn't dare say it. He'll think she's gone crazy, that she's lost her mind. She knows what an obligation he has to the kingdom, and the debts that they have to pay. And she couldn't do it to his parents or to hers. They're not twenty-year-olds; they're adults with obligations and commitments, and there is no place in their lives for crazy fantasies.

And as the lights and voices continue blaring out of the television, she realizes that they're no longer building the foundations of their future. This is their future. This is her life, their life, and it's not something on the way to somewhere.

This is her husband, these are her children, and this is her. Now, she's at that part of the story that arrives after the climax. After the sunset. That part of the story that no one bothers to write. That no one bothers to tell. The part that comes after. After the end. And after the end, she knows, there isn't much chance that anything exciting will happen. Because this isn't the exciting part of the story, of life. And she hopes that he'll see the tear that falls silently on her cheek, and hopes that he'll say something.

She remembers all those times that he offered to take her on a romantic vacation, just the two of them, and how she refused. And after so long that she hasn't felt this way, she wants him to hug her, to run his hands over her lustfully, like he used to, just so she can remember how she used to feel. She knows that it won't happen. Because that's not how they do it. Only when they go to sleep, when both of them are in bed, does he reach for her. She's refused him too many times. She's said yes too few times, and when she said yes, there were too many times that she said yes just because there were too many times that she'd already said no. And she knows that he'd be happy if she made the first move, but she no longer remembers how to do it. And she no longer remembers how to want it. And she can't find the words. And she doesn't know how to suggest. They've been role-playing for so long, playing a game in which he wants and she doesn't, in which he is silent and she is upset. In which he is disappointed and she is disappointed too. And there is silence. And the only voices heard are blaring from the television.

> Every woman I meet, who has less than a minute to talk, deals with the exact same issues and complains about them. I've been a nurse for 18 years. Occasionally, I let off a load of complaints about work, about my children, and about the obvious - my husband, may he live a long life (yes, sometimes I'm not opposed to his staying alive and I even want him to).
>
> Yesterday, I was at the emergency room and a woman with frightened eyes and a baby in her arms arrived. Her husband went up to fix something on the roof and fell from a great height. I think that all she wanted at that moment was to return to her boring routine, to a husband lounging on the sofa (the husband who isn't exactly the friend and lover that she wished for), to the children screeching in the living room.
>
> I see tragedies every day, and it puts things into perspective. This morning, I called all my belligerent girlfriends and told them that they should say a prayer of thanks every day, three times a day, for almost everything and especially

```
for what they take for granted. It's a shame
that we need a tragedy in order to know how to
appreciate things.
Daphna
```

Twice a week, we went with our little girl to a place where they treated children like her. There, we met parents like ourselves. Parents who, one sunny day, had a block of concrete fall on their heads, and they, like us, didn't know how to carry on. Apart from my man, these were the only people who understood how I felt. In this entire world, out of all the people with whom I was previously acquainted, who mainly had no idea what to say, who saw my pain but were helpless and tried not to look into my eyes, these were the only people who understood. The only people who were as angry as I was. Who were as lost as myself. And I wanted to be only with them. Because I wanted to talk about it. Especially with the mothers. And I held on to them. And these days with them were what kept me afloat. Just like the group of mothers in the park had kept me afloat when the children were tiny. Because I could talk to them. Because they understood. And I held on to the group with all the strength I had in my ragged nails. And I waited for these meetings like a person waits for oxygen.

Once every two weeks, we, the parents, met at a support group. One time, the facilitator started the meeting by suggesting that we not talk about the children. That we talk about our hobbies. A silence descended on the room. A terrible silence. It was the most inappropriate offer, in the most inappropriate place, at the worst moment of our lives. A moment in which none of us remembered if we had ever even had hobbies. Or remembered if we had ever done something for ourselves that didn't include survival. I felt my blood boil with fury; I felt as though in another minute I'd explode on all the walls, and especially on the facilitator's head. And I couldn't keep silent. I yelled that we didn't have hobbies anymore. Because it didn't matter what we had before; now we were one thing only. I was one thing only. I was the mother of an autistic child.

Suddenly, without understanding how or why, we all burst into a crazy, huge laughter. All the parents there laughed. We laughed for the first time. And then we started going out together in the evenings. Once a week, we went out, to laugh together, to cry together. And apart from those evenings, I didn't laugh at all. For a very long time.

15

Wash thyself therefore, and anoint thee,
and put thy raiment upon thee...

(Ruth 3:3)

The prince's work announces a big event for the employees on the occasion of a change of CEOs. The prince tells the princess about the party, and knowing her, he immediately adds that he knows that she doesn't have the patience for these events, and he'll understand if she doesn't feel like going. But the princess says that she'll be glad to come. *He reacted to that somewhat strangely,* she thinks to herself the next morning, *not very happily,* as though he's a bit disappointed that she wants to come. And it confuses her. He's always expressed such a desire that she come with him to company events, always pleaded with her, and it's true that most of the time she stayed at home and he said that he didn't mind going alone, that he's used to it by now, but he always has much more fun when she comes along. She's probably mistaken, she soothes herself. He was simply surprised by the joy and exuberance with which she jumped at the opportunity. Then she scolds herself; she shouldn't have shown him how eager she was. That's what confused him – that she wasn't subtle about how much she wanted to go.

And she really does want to go, because ever since that evening in the living room she's been doing a lot of thinking about them and about herself. About what she's turned into. She decides that it's about time she get out of her sweatpants, and for the last few days she's been chopping herself a finely cut salad, hasn't touched her children's potato chips, and hasn't finished the meatballs that they left on their plates. She remembers the gym subscription that she signed up for and decides that she'll renew it at the first available opportunity. She decides that she's going to stun them all at the party.

> We read, we internalized, and this is what came out of it: yesterday evening, while the sea was high, us girls went out to celebrate International Women's Day (even though we're Israelis and not international). We decided to exceed the boundaries of stupid behavior considered legal for mature adult women like ourselves - and of course, the more stupid we were, the more we felt liberated and alive. Since we *are* women, we decided to start the evening at the mall and tried on clothes. After that, we raided the cosmetics counters, and then we continued to a club. At the Whisky a Go Go Club they didn't want to let all of us in, so we went to Shablul Jazz Club. The level of frivolity increased with the level of alcohol, which made the evening more enjoyable.
>
> So we didn't burn our bras and didn't grow mustaches, but we made a statement that we're here. To whom? Mostly to ourselves, because in life's race, amongst the diapers, homework, and gourmet cooking, sometimes we forget that we can have fun, just us girls. And that sometimes we need to be alone. Thank you.
>
> Gabi

During her not so distant youth, the princess did it so easily. All it required was another tiny effort, to wear high heels that added the desired inch, and to fix up her hair. She could enter any room and cause all eyes to turn to her. The prince would put his hand on her shoulder, with proud ownership, as if saying, *she's mine, eat your hearts out*. And she plans to make that tiny effort that she hasn't made for a long time. So she hops over to the nearest mall. She tries on clothes and takes them off, and tries on more, and after several exhausting hours, she goes back home. The next day, she goes to the mall again, this time to a different mall, and once again, she tries on clothes, and every dress or shirt that she throws on the floor pains her. In the afternoon, she goes down to the gym and asks if she can renew the subscription that she froze several years ago. They are gracious and agree on condition that she add a token payment.

The day before the company event, she goes to wax her legs and mustache and have her eyebrows plucked. On the day of the event she goes to the hairdresser, has a pedicure, manicure, and highlights. And when the prince comes home, he remembers for the first time in a very long while how pretty she is. How pretty she can be. "You look wonderful," he tells her, and can't make up his mind if he should tell her that the dress she's wearing is a bit too glittery, because he knows the women with whom he works, and knows that they'd never wear something so glittery, and certainly won't come with long dresses. He decides not to say anything, because he likes the way she looks, like a princess, and he doesn't want to say or do anything to ruin her rare good mood. The few times she's come with him to his office parties, she sat with a bored and sour expression and didn't even try to get to know or befriend anyone, and he's pleased that this time she's made such an effort.

When they arrive at the event, everyone is happy to see the prince, and casually shakes her hand and coolly says, "Pleased to meet you," and in a matter of seconds, they surround him, and his hand leaves hers, and she's left standing there, alone. She gazes around and sees all the other women, who have just thrown something on themselves, and casually wipes her face in order to rub off some of the makeup on her face, trying to erase her exaggerated efforts. If only she could tear off, one by one, the sequins that decorate her neckline, which in the dressing room illuminated her face with a glow, and now look as cheap as confetti. The prince, who stands several steps from her, is encircled by people who chat and laugh with him, and she remembers how she used to love it that people always tried to get close to him and loved him without him having to lift a finger for it. And she can see how much they like him, and how all of them, the women as well, touch him, slap him on the shoulder, laugh at what he says, whisper secrets in his ear, and he laughs that big laugh of his. The laugh that turns his eyes into two narrow slits of warmth. A warmth that has always drawn people to him so they could bask in it, in that laughter that she thought, especially during recent years, was a bit too loud and coarse.

And that man whom she saw only several days ago by the cold light of the television suddenly looks not so tired, and not so gray, but just a little older. And she stands there, immobile and glittery, and doesn't know what to do with her hands. She realizes that she doesn't know a thing about these people with whom he spends his nights and days, and that she hasn't even heard most of their names, and certainly can't make the connection between their faces and their titles, and is confused by the fact that her prince is encompassed by an entire world that loves and appreciates him.

And is interested in him. And he's interested in them. And she discovers that she is unraveling a thread from the cheap evening purse that she bought to match the dress. And the fact that it is such a perfect match mortifies her.

The host of the evening calls everyone to sit down, and the prince searches for her with his eyes and with a big smile, he leads her to their table, and briefly introduces her to everyone. She nods and knows that she won't remember even one name, even if she tries, because she is making such an effort to nod charmingly and hold in her stomach that she can't breathe. To the sound of wild applause, the new CEO gets up onstage, and her prince yells something and everyone there laughs, and she remembers how he used to make her laugh once. She tries to imagine him standing there on the stage, and she knows that he could have been the one standing there, but he isn't pushy enough, he didn't fight hard enough, didn't really comprehend office politics, those that she understands without words. Perhaps had she helped him a bit more, he would have been promoted faster. And she remembers all those times that she tried to tell him something, and how he didn't listen, and it pains her.

When the food arrives, everyone around the table chats and argues, and talks about work matters, and gossips about the people sitting around the other tables. And she sits there, a polite princess smile frozen on her face, and doesn't say a word. She doesn't have anything to contribute or say. And then someone approaches her and says, "Pleased to meet you," and tells her that she's new on her husband's team and she's so happy to finally meet her. The princess is surprised by how young and pretty she is. And then the new girl asks the princess what she does. The princess says that she has little children and that she's at home with them.

The young woman says, "Sorry, I didn't know that you just recently gave birth. He didn't say a word."

And the princess mumbles that her youngest is already four years old but she still needs her.

And the new girl says that she's sure she does, and that it was fun meeting her, and moves along.

> I'm 33 years old, married with three kids. I have my weekly custom: Friday evening, after my children go to sleep, I allow myself to overeat a bit and read your column. Right now, I'm getting my driver's license. I'm having a hard time with the theory. I've flunked five theory exams. I'm desperate. I'm tired of studying. I can't open the theory book anymore. My husband helps me, my driving teacher sits with me, but then I go to the licensing office and feel as though my head is about to explode, get nervous, and flunk. I wanted to ask if you have a tip for me about how I should approach the entire matter.
>
> And here's something for you. A recipe for a wonderful chocolate cake. Four eggs, a cup of oil, a cup of sugar, a cup of flour, a teaspoon of baking powder, a cup of cocoa, half a carton of cream. Mix all the ingredients. You can use a large spoon; you don't have to use the mixer. Preheat the oven to 350°F and bake. For the chocolate frosting, you need half a carton of cream, three and a half ounces of dark (semisweet) chocolate. Heat in a pot until it melts and pour it on the cake while it's hot.
>
> Abigail

My man, who saw me being sucked into a maelstrom of grief and anger, spinning inside it without even attempting to break out, without believing that I could climb out, tried to save me from sinking even deeper. He stood there for me, and for our little family, like a steady rock of strength, which he drew from God knows where, and insisted that we try to move forward. That we continue with our lives, do things that couples and families do; he wanted to go on trips, go out, be happy. He wanted me to be happy. He insisted on trying to explain to me that there is a meaning to life. He tried to take me on vacations, just the two of us, so that we could preserve the wonderful thing that we once had, that was only ours, and belonged just to the two of us. Because during those lone moments in which he managed to take me away, and when we were alone, even for an hour, we loved each other so much. But there were only these lone moments, because I didn't want more. And I wouldn't let him.

I didn't want to enjoy myself. I couldn't understand how I could. Or why I should. Or what was the point of it all. I wanted to sacrifice, to give myself, all of myself, as if only by suffering I could help. I didn't want to think about myself. I didn't want to be happy. And I didn't want to go away. I wanted us to be by our daughter all the time, checking, supervising, because maybe a miracle would occur, and maybe I'd notice something. I was afraid that if I wasn't by her side for one minute, something awful would happen. Something that I'd regret later for the rest of my life. That would scar her. I wouldn't be there and someone wouldn't understand her. And she'd withdraw even more into herself. But in the meantime I withdrew into myself, into my sorrow, entrenched in my pain, unable to see a thing except my hurt.

In a pathetic attempt to reward my man, who tried to protect me and our family, and make me happy, I tried to spare him the knowledge of how miserable I was. How sad and hurt I was, and how I didn't know how to continue.

And neither of us was very successful. He knew how miserable I was, and I couldn't find a reason for joy.

■ ■ ■

The princess can't stop thinking about the party. She remembers the women there, their lightness, their smiles, their wild laughter, the confidence with which they walked, and the looks that they sent her prince. They looked at him as she no longer can. She knows too much about him. She knows the snorting sounds that he emits at night, his nose-blowing in the mornings, how he pulls in his stomach when he tries to look better, and the smell in the toilet after he leaves it. And he knows too much about her, as well. He sees the tampon wraps in the garbage, the razor that she uses to shave her armpits, the stretch marks on her stomach, her smell when she sweats. She remembers how that young woman looked at him, and that condescending and cheeky look comes back and bothers her and stabs her. But it's also her wake-up call. It makes her realize that she's not the only one who sees herself as some sort of discarded leftover. Others see her like that as well.

One evening, it's her turn to host the girls' night out, and they arrive, all her girlfriends, all of those who never stop, who keep constantly moving on in the race, working and growing. One is a psychologist, one is a doctor, and one is a teacher. Without even noticing, they scatter around stories of success, of achievements, of failures, of struggles, of an exciting life, of wild, unapologetic shopping sprees that they don't have to justify to anyone, of exhilarating trips abroad, and all the while they compliment her on her lovely palace, her tidy children, and her tasty dishes. Compliments that until recently were her adequate compensation, a source of pride and satisfaction, a sense of achievement and success, and suddenly seem to her like empty shells. This palace, which she licks clean, the children whom she nurtures, the dishes that she cooks – all these things that she puts her heart and soul into, that she dedicates all her time to – suddenly seem so unimportant.

Yes, okay, the house is clean, there's hot food, and the children are attended to, but they don't seem much happier than her friends' children. And not much more successful than them. She, who had no less potential than them, if not more, who was supposed to prance around the world wearing designer gowns, who was supposed to buy whatever she felt like buying, who was destined for greatness and success, is now receiving compliments on her clean house. On her cooking. And now, these compliments of theirs insult her. Anger her. She feels as though she doesn't deserve compliments. She hasn't achieved anything unique; she knows that each and every one of her friends could have a house like this, were they sitting at home all day and licking it clean. And she can no longer lie to herself. She can no longer say to herself that she's happy. That she's content. That she's doing the most important thing in the world.

> Can it be that we've really reached a stage in which everything is more important than myself? After ten years of marriage and two children, I can barely understand what I want. And even when I express the slightest interest in something a little bit unusual, it always scares me to try.
> Betty

On Saturday, I was at my parents' place. It was just another Saturday like so many other Saturdays, when I showed up in sweatpants and slippers so I could crash there. So I could tune out. It was my sanctuary and my shelter. A place where I could analyze for hours every sliver of progress, and remain silent when there were regressions. A place where my son was a king because my mother was completely overwhelmed by her love for him. A place where my wonderful father, who was connected to his granddaughter with all his soul, always had the strength to go out with her, lift her on his shoulders, encourage her, and gather the mess she left behind her, spilling, breaking, tearing to shreds the pages from the precious books organized on the shelf. The only place where I could go to sleep peacefully knowing that someone else would worry. The only place where I didn't have to hide, run after her and cover, explain, and apologize. The only place where I could cry.

That Saturday, I cried in my father's arms, and for the first time I dared ask him why.

Why did it have to happen to my baby girl?

And he was silent, and then he told me that there wasn't a better place in the world for her than with us, and that no one understood her like we did.

And then he said something that I'll never forget. He said that this is probably my role in life.

And I knew that he was right.

And he also said that I was a wonderful mother.

And that was the first time. Five and a half years after I became a mother. For five and a half years all I had done was take care of everyone, and worry, and give, and I wasn't interested in anything but my children; and for four years nothing had interested me but my daughter, and all I had felt was sorrow and anger. And now for the first time, I felt that I wasn't a failure. That maybe I was even doing okay. That I was a pretty good mother.

And it was the first time that I realized that I was crushed. That I was shattered.

If my life were a movie, I'd dismiss it on account of implausibility and excessive melodrama. The reason that I'm writing to you isn't completely clear to me. I've been thinking about taking up writing, because I want to write about what I'm going through, but I don't know how to begin. I'm intimidated by the blank page.

I'm 33 years old and I have two daughters. The oldest is four years old. She's an amazing and mature child who was diagnosed with a rare blood disease at the age of eight months. Her immune system attacks the blood cells and destroys them. She's treated with medication that suppresses the immune system, and therefore can't go to preschool and is at home, with me. Needless to say, I've left my job. We're at the hospital two to three times a week. Our entire life has been disrupted and instead of the calm mother I used to be, I've become a stressed and anxious one.

After many deliberations and consultations with doctors all over the world, we've decided on a bone marrow transplant donated from her sister – a difficult decision that the doctors placed on our shoulders. One month ago, a few weeks before the intended transplant, unbelievably, I was diagnosed with breast cancer. I had surgery and now I'm supposed to start chemotherapy and radiation treatments.

That's basically the whole story. What a world. Several weeks ago I couldn't stop complaining to my friends and husband how sick I am of spending all my time in the hospital, and now I'll probably spend twice as much time there. I was also bothered by the question of how I'd tell my daughter that her hair will fall out, and now I can give her a live demonstration. Currently, the transplant is on hold, because a person can't cope with so much all at once, and I'm just trying to remain sane and draw strength from God knows where.

I'd appreciate it if you could give me some advice about writing.

Yael

I was thinking about what the group facilitator asked us. About hobbies. And I remembered that once, I had dreams. Not just about children. Not just about my baby girl. Once, before everything came crashing down. Before nights turned into days. Before teachers filled the house and worked with her in her room and my man and I sat on the other side of the closed door, listening to her cry, torn apart by how difficult it is for her, and I curled up in the circle of my beloved man's embrace wanting to scream, and wanting only to wake up from this nightmare. And I remembered that before all of this, before this dizzying cycle of awful exhaustion and anger and heart-wrenching sorrow, I had dreams about myself. Dreams that I hadn't dared dream for a long time. That I was ashamed to dream. Because how could I even dare to want something for myself when I was supposed to think only about her? And I started realizing that if I didn't have dreams to escape to, I would fall apart.

16

Wherefore she went forth out of the place where she was...

(Ruth 1:7)

I decided to resume working on my book. And I tried to find the time to write. Like tiny shards of a smashed crystal goblet, I gathered my time, assembling piece after piece. Another sentence, another paragraph, erasing one sentence, struggling with myself, between my desire to sleep and my desire to write, trying to make up for my sleep deprivation, while briefly napping in the waiting rooms in the occupational and speech therapists' clinics, collapsing, stealing half an hour here and fifteen minutes there, and I felt like an escaped criminal. I felt as though these moments during which I sat at the computer, conversing with the characters from the book, living their lives and not mine, were an escape. An escape to a tiny, secluded island, where there is a different set of rules, where there isn't constant pain and there isn't any sorrow. Because there, in front of the computer, in the laundry room, with the monotonous sound of the washing machine cutting me off from the confusion and noise all around, I could tune out a bit. But the island was small and I barely found the time to escape to it.

After more than a year of collecting the minutes and seconds, I completed what I had once begun before my world fell apart, and I held in my hand something that looked like a book. I sent it out to a publishing house. After a month, I called them and they still hadn't read it. Two weeks later, I called again, and they still hadn't read it. Four months passed and they still didn't give me an answer. For months I checked my messages every few hours, crossed my fingers, jumped every time the phone rang, and then, I finally received an answer from the publishing house to which I had sent my book.

They said that they weren't interested. Thanks, but no thanks.

And something happened to me that hadn't happened in a long time. My heart started beating again. My veins swelled. Because I believed in it, in this book, and I wasn't prepared to give up, and I wasn't prepared to listen, and suddenly I had ambition and I remembered this feeling. This feeling that there's something I can win at. Something achievable. After so long, I felt something similar to the feeling of life. And I yelled that they're idiots, that they don't understand, that they're making a mistake. Finally, my story had a bad guy. I had someone to be mad at. I had an enemy. I had someone I had to defeat in battle and there was a chance that I'd win.

> I wanted to share something and say that during these last months, since the birth of my second son, I have finally started believing that I am allowed to enjoy, and not only to sacrifice for my home, husband, and wonderful (and demanding) children. I have just returned to myself, to moments that are just for me, even though they are supposedly "at the expense of" my loved ones. I have to mention that my husband constantly urged me to have fun and take some time for myself.

```
He claimed that it would be better for everyone
involved. I didn't believe him. He was right.
    I hate being wrong.
    But this time it's a pleasure.
    P.S. My mother, a chronic sacrificer, finally
divorced my father this year, and she's at the
height of her glory and joy of life. This divorce
proved to me that every person or subjugated
people will eventually revolt. No doubt about it.
    Shelly
```

When the princess tidies her house, after her friends leave, she knows that she wants to do something. To be someone besides the one taking care of everyone all the time. She never thought that she'd be a full-time wife and mother. That's not why she studied. She's capable of much more. She wants to be something. She feels that if she goes out to work, she'll find her place again. At home as well. A place of respect. Of appreciation. And she wants that appreciation from the people surrounding her. Most of all, she wants it from him. From the prince. She wants him to look at her like he looked at those women at the party. The women who work with him. And she also wants to earn money. Because these conversation that they have, she and the prince, every few months, about her expenses, always leave her somewhat embarrassed, and sometimes even humiliated.

One evening, the princess notifies the prince that she wants to go back to work. The prince turns off the television and looks at her, surprised. "But it's so hard for you to manage everything and you're so tired."

And he's worried. As it is, she's so exhausted all the time, tense and nervous. She's liable to have a nervous breakdown if the heir spills some ketchup down his shirt or the heiress is five minutes late for her ballet class. How can she even think of adding work to all this? He imagines an entire new world of complaints about to crash down on him, and now she'll probably want him to help out even more at home and he was barely coping with all the stress at work, with all the dismissal letters flying around, beheading various employees. And he feels as though he can't breathe.

"Yes," she says, "but the children have grown up and I have time in the mornings."

And she also says that the money she'd earn would help them.

I wanted to tell you that there's a different kind of poverty. A quiet poverty that doesn't come across well on television. You'd see a person suffering from this kind of poverty in a soup kitchen only as a volunteer. This kind of poor person wears jeans bought in second-hand shops, and smiles, and wears her teenage daughter's outgrown sneakers, and smiles. And goes out to work and returns to a tiny rented house (500 square feet of father, mother, and two teenage daughters) in a green setting that raises new generations of salt of the earth.

This is a poverty that starts because the industrious, hard-working parents really didn't receive any help, and thanks only to waitressing, cleaning, and babysitting, managed to graduate. And back then, the smile was genuine, with a mouth full of teeth and dimples full of hope. This is a type of poor person who has been working every single day, from the age of 14, and finds time for volunteering. And has never asked for a favor, or a donation, or help, and who is now collapsing.

Fifteen years of love and marriage have passed by, during which anniversaries weren't celebrated; and so many debts have been paid off, yet we don't have a house of our own. And it seems as though we'll never have one. And it's true that we celebrate the shedding of a leaf in the fall, and the first rain, and we smile and love.

So that's how it is: a father, mother, two girls, and a cat, and with the approaching New Year holiday at the end of the week, I'm afraid that I won't have it in me to give the little extra push that will help them study without any concerns, that will enable them to learn how to dance or play a musical instrument, my two wonderful and talented teenage daughters. And I'm so scared that a day will come when I won't be able to work and won't be able to pay the rent.

I didn't think that this was how things would work out. And maybe the good Lord did forget me, or maybe He's just very busy because there are the ill and the orphaned and there are always people worse off. I thought that at the age when the dimples become wrinkles, life would be more peaceful and secure. Yet, I'm starting the New Year and I'm scared to death.

Ruthy

The prince feels as though she's twisting a knife in his belly. They've tried not to talk about it until now, not to say it. And now it's here, out on the table between them, the fact that he, who had promised her a palace and a fairy tale, who promised her the life of a princess, and happily ever after, hasn't kept his promise. He failed to pave her life with indulgences; he failed to provide her with a life of real luxury, not to mention living without a care, just like they once dreamed, like she once dreamed and like she deserved. And he feels pathetic. And it burns his heart, that sentence of hers, that the money she'll earn will help them.

He wants to shout that she doesn't know how hard it is out there, and how hard he tries, and he deserves a kind word for nevertheless succeeding. Because, after all, he provides for them adequately, even if he isn't a hotshot provider like her girlfriends' husbands or a bunch of the guys he grew up with. He drives to work every morning in his little white company car, and looks up at those women in the huge, shiny jeeps stuck in traffic with him. And this sour sense of failure – that he's not good enough, not man enough – chokes him and he says that if it's for the money, then she doesn't have to. He'll probably get another promotion soon.

And she says that she wants to.

"And it won't be too difficult for you?" he asks.

"So…it will be a bit difficult," she says.

"Okay," he says. "It's your decision."

And there's a silence. She waits for him to say that he'll help. He doesn't say it. And she understands. She understands that not only has he left her the decision, he's also left her the responsibility. Just as they promised each other that they wouldn't. Once upon a time, when they decided about things together, when they had a shared goal. Now they are two people standing on different sides of the barricade, each of them trying to shove the border just a few more inches into the other's territory, to gain a little more maneuvering space for himself or herself, to shed the responsibility, get some relief. And it angers her. She wants to remind him that she isn't doing this only for herself. But she doesn't.

And he tells her to do it if this is what she wants.

And this is how the priority of her work is defined in their lives.

The princess doesn't go out to work because she has to. They can live without the money she'll earn. Frugally, as they've lived up until now. She's going to work for herself. Because she wants to. It's her decision. For herself. She hadn't realized that these words – that she doesn't have to, she *wants* to – would place her work second in its importance. Or maybe third, after his work and the children.

17

And [she] said, If it please the king...

(Esther 8:5)

My girlfriend invited us to her son's birthday. "It'll be fun," she said. "We've invited all the children from the preschool, and some friends of mine you've already met." I hated these events. Events with children and a lot of people I didn't know. But I didn't want to bail out because I wanted to do the right thing. For my girlfriend, to whom it was important; for my son, who would probably have fun; and for my daughter, who also loved these events. Or at least, that's what I told myself. And I went. I cursed myself the minute I walked into the room. I tried to ignore the stares the other mothers gave my daughter, the misunderstandings, the whispers – and the brave ones, those who asked interested questions, who forced me to explain, smile, play it down. I also tried to ignore the other children, their sweetness, the ease with which they conducted themselves, asking for potato chips, cooperating, playing with the surprises and knowing well enough not to eat clay.

"She's eating the clay!" one of the mothers shouted and swooped down on her, on my daughter, with two others, trying to extract the tiny morsel out of her mouth. "Leave her alone!" I shouted. "Don't touch her!" An uncomfortable silence descended. I didn't tell them what other strange things she eats.

I apologized to my friend, and asked her to let me off the hook in the future. And from then on I avoided going to these events. Joint afternoons with other children weren't good for me. Neither were the apologies for the mess my daughter left after her. I think both sides were relieved.

Slowly, most of my friends had become mothers. Each of them was immersed in her own world and in her diapers, and the relationships dissolved. With this particular friend, and with several others that I can count on one hand, I kept in touch, but only in the evenings. Even though we were few, it still required endless exhausting coordination. This one doesn't have a babysitter. This one's son is sick. This one has to go with her husband to some event. And this one has a ton of work.

Usually, we'd meet at one of our houses, and once in a long while, on festive occasions, we managed to find a stolen evening, dress up in our best clothes, and go out to a bar to have a drink. Four women who were destined for greatness in their youth; four women who could move mountains if they just wanted to: four mothers. And we'd sit and talk. This one talked about problems at work, this one about confrontations with the boss, this one about childrearing problems, all of us about problems with teachers and nannies, and about the husband who didn't understand, or wasn't sensitive enough, or romantic enough. This is what we met for. This was what we needed. To share with each other the tiny details that no one else had the energy or strength to follow, or to examine; to go on and on about the little encumbrances that bothered and worried us, and in exchange give each other a shoulder to lean on. We met in order to get a load off our chests. So that someone would listen to the difficulties and problems, listen to that awful thing that happened to us, or what our mother told us, and how dare she, and to confirm that even though we're miserable, we're surviving, and coping, and we're so brave.

And I knew that they got together with other mothers in the afternoons, with their children. Because that's what other mothers of little children are supposed to do.

> Maybe I'm laughing from fear, because of something that just happened at our place. I told my husband that I want to invite my oldest son's friends because he seems a bit lonely. This, of course, involves entertaining children who are part of Attila the Hun's group, which means parting with several precious articles in the house. But I'll do anything to get a smile on the lips of my sweet boy. My husband stared at me with disbelief and asked, "Where are you getting this from? Can't you see that the boy is happy and content? What party? What do you mean, 'lonely'?!"
>
> "I don't know," I stammered, and searched for an answer for myself.
>
> Now I understand why I don't earn more. Because instead of investing all my hours in paid work, I spend them, with so much love, joy, and cheerfulness, clucking around my children's desires. Oh, now I get it. Thanks for the enlightenment, Buddha.
>
> Talia

The princess starts looking for work. She sits down and goes over the ads in the newspaper and on the Internet. Among all the ads and job offers, she crosses out the fields of industry and manufacture, engineering and technology, security and cleaning.

She's looking for something in the humanities. That's what she loves and that's what she studied. She examines the small print that appears under education, instruction and caretakers; marketing and sales; fashion, textile and beauty.

Energetic and responsible person needed to market cakes: base + percentage + car. Full-time job. She's energetic, she's the champion of cakes, but a full-time job is out of the question. And it also doesn't have the same area code as the palace.

A garage needs an experienced secretary, computer-oriented, with a desire to succeed. Full-time job. She isn't really all that good with computers. She has the desire to succeed, but how successful can she be as a garage secretary? And it doesn't really open any options for the future.

And experience. Everyone wants experience and she isn't experienced. Import company needs field agent. Experience mandatory. Full-time job. Fashion chain needs district manager. Experience in leading fashion chains, fax CV. Well, she does have the desire. Secretary/student for law firm, afternoons, Word proficient. Full-time. Full-time for afternoons? That means all night. No wonder they're looking for a student.

Agent, sales-oriented, credibility, highly industrious, independent, must own a car, 30+. That looks pretty good. She writes down the phone number and thinks of all the things she once dreamed of doing. She dreamed of becoming an art teacher. She even has a degree, but she doesn't have a teaching diploma. She dreamed of running her own business, but for that one needs a financial investment, and it's too scary, and who would invest in her anyway? She doesn't dare think of asking the bank for a loan. A loan for what purpose? What would she say? She has no idea what she knows how to do. Design. She has great taste. She could have been great at interior decorating, but she'd have to study for that. Besides, she's already studied; she won't go now and study for four years, and then work another two or three years in an architect's office from morning till night. That's for young women. And she's not at an age for new beginnings. She's a thirty-three-year-old princess, and she has a useless degree that's gathering dust somewhere and doesn't interest anyone. And she has no experience. And nobody wrote in their ad that they're looking for a princess. No one needs princesses nowadays.

My name is Tamara. We corresponded once on the subject of work. I asked for advice and you gave me emotional support. It was good. And lo and behold - once again I've returned to the circle of job-seekers. I accept it being a long and draining procedure, but what makes it really difficult is the procedure itself.

A company advertises an open position through a manpower service. Tamara makes the effort of sending her resume and a relevant letter. The HR manager makes contact and conducts a phone interview, during which she questions me about my positive and negative traits and summons me to the evaluation center. The big day arrives. Tamara wears her best clothes, pays her hard-earned money to the nearest parking lot attendant, and enlists her most upbeat energies for this wonderful day.

Now the big moment arrives: group dynamics. A group of adults with employment experience constructing paper airplanes, preparing presentations, and conducting negotiations over

the paper planes. It isn't enough that I have to
market and represent myself every time anew. When
will they understand that adults, not children,
are standing behind these resumes?

Hey, if you hear about a job opening in
marketing/public relations, etc., I'll be more
than happy to show you how I build paper planes.

Tamara

There was only one thing that inspired me more than writing and
made me happy. One big ray of sunshine that during all those
darkest, gloomy moments illuminated my soul. My oldest child.
My sweet boy with his big blue eyes, and his thumb in his mouth,
who from the age of two and a half accepted the fact that his sister
could tear up any one of his drawings, break any one of his toys,
and wake him up at night. Who knew that he had to be considerate
toward her, that we had to watch out so that she wouldn't get lost,
who knew that the entire world revolved around his sister, who
doesn't speak and doesn't answer. He lived with all these people
walking around his house, and he never complained. And he was
never mad at her. He never hit her, pushed her, or yelled at her. He
was the best little boy in the world. Only in the morning, when
he had to go to preschool, he would cry terribly. Cry and ask why
he had to go to school, why he couldn't be like his sister. And stay
at home.

18

Who can find a virtuous woman?

(Proverbs 31:10)

The princess, who runs from one job interview to another, starts realizing that it won't be easy finding a job in which she can pick up the heirs from preschool at one o'clock. She, who up until now was part of a small group of mothers who reported every day at midday to pick up their children, the proud group, the wonderful group that doesn't joyfully throw their children into the preschool for eight hours, knows that she'll have to give up her exclusive membership in this lovely association: the Association of Dedicated Mothers. Those mothers, who arrive first and converse briefly with the teacher, and then leave the preschool while glancing pityingly at the children who have to stay until four o'clock; those mothers who prepare a nutritious lunch every day, sit down with their children and patiently listen to what happened to them, involved in their lives and in the community.

And she is a woman who up to the present moment has believed in what she is doing, in the fact that she's giving everything she has to her children, that her sacrifice is the highest level of love and motherly dedication. Now she discovers that in order to go out to work, she'll have to shove aside everything that she has considered holy until now. She'll have to switch sides and become part of the group of mothers whom she didn't understand until now: the group scorned by herself and her friends in their exclusive and amazing group. Because she'll either have to leave them at the preschool for several more hours or find a nanny. And not for her dream job. Not so she can become a brain surgeon, or a tower-constructing architect, or a high-income manager in a high-tech company. She'll be doing it for a pretty dreary job, in a pretty dreary office, that maybe, one day, in several years' time, will lead her to something that comes close to being interesting. And she decides to leave the heirs in the preschool, and swears that she'll do her job quickly and efficiently, and pick them up way before four o'clock. That way, they'll only have to stay another hour, two hours max. It won't be so bad.

> I have a daughter in preschool and a son in first grade. Three times a week he finishes school at 1:40 and she finishes at 1:20. Paying for two after-school activity day care centers eats up my entire salary to the last penny. This is a problem that can be resolved when a mother works part-time. Then, she can help with homework, and experience preschool and school with her children. Unfortunately, it's very hard to find part-time jobs. I can't look for a job that exceeds the 8:00-1:00 hours, and it also has to be close to home, otherwise the nanny will earn more than I do during the extra hours that I've added to the job.
> Adina

I knew that I wouldn't succeed if writing continued being a hobby. I realized that if I really wanted my story to become a real book,

I'd have to give it everything I had – really submerge myself in it, with all my soul, with all my heart. And I didn't have time, and I wasn't even sure if I had any place left in my soul.

I was an angry and bitter woman, sad and desperate, who had become addicted to struggling against demons and dragons on a twenty-four-hour basis. To make time for writing, I had to search my soul and find the resolve to change the priorities of the entire household, of the entire family, and I was scared. Would my family have to pay a high price for no more than a hopeless and desperate attempt at trying to make a crazy dream come true? I was afraid of what would happen to my little girl if I wasn't there to give her my heart and soul, what would happen to my oldest child, what would happen to this family, for whose survival and function my man struggled with all his might. This was a war in which I dug the trenches and manned the line, but I didn't give it even one moment of hope or contentment. I dragged all of us down with it, and forced everyone to be sad and hurt. And I knew that for several hours a day, I'd have to pull myself out of it, out of there. And for the first time in a long time, I realized that if I didn't have a dream, if I didn't have something of my own, I'd destroy what we *did* have. And I decided that I wasn't giving up, that I was fighting for my book.

After two years during which my little girl was home-schooled, and I insisted on supervising her every second, every minute – during which I heard every peep she made and was proud of my dedication – I dared suggest the idea that we send her to a preschool for children like herself for half a day. I told myself that it was for her own good, and that she'd get what she needed there, and that they're experienced and know what they're doing. And my man also said that he thought the time had come, and that it was the right thing to do. And I didn't know if I should believe him – or myself. I didn't know if he was saying that because he thought I couldn't handle it anymore. And after all, maybe that's what I was saying myself. And I felt as though I was sending her to preschool just so I'd have several hours in the morning – that I was sending her there just because I was weak, because I dared think of myself – and I was ashamed.

She started going to preschool. At night I was awake with her, in the morning I worked, and at noon I was with her again; in the afternoon I ran around with both of them from one after-school activity to the other, enrichment activities, occupational clinics, speech therapy clinics, the doctor, and errands, and I was exhausted and bleary-eyed, but I didn't allow myself to miss one minute with her. And even though I hired a nanny to come and help me out, I still couldn't manage. And I felt spoiled for not managing. For not being able to go out alone with both of them without something happening. Because all it took was for me to turn my head and let go of my little girl's hand and she'd immediately get lost. In the shopping center, in the mall, in the supermarket, everywhere, she could just disappear. And there was no point in calling out for her, because she didn't respond. It happened to me again and again. When I took out my purse just for a second to pay for ice cream, or when my son asked me to unwrap something for him, that was it. And if there was a road, then I'd immediately run to check that there wasn't a little girl who had been hit by a car. And my oldest, only a little boy himself, was already experienced and knew how to warn me, "Mommy, she's going," and knew how to run after her, and hold her, and help me search for her. Search without yelling her name. Quietly we'd search.

These moments when she was lost and my heart would beat erratically scarred me with the notion that I wasn't good enough or responsible enough. And then there were the stares of those people, who stood around a sweet, smiling four-year-old child, trying to ask her name, and asking her where her mommy was, and when I came, they looked at me as if I was a failure. A mother who loses her child. And I felt like a failure, even though holding her was like holding quicksilver. My son was already five and a half years old, and whenever he was with me, she was there too, and she was the center of attention, and the only places we could go to were places where we could take her as well, where there weren't many people, and there weren't any roads, and she couldn't get lost. And that's how we'd wander around in the afternoons, together. A mother, two children, and a nanny. Because the mother couldn't handle both of them alone. A mother who doesn't work, and doesn't earn, and employs a nanny. And still can't cope.

■ ■ ■

The princess finds a job. Part-time as a secretary in a real-estate agency. She takes the job because she knows that she'll be able to make progress from there. She has a tidy plan. She'll work there for several months, learn the business, because she's a fast learner, and then take a course, and become a realtor herself. All she needs is to sell one apartment a month. What's the problem to sell one apartment a month, with her outgoing, personal charm? Who can resist her? And that will be enough to change everything. Maybe she'll even open her own agency. They'll go on vacations, go out to restaurants and order without looking at the prices on the menu, and one day, perhaps they'll even replace the derelict palace and move to a larger apartment. Which she'll find at a steal. Within a year or two, she believes, she'll already strike out on her own. And she starts working.

On her first day she wakes up way before the alarm clock and gets dressed, having prepared her clothes the day before. She brings her children to preschool, the teacher compliments her on her appearance, everyone wishes her luck, and then she goes over to kiss the heiress, and reminds her that she's staying today at the afternoon day care center, just to eat lunch with all the children, and then Mommy will come to take her home. The heiress bursts into heart-wrenching tears. "No!" she screams, "I want to do what we always do, I want you, I don't want the yucky food here, I want to go home. I want to go home now!" And the princess strokes the heiress, and promises her that everything will be just fine, and that the food is delicious. And the heiress says that she was the one who said that the food is disgusting, and the princess promises her that she'll come as fast as she can, and she looks at the clock and knows that if she doesn't leave now she'll be late, and the preschool teacher sees her glancing at the clock and tells her, "Go, it'll be fine, in a minute she'll forget all about it." And she walks backwards, trying not to turn her back on the heiress, blowing her kisses while the preschool teacher holds her with all her might so she won't run after her, and the heiress cries like she's never cried before because the princess has always stayed with her until she agreed to let Mommy go and shouts after her, "Mommy, Mommy!"

The princess, who had applied her makeup so beautifully, looks in the little mirror in the car and sees how her tears have smudged all her efforts. She repairs some of the damage and goes to the office for her very first day, and her main occupation all day is to ignore the lump in her throat and make an effort not to glance at the clock every minute. But she does look at it every minute, and time stands still. Half an hour, and another hour, and she feels that the pain of the abandoned heiress is racking her entire body. She curses herself for causing her such pain – who knows what scars this day inflicted upon her – and she barely hears what everyone is telling her, what they're trying to teach her. And the minute the clock strikes one, she smiles at her boss, hitches her bag on her shoulder, and says thank you. And he also looks at his watch, and she smiles apologetically, aware that she's making a mistake, and that she should stay until he tells her to go. But her heart is in shreds of agony because of the heiress's misery – she's probably been crying for hours – and she says that she'll see him tomorrow and leaves the office. And she runs to the car.

> When I was a child, I was once walking with my neighbor down the street. On the way, she approached a woman I knew who ran an appliance repair shop on the street where I grew up. I have no idea what the neighbor said to her, but I'll never forget what that woman answered my neighbor. "She's a street child." Yes, that's what she said about me, because I'd wander around with a key hanging around my neck because my mother was at work. But I think that this is the reality that shaped my life and I'm grateful for every minute of it. Because this sentence generated a lot of thought in my adult life, as well as my enormous capacity to give.
>
> Libby

I began realizing that I'd been so concerned about my little girl that I hadn't spent time with the others. I hadn't sat quietly with

my stepson, just me and him, for such a long time, and once we
used to do this a lot, and we were so close, and I knew that I
didn't want to lose this relationship, and that I had to carve out
a place for it. And it hurt me that I hadn't seen it before, that I
hadn't understood it before, and I was angry with myself. And I
realized that I didn't spend time alone with my son at all, and that
I should spend more time with him, just me and him. He needed
me, my oldest child, who was really so young. And he needed not
to always be around his sister, and not to be with me only when I
was concentrating on her. He needed time during which he didn't
have to be considerate and helpful and shoved aside. I was angry
with myself because he was such a good boy, so accommodating.
And I was tormented. I decided that twice a week I'd spend time
with him only. And twice a week, when I was with him, I sent the
nanny to the pool with my little girl.

My little girl had always loved water. I hate pools, yet my little
girl loved them. During the first years, the pool was a place where
I could be with her, hug her, touch her, and feel that we were
together. And I taught her how to swim. At the age of two and a
half, she already knew how to swim. That's why, when I realized
that my oldest needed some time alone with me, I decided that
the best thing to do was to send my little girl to the pool with
the nanny. She couldn't get lost there either. After several months
of this arrangement, one day I brought her to the pool myself.
Suddenly, I felt the stares. The life guard, the swimming teacher,
the other mothers, even the guy from the refreshment stand all
stared at me. I felt their glances like knives in my back. *Here's that
mother*, the knives twisted, *who sends her daughter only with the
nanny, who doesn't really care about her child.* And I wanted to yell
at them that they don't see me during the other days – and there

were so many other days – when I was only with her, when I took her wherever she felt like going, and turned off my cell phone, and sang all the words to her children's songs at the top of my lungs, clapping hands with her enthusiastically.

I'm an amazing mother, I wanted to tell all those stares. *I just can't stand swimming pools; I can't stand walking around in a bathing suit, even if my little girl really loves to, and I did it for so long, and the fact that I stopped doing it doesn't mean that I'm a neglectful mother. And anyway, my son needs me. Needs me a bit for himself.* And their stares hurt me, so I decided to come more frequently with my child to the pool. So that everyone would know how dedicated I am. How wonderful. I reported at the pool a week later. And I sat outside the pool for an hour, looking at her. And I felt like an idiot. I felt as though I had wasted an hour on something superfluous. An hour during which I could have spent time with my son, who needed me so much. And instead, I made an appearance. And I sat there and got mad at them. For making me play this game. This stupid game that we had going between us. Between one mother and another. An international competition of sacrifice and investment. A competition in which the dedicated mothers stood on one side, and the working mothers who juggled between work and family stood on the other side.

And this competition sizzled and raged, and the dedicated mothers were condescending toward the working mothers, who in turn, were condescending toward the dedicated mothers for choosing to raise children and not to work, and said that they spent their entire day in cafes. It was a struggle of justification, because each side justified itself by condescending to the other side, who had chosen differently. It was a war that left the women on both sides with the feeling that they're not good enough.

A war in which everyone was left bruised and bleeding and feeling like a failure. Feeling as though they'd sacrificed. And I didn't understand how I hadn't seen that those women I once thought were my friends, my partners – my support group – were actually a judging team. They supported only those who had chosen as they did, but judged and criticized all the others and thought they were better than them. And I was angry that I even cared about this game of appearances, the stupid, dizzying game of *what will everyone say*, only so other mothers, neighbors, grandmothers, teachers, counselors, and random women won't think that I'm a bad mother.

And no one, not for a minute, would have thought that my husband was a bad father because he didn't sit at the pool twice a week and waste an hour watching his daughter swim. And I kept silent. I choked, but I kept silent.

> Why is it that we, the women, are the ones who always have to go to seminars? Why are we the ones who complain? Why do I have a feeling that men don't understand us? Why is everything so simple and clear for men? Grrr!
>
> Batya

19

As cold waters to a thirsty soul...
(Proverbs 25:25)

The princess arrives to pick up the heiress from preschool and finds her napping on one of the small, thin mattresses in a row with all the other children of the working mothers. The row that she was so proud that her children weren't part of. The princess asks the teacher, fearfully, how the heiress held up, and the teacher tells her that she stopped crying several minutes after she left and that she was really fine. Like always. The princess doesn't know whether she should be glad or sad, and says that she was so worried, and the teacher says that she doesn't understand why she was worried. And the princess takes the heiress and goes to pick up the heir from kindergarten.

After a while, the heirs grow used to eating lunch at school, and gradually, the princess starts learning the work and befriending the realtors. Everyone appreciates her and counts on her and consults with her, and sometimes they even call during the afternoon to ask something, and she always answers gladly, and she goes out of her way and manages to get through the summer in one piece, paying her entire salary to summer camps, and in addition has to ask for help with the heirs from the queen and her mother, even though she hates asking for help – not only from them, but in general – but she swallows her pride. And the moment comes when summer ends, and the heir starts first grade. And when she sees him with his large schoolbag, she can't help but cry. The prince is also very excited.

And she knows that the time has come.

The princess asks for a meeting with the office manager, and tells him that she wants to start a course and earn a certificate and start working as a realtor. He tells her that he thinks she'll be great and asks her not to leave the office. "We can't manage without you," he says, and she's so proud. She says that it never even crossed her mind to leave, that it's only twice a week. She'll manage. She leaves the meeting, and she's so happy, and she tells all the other realtors that she's starting the course, and she's surprised that not everyone is as happy for her, and one of them even says that it's not for her. That she's too nice for the job. She's slightly insulted, and then she realizes that he fears for his job. That he's afraid she'll take his job away from him. He's afraid of her. And she'll no longer receive all the support that she has received until now as the beloved secretary. Now, she's a competitor. She's in the race. It scares her but she knows that she's good, and that she can do it, and apparently, so do they, otherwise they wouldn't be afraid. And twice a week she leaves the children in school until four o'clock and participates in the course.

■ ■ ■

I continued writing during every spare minute, and I went to another publishing house.

But this time, I prepared myself differently. I lowered my expectations. I tried not to even hope that they'd like it, even though deep inside I dreamed that they'd faint, and I told them that I was ready to hear everything, every comment, to write and rewrite, but I just didn't want to hear no. I asked them to please notice that there was something there. To try to see, in the forest of words, that there was a good story there. And they did notice. They said that it wasn't bad, that it was actually pretty good, but that it needed work – a lot of work. And as painful as that was, the feeling was different. It was different because I knew that this wasn't an abstract dream, but something that could really happen, because someone believed in me, and someone was with me, guiding me, and I started feeling as if it could really happen. My dream could come true one day. And this publishing house signed a contract with me. I received an advance payment. I made money after years that I hadn't. I was on the right track. It wasn't just a dream after all. I was right – I wasn't just amusing myself – there was a good reason for which I had painstakingly collected all these fragmented hours, for which I had fought and worked so hard. And for the next six months, I continued writing.

> Lately, I have a growing suspicion that I've been cheated all the way. Cheated by how I've been educated, by how I've been led to believe all those theories that you've described. I'm not like that. It's not nice to push. I should wait until someone sees how talented I am. I should be gentle, kind, modest. You described everything so beautifully and with such accuracy and pain. The truth is that I was slightly surprised because you look too young to have grown up in the same atmosphere in which I was raised. Anyway, you look very young. I hope the younger generation

```
has more brains, and that the young women are
different from my generation.
    Aviva
```

One day, as the princess is driving back from the course, she gets stuck in a traffic jam. She looks at her watch and knows that there's no chance that she'll arrive in time to pick up the children. And she's angry with herself for staying that extra minute. She shouldn't have. But she thought it was important just for once to stay back with the other students in the course, who always go together to drink coffee, chat, and compare agencies. She knows it's important to make contacts, and not always grab her bag and rush out of the classroom, because as it is, she's something of an eccentric, slightly older than everyone, always in a bit more of a rush than everyone else, and she knows that it's important that she sometimes stay a bit longer and make friends. But now she's alone in the car, stuck in this infuriating traffic jam that won't budge an inch, and time isn't standing still.

3:52. No chance that she'll make it. And she can already imagine her heirs waiting for her with big eyes overflowing with sadness – children whose mother didn't come to pick them up. The only ones whose mother forgot them.

3:57. *She doesn't love me*, they're probably telling themselves, *she doesn't care about me, I'm not important to her*, and guilt racks her, etching scars in her heart, which are now also carved in the little souls of her young heirs, scratched and bruised for all eternity, teeming with fear of abandonment, irreversibly scarred. And she phones another mother, asking her to take her little girl. She's already left but she'll go back for her if that's what she wants. "No, no big deal," she says. And she calls another mother, who says that she's already in the park and that they should join them later on.

3:59. Now she'll get those glares, from the heiress's assistant teacher, and the woman in charge of the after-school activity club in the heir's school. Those glares that say, wordlessly, what they think about mothers like herself. Confused mothers, who forget life's priorities, that children come before careers, and she feels so selfish and wants to say that she's trying, that she's well aware of priorities, but sometimes things go wrong, sometimes things happen, and not because she doesn't care, but because of the fucking traffic jam, and she feels as though she's about to faint.

4:00. She calls the woman in charge of the after-school activity club. "I'll be there in a couple of minutes." And a call beeps in from the heiress's preschool. "I'm on my way." And one more traffic light.

4:03. She wants to scream and cry, and she remembers that look she got at work when she went out to her course, and the looks that she got at the course when she left while everyone was still standing around chatting, the young women and men, who can come home in the evening, which she can no longer afford to do, and she thinks how much more of an effort she'll have to invest in order to work. She knows that there are people who have time to see apartments only during the evenings, and there are those who will want to view an apartment at five o' clock in the afternoon, and she doesn't know how she'll manage, because her children are still small, and as it is, real estate agents fight over every deal, and if she doesn't give everything she has then she won't make it, and maybe he was right, maybe she doesn't have what it takes. Because she sees them, those other realtors, most of them men. They're always available and can always meet everyone's requests. They aren't time limited; they answer their phones like junkies. There's this one woman realtor who's just like them, who works around the clock. But she knows that she isn't like her, that she knows her priorities, that the heirs' young souls are more important, and she realizes that as much as she tries during the day to be as efficient as possible, and just as wonderful, and to achieve as much as she can in minimum time, she'll never be able to keep up with them. With those people who give everything they've got. Because occasionally, she's going to get a phone call notifying her that her son isn't feeling well, and she'll have to go pick him up, and she'll let someone else take care of the client, and it won't be her sale. And she presses on the horn, knowing that it's futile, that it won't help move the traffic jam, and if only she could stop time, stop the clock. Stop it. Freeze it.

4:04. So it will just stand still for a moment and let her catch up. But the clock doesn't stop. And no one stops, and she starts realizing that no one even sees it. No one knows how hard she's trying. And now her heir is crying. And everyone can see how she's screwing up. And she feels dizzy. She feels as though she's on a merry-go-round ride and she can't get off in the middle, and it's stirring everything within her and causing her a bitter, oppressive nausea of failure. And she feels so alone. She feels as though her shoulders are too narrow to carry this burden, to carry this responsibility all by herself, and she knows that no one is truly aware of what she's doing, of what she's going through, and the price she's paying for trying to do everything. And she remembers that lovely evening, at their wedding, when she spun around with her white ball gown, with her hair that had been tended to for hours, and her makeup, floating on clouds, expecting happily ever after, and how she felt as though she were a real princess.

And she furiously presses the horn again and thinks how easy it is for the prince. How much quiet he has when he goes to work; he just goes. And how easy it is for him to work. He doesn't have to worry who'll take the kids, who'll pick them up, what they need, what they ate, why they cried, what has to be bought, and more than anything, he doesn't ask himself if it's okay that he went. Because the prince will always have her, and she's the one taking care of the children. They're her responsibility. And she can't understand how this has happened to her, to them. How did they turn into one of those couples that they swore not to turn into? Those couples where the woman takes care of the children, and the husband goes to work. And she knows that if she continues working, it won't be the last time she's late to pick them up.

4:05. And she can't breathe.

> I'm married and a mother to a first-grader and a two-year-old, and I work full-time as a manager in a company. I cope, like everyone else, with the imbalance of being a working mother. Every night, I go to bed and pray that tomorrow, everything will be different, and I'll succeed in what I want. I want to get up at 6:00 when the alarm clock rings, and not stay in bed because I'm too tired to move. I want to be patient in the morning without nagging, "Come on, already, wash your face, eat, we have to go." I want to pick up my youngest from preschool (which doesn't always happen) and get home by 5:00 at the latest. I want to take them to a playground once a week, to friends once a week, to have friends over once a week, and once a week just to sit with them at home and play (without the television blaring in

the background, and the laundry, and the dishes).
I want to prepare a healthy dinner (not frozen
pizza or microwave meals). To stop giving them
too many snacks and candies. I want to come home
and bake fancy cookies and bring them to the
office. I want to sit a bit more with my oldest
on his homework, take him to his after-school
activities and not only bring him back from them.
I want to exercise twice a week and not only run
up and down the office stairs. I want to get up
early on Saturday, drink coffee, travel, and not
only think when I'll find the time to sleep. I want
to sit with my husband in the evening, cuddle
with him, talk, and not fall asleep on the sofa
exhausted. I want to go on a weekend retreat,
without the children, recharge my batteries
and energies. I want a little more money in my
bank account; it would help me breathe easier. I
want to get together with Sharon, and Reva, and
Hadar, whom I haven't seen in a long time. I want
quality time with my father and my mother. I want
to smile at the children, and not get upset at
what they're doing, because all in all, they're
lovely, and I'm the one who's exhausted, angry,
impatient, and waiting for them to go to sleep so
I'll have some peace and quiet for myself. But
my youngest won't fall asleep if I'm not sitting
next to him. I want to do a boot camp week to
teach him how to fall asleep by himself, during
which he'll cry bitter tears. And yet, I derive
so much strength from how he cuddles into me,
kisses me on the mouth and cheek, and the special
way he has of saying, "Mommy, I love you." I want

to pursue my dream of making a sister for my
boys. Mostly, I want.

Karen

I finished the book and it was just about to be published. Even though I knew that I shouldn't expect too much, because so many books are published every year, and so many of them disappear, swallowed up or forgotten, I couldn't help dreaming that it would become a runaway success, and that many people would read it and respond, and listen. And my life would change and at least in one thing I'd once again become successful and I'd know that I did it, that I won, I arrived, and that I have a place of honor and significance. I believed that there was something in this book, and if only it succeeded, I thought, it would grant me my desired place in the world. I'd be somebody. And one day, I opened the door to my house, and a box was waiting there for me. Inside were twenty copies of my book, containing four years of struggle, of accumulated minutes and moments, disappointments and hope; and I stroked the cover.

That evening we were invited to friends. I brought them a copy of the book. There were all sorts of people there, and everyone congratulated me, and I felt on top of the world.

Someone I didn't know read what was written on the back of the book. "Isn't it intriguing?" I asked.

"No," she told me. I must have looked pretty surprised, because then she said, "Sorry, but I always say the truth."

20

Why weepest thou? and why eatest thou not?
and why is thy heart grieved?

(1 Samuel 1:8)

The prince comes home one day, this time pretty early and in a good mood, because he found out that he got the promotion he's been waiting on for so long. When he enters, the princess is just giving the heirs their bath, washing the conditioner from the heiress's head, and when she hears him put down his briefcase, she immediately yells out to him, "You're here at last, come and take them out," and she dries her hands, and when she leaves to make room for him, she reminds him to wipe them down thoroughly because the heir has a bit of a cold, and the heiress likes now only the pink pajamas, and if he's already at it, maybe he can read them a story, she says to him, and adds that she's going to the living room, that she needs a moment of peace, because she had a terrible day, and he can't imagine the traffic jam she got stuck in, and she starts telling him about that horrible traffic jam, and how she was late for their poor children, and she wants to talk to him about something because things are really hard for her, and she thought about it and she wants him to arrange one day a week when he'll be the one to pick them up at four, and he says that he can't and it's actually related to something good that he wants to tell her, and she asks him about what, and he says that they'll talk later, and she says tell me now, and he tells her that he got the promotion, and she asks why he didn't call her sooner, and he says that he didn't want to tell her on the phone, and the heiress starts crying that she wants to get out, and that she needs to wipe her eyes because she's got soap in them, and it burns, and she cries terribly, and the princess says to him that she doesn't understand how he didn't want to tell her the news immediately, and the heir wants to get out too, and the princess tells the prince that they'll talk about it later, and the heir climbs out and drips water on the floor, and the princess tells the prince to look how the boy is dripping water all over the house, and she's so tired already, and the prince tells her that she doesn't have to work so hard, and now he'll definitely get a raise, and she turns to him and tells him that it would be foolish of her to give up on it now, and she also raises her voice a bit, because in just a short while she'll get her certificate, and she'll earn a fine salary, and she wipes down the heir, and besides, it's not only because of the money, she says, it's the fact that the children barely see him, and he isn't involved enough in their lives, and she asks if he's going to be working longer hours, and he says, and his voice is also approaching a shout, that his father also worked like this and he doesn't remember his father ever picking him up from school, and it didn't make him feel as though his father had neglected him because his father provided for them, and he's also providing for them, and she tells him quietly, not in front of the children, we'll talk later, and she goes to the living room and collapses, because she still hasn't pulled herself together from that traffic jam, and for the first time that day she sits in peace.

And she thinks about the fact that it wasn't even important enough for him to call her and announce his promotion. And she thinks about how she needed someone to give her a kind word when she was stuck in the traffic jam, and she didn't call him either. And she understands that he's no longer really her friend. Not like he promised to be. And she's not really his friend. They only have shared children, and a joint address on which they haven't even finished paying half of the mortgage.

> Your man is interested in soccer, but he'll never notice if the children don't have a winter coat, or if last year's shoes are already small. That may be true about men like my father, who is 78, may he live a long life, but things have changed since then. I know that my situation doesn't represent everyone - I am singlehandedly raising my teenage son and daughter, and yes, this week I went with them to shop for winter clothes, without any woman sending me to do so, because there isn't a woman in the vicinity to take care of them (or of me).
>
> I work hard, get home in the evening, and then my daughter announces that tomorrow she has an algebra test and that I have to help her study, and my son has an English assignment, and dinner has to be made, and they fight a little, and to make a long story short, when I finally sit down (collapse or dive into semi-consciousness would be more accurate) at 11:00 in front of the television, I don't even see what's running on the screen. I just enjoy the quiet for a bit.
>
> I was a good husband. I loved my wife. I enjoyed spending time with her, talking with her at the end of the day, seeing a good movie with

```
her, and we laughed a lot. In the end, she left me
and the children and went off with someone who's
the exact opposite. A bad character who makes his
woman miserable (in short, the bad boy). But try
figuring out women and what they're looking for.
Danny
```

The prince takes the heirs to their rooms, dresses them in their pajamas, tells them a story, pulls the covers over them, and kisses them. And then he stays with them some more. Enjoying their sweet scent of pure cleanliness and listening to them breathing. And he doesn't even feel like leaving their room, leaving the quiet and the warmth. He isn't up to the conversation that will start now with the princess, an inevitable conversation whose end he already knows. And he doesn't understand how it happened that instead of celebrating his promotion, they managed to have a fight. He desperately wanted to celebrate with her; he wanted her to be happy for them, for both of them. And he wanted her to be happy for him, because she knew how hard it was for him to achieve this, and how he waited for it, and he couldn't believe how he even thought, all the way home, about the way she'd look at him when he'd tell her about the promotion. He couldn't believe that he hoped she'd have that look he hasn't seen in so long, that look she used to give him.

And he realizes that he's waiting for morning. He's looking forward to going to work. Because with all the difficulty and the challenges there, there's also laughter and action, and camaraderie, and people who appreciate him. And especially her, the new girl, who smiles at him every morning, and laughs brightly and heartily at every one of his jokes, and he realizes that that's what he's waiting for more than anything. Her looks and her smiles. He knows that they're flirting. And he knows that it isn't a good idea but she's the one who started it. She's the one who brought a cake one morning and sent him slightly vulgar e-mails; she's the one who told him about the dreamy massage that a masseur gave her and recommended that he get one as well; she's the one who told him on her birthday that she doesn't want him to bring her anything but himself and he's well aware that he likes it. He hasn't felt like this for a long time, and he feels so good; it feels so pleasant to him. Much more pleasant than coming home and fighting again with his frazzled and unsatisfied princess who finds hardship in every day.

21

Things too wonderful for me, which I knew not.

(Job 42:3)

My book succeeded far beyond expectations. It succeeded even more than I had dared dream. It was a best seller. After two years of unsuccessful pregnancies, seven years of motherhood, four years of raising a special child, which together constituted almost a decade of giving, investing, rescuing, caretaking, wars, survival struggles, keeping promises made to others, and trying along the way to keep some of those promises made to myself; after four years of writing born of a desperate struggle for every second of free time during which I ran to the computer, of the attempt to also be a wonderful mother, a lovely daughter, a wife, and a friend, while stumbling and failing in every one of these things, scratched and bruised from feelings of guilt, agonized but reminding myself that there was a large and important goal, and that if I succeeded then one day I'd reach that place of accomplishment and peace and joy that I yearned for so desperately, I had done it. I had reached the moment when I was supposed to dance on the top of the world, celebrate my success and the fact that I was earning money once again, that I had done something real, that I had made it. That was the moment in which I was supposed to touch happiness. And my man hugged me and told me how wonderful I was, and I went out for a drink with the girls, and my mother was proud, and the check was deposited in the bank account, and that was it. That was just about it.

I had waited for this moment for so long, and now it was here, and everything stayed just the same. I was an adult woman, exhausted, angry, with a sour face, the corners of my mouth slanting downwards in a dissatisfied expression, with a deep line of worry dividing my eyebrows, joining other wrinkles in a hard, irate visage; a woman who hadn't laughed for so long, who hadn't been simply happy for so long, who constantly ran and worried and was troubled, and in a rush and late, and was afraid that she was screwing up, and *knew* that she was screwing up, and couldn't see any kind of tranquility on the horizon, couldn't see any peace, couldn't see the end of the road. There weren't any firecrackers flying around me, and I wasn't carried on anyone's shoulders, and I didn't become prettier, and those who knew me didn't change their attitudes toward me. I still had to run errands and take the kids to their afternoon activities, sit down and wait for them, drive them, pick them up, ensure that the house was functioning and that there was fresh bread at home, and milk.

Nothing changed in my relationship with the world, or with myself. I was the same woman, and my life looked the same, except I found it slightly easier to spend money on shoes and I had a bit more time. And it was so confusing, so I told myself that I'd write another book. I thought that if I wrote another book, I'd be a real author, and people would really think of me as an author, and then maybe it would truly happen. Maybe then, something would move and I'd feel as though I was doing something – that I'd achieved. That I'd succeeded. So I sat down to write another book. And I returned to the exact same situation, because once again, I didn't have time. And I sat, and wrote, and erased, and sat some more, writing and erasing, gathering moments, fighting for minutes. And after several months I sat down to read it and realized that it wasn't good. I realized that nothing was going to come out of it, that I didn't have the energy, that I had nothing to give and nothing to say. And I turned off the computer. And I quit writing. Because suddenly, I realized that it didn't really matter. It held no significance whatsoever, not to anyone, not even to myself. I realized that if, after achieving my biggest dream in the world, I was still in the same place, then there really was no point in making an effort. And that was when, just when I was supposed to be happy, I shattered.

> I wanted to tell you that it warms the heart to feel from afar that there's a feminine truth, reaching and embracing through the glass walls closing in on all the mothers who want to be part of the world that's outside (you know, combining work and children), yet at the same time wanting to maintain and nurture the world within: the house, the children, the husband. That there are other women who feel and experience, and kick, and agonize, and question, and check, and fear, and rejoice, and sparkle. And I get up every day with a prayer to get through this day in one piece, to manage to be myself, and be there for them, and for him, and be smart and victorious, and right and successful, and thin and happy, with the will and strength to be all those things tomorrow as well. And the day after tomorrow. And the day after that.
>
> Daniela

I didn't understand how no one had told me. How had no one told me that this was what I should anticipate? How had no one warned me? I felt cheated. Because as I was growing up, I was promised – the world promised me, life promised me, my fucking potential promised me – that if I tried hard enough, and if I worked hard enough and fought and gave everything I had and my entire soul, and if I was kind and wonderful, then one bright day, I'd reach a place where the birds sing, and butterflies fly, and there is just peace and quiet. And I was told that it was all up to me, and I gave everything I had to get there. All my energies, everything that I had in me, just to find out that it doesn't work like that. To discover that in real life, there is no suitable compensation, there isn't reward and punishment, and things can always get worse. That after every success, you have to get up in the morning and try again. That after every vacation, you have to return home. After every pair of boots you buy, there's another shirt you want. After every pound you lose, there's a holiday rich with delicious food.

And with every cake that I ate, and every second in which I didn't do my best, I felt less successful and more like a screwup; less triumphant and more like a failure. Because despite everything I did, it was never enough. And I mainly understood that I couldn't save my little girl. Even if I were to slay all the dragons, and run to all the therapists, and even if I did everything – everything they'd tell me and recommend that I do – I wouldn't be able to save her. So I did the only thing left to do. I fell apart. Because I had hoped so much, and believed so badly, that in the end, I could only fall apart. And I knew that I no longer had any energy left. For anything. And from within this abyss into which I had been sucked, I saw her wave to me, that woman to whom

I had already said goodbye once, before what seemed to me like an entire lifetime ago; I had already said goodbye to who I was, that girl who laughed, who loved to go out, to have fun, who was interested in the world around her. And not only did I lose myself. My man lost his friend as well.

> I'm a mother to four young children who are very close in age, and it's not easy for me. I'd be grateful if you'd provide information about recommended seminars on the subject of couples therapy, and also if there's a seminar on the subject of anger management, which, unfortunately (I plead guilty and I'm racked with guilt), is part of my life because of the pressures and the intensity of numerous confrontations related to childrearing and my husband's involvement (or lack thereof) in all the fun.
> Hannah

And it had already been three weeks that my man and I were no longer living in the same house.

22

So that two of them were not left together.

(1 Samuel 11:11)

I went out for a drink with the girls. This time we celebrated. We sat on the bar and I told them all the details about my new job, writing a column for women in the newspaper, and we immediately proposed a toast, and everyone wished me luck, and after that we talked a bit about my situation, and then about their situations, but then the alcohol started kicking in, and we laughed a bit, and only one of us was more quiet than usual, and we loosened up, and someone else asked if we weren't supposed to be at an age where we have more desire than they do, and we laughed. Yes, that's what's written in the books, that now we're supposed to want it more than they do. And it's not that we don't want it, we concluded unanimously, it's just that at the end of the day we're already exhausted, and for sex, we almost always have to get rid of a child sleeping in our bed, and in order to give the sex its due investment, we have to dig through all the dolls and kiddy CDs in order to find the toys that we bought each other for our birthdays. And for the sexy negligee we have to wax, and in order to wear only a thong without looking ridiculous, we'd better lose a few pounds, so we decided to postpone it for tomorrow or some imaginary tomorrow that we hope will arrive someday, or a romantic vacation with just the two of us, alone, relaxed, and mellow after a good massage.

But the romantic vacation never arrives, because how will we go on a vacation without the children, when both of us work so hard and hardly spend enough time with them, and eventually, it always ends up being at some child-friendly hotel, where we run after them from one activity to the other, where we share the single bedroom with the children, and imagine what we could have been doing had we been there without them. And we imagine it alone. Each one to him or herself. Not daring to voice it out loud. And this girl talk of ours, on the bar, about sex, was so far from what it was supposed to be, wrapped up in so many layers of disappointment. Too much, not enough, he wants, I want. I'm tired. She's tired. He's tired. And even the alcohol couldn't keep at bay the bitter feeling of a missed opportunity.

When the bill arrived, we divided it in five, just like we divided the salads that we ordered and nibbled at listlessly, counting calories, counting hours of sleep, because how could we get up for work tomorrow morning, to another day in our measured lives, laden with details, in which we had lost not only the joy of sex, but almost all of our joy. And none of us talked anymore about what she'll do when she becomes a minister. Or the prime minister. Or queen.

> I'm the owner of the shop *Blue*, up north. If you
> ever visit the north, I'd love to have you visit
> my shop, which is very special (yes, I know I'm
> subjective, but I'm not the only one who thinks
> so)and I'm very proud of it. I'm also a single
> mother to two beautiful boys. My wet fantasy
> (one of several not yet realized) is that the

```
preoccupation with sex and sexuality will become
a legitimate and varied cultural experience. I
also founded in the city a forum for businesses
run by women. The forum provides services for
the benefit of the participants and helps out
enterprises run by women, mostly single mothers.
I'll be so happy if you ever feel like dropping
by for a cup of coffee.
Sigal
```

A minute before we dispersed, after everyone made sure that I'd be fine returning to an empty house, and I hid the fact that I wasn't, a big tear suddenly fell from the princess's eye, down her pretty makeup-free face, in which fine wrinkles had started etching their mark.

Surprised and frightened, we tried to ask what was going on.

The princess took a deep breath, and then said that for several days the prince hadn't been living at home, and while wiping away the tear with a quick movement, she added that tomorrow a truck was coming to pick up his things. They were separating.

Everyone looked at me, expecting me to say something, and I couldn't find anything to say; I was totally surprised. So I gathered her into my embrace, and while she was there, the thoughts ran through my head, crashing and contradicting, and I wondered how I hadn't realized, how amid all the little complaints that she had about him, about their life, about her life, the complaints that she scattered during our meetings at the bar, and during our conversations on the phone when she was on her way somewhere and I was on my way to somewhere else, how I hadn't realized. And she embraced me tightly, and I was furious at myself for being so busy falling apart, my entire life collapsing with me, that I hadn't seen it happening to her. And for a minute, I was angry with her, for not saying that these weren't small things, for not yelling, for not calling out for help. And her silence wasn't the only thing I was angry about. I was also angry at the ease with which she was breaking up – both of them were breaking up – their wonderful family, so successful and healthy, my dream family. And I released her from my embrace, and she tried to smile at me and it was even sadder.

And then I realized that it hadn't been easy at all. And I knew that I preferred to believe that there were fairy tales; that I preferred to believe that I was the only one who had been expelled from them, by the force of destiny and statistics.

And another tear fell, and she told me that two weeks ago, they had a fight, and at a certain moment – as it sometimes happens in the middle of a fight, when one loses control, and things come rushing out – he suddenly yelled that he doesn't deserve to live like this. And she also yelled that she doesn't deserve to live like this. And there was a silence. And he said that maybe they shouldn't live together. And she said that maybe they really shouldn't. And he slept in the living room. It wasn't something new, she said, it had already happened to them several times before when they had a fight and he preferred the sofa, but this time, after several days of not talking to each other, during which they just exchanged a word here and there about the children – when he has to pick them up, when she does, when he plans to be home from work, when she does – he went and two days ago he rented an apartment.

And we stood there, outside the bar, with our princess, the most successful girl in our group, who married the cutest guy, who had the most charming house and the prettiest children and was always the one we looked up to, who knew how to entertain, who always put so much thought into each present she bought, who never forgot an important date in our lives, be it birthday or anniversary, who produced every dinner or special event in the most perfect and glamorous manner, who was so smart and wonderful that we couldn't help but envy her occasionally, who always knew what she wanted and how things should be, and whom we loved more than anything because you couldn't not love her, and she didn't look us in the eyes and we were quiet.

And then she said that maybe it's better this way because she hasn't been happy in quite a while, and she deserves to be happy.

And we surrounded her, our beloved princess, who up until now kept the faith for us, who held on with her teeth to the fairy tale so it wouldn't just fade away, and we knew that this was the moment. The moment after happily ever after, after the end of the story. The moment that isn't mentioned in the fairy tales.

> After 15 years together, and toward the end of my thirties, I feel burned out. And it hurts. The partner who lives with me is the father of my children. He's a lovely man. He's gentle, understanding, and smart. He's loving and he's all that I've got. But I'm distant. Because he forgot how to woo me. Am I the only woman who needs to feel that wonderful feeling, when your man makes you feel as though he thinks you're the most beautiful, the smartest, and the most talented woman on earth? Are there women out there who live without getting this feeling from their man and think that it's just fine?
>
> I think I'm all right: witty, smart, and looking at me is certainly easy on the eyes. And

it's not that I need someone to tell me this;
I just need some guarantee that that's how *he*
feels. Because, at the moment, I feel like his
roommate and his partner in childrearing, and
that romance is dead.

   Well, I refuse to bury it! I'm not going to the
funeral and I'll fight for its life fearlessly.
I want those butterflies in my stomach again! I
want to smile that stupid smile, for no obvious
reason, in the middle of the day. I want to feel
outrageously sexy.

Talia

And I walked with the princess to her car and asked her if she was sure that it was really over. If they had really tried everything.

And she said that she really tried. That she tried to see the good and ignore the bad, the difficult, but she could no longer ignore the fact that running down the middle of the photograph of their life, there was a scratch. A deep scratch. And for a long time, this was what she'd been seeing when she looked at the photo: just the scratch.

I got into my car, and I thought about the prince and the princess and me and my man, and I tried to understand how it happened to them. How it happened to us. And on the way I remembered something that the prince told us one evening when he came to watch soccer with my man, and I joined them after the game and we chatted a bit. And I laughed at them, about how you can put them in an armchair in front of a green screen with little men running around, and they're blissfully happy. And the prince said that that's the way they are, that that's what we don't understand about them, that they don't need a lot to be happy.

"Just let us come home from work," he said, "come in the house, and have our woman smile at us. We don't need more than that. That's what we want from our woman. A smile at the end of the day."

And I laughed when the prince said that. I laughed because I knew what we want from them. How much we want from them. We want them to help us more, to spend more time with the children, to care more about the house, to spoil us, to be romantic, to initiate vacations, to listen to our troubles, to console us, to talk to us about what's bothering us and about what's bothering them, to ask for our advice, to enable us to live in financial comfort, to encourage, support, fix, buy, compliment, fulfill all our most secret wishes, to understand without words, to give without us having to ask, to know when to hug, to flirt with us, to save us, and finally, to remember to buy milk.

And sex, I asked him, what about sex?

"There's nothing less sexy than a complaining wife," he said, "and a sour, angry woman."

And I laughed again.

And the prince said that it wasn't funny.

And I said that there's no way that this is all they want, a woman who smiles.

He lowered his gaze and was quiet for a second. Then he told me, almost in a whisper, how every evening, when he gets home, the princess has some sort of complaint: that he came too late, that there's something that he didn't do, or did do but not like she wants him to, or not enough, or he forgot, and how he's discovered that before he enters the house, he stands by the front door and takes a deep breath. Before he enters his own house, which is supposed to be his sanctuary from everything out there that's so difficult, and which has become a place even more difficult than the outside world. His house has become the last place where he wants to be. And he said that he tried so hard to satisfy her, but she's always unsatisfied. Dissatisfied with him. And he just doesn't have it in him anymore, and he doesn't feel like trying, because as much as he tries, it's never enough. And he tried to make her happy, but nothing he does makes her happy. And then he said, "When your woman gives you the feeling that she's unhappy with you, that you're not good enough – when she gives you a feeling that you're a compromise, and that she's stuck with you, and she'll just have to make the best of it – you start feeling like shit. Because no one, man or woman, wants to live with someone who makes them feel like that. Makes them feel that they're not wonderful, and not great, and that they're guilty. Guilty for not being good enough." And he's tired of feeling guilty, he said. "It's not my fault that she feels like shit. I don't know why she's so unhappy."

> When my husband came home, he always got a smile, a big hug, and a warm, wet kiss. I swear. After this reception and the hot dinner waiting for him, we celebrated together in the bedroom. It happened many times. It also happened that some pleasant surprises waited for him. Wine, candles in a darkened room and a half-naked woman, or a beautiful song that I sang to him. I remember only two times in our lives that I didn't welcome him when he came home. Once, I was in the middle of frying and I almost burned something, and another time when there was some issue with the children. You have no idea how angry he was with me later. You can't even imagine.

I did all this in order to keep my marriage and a husband that I loved. And not only that. I also stopped teaching; I didn't sleep during the day after night shifts. Nothing helped. There are those who get used to having it good and after a while, they no longer notice. Do men remember how to smile and tell a woman frequently how beautiful she is? Do they really see her? If they saw her, the need to "demand" pampering wouldn't arise, or that they initiate vacations or help at home, and there certainly wouldn't be any disappointment concerning the fact that they don't listen to our troubles. Because if they really saw us, all the aforementioned would happen naturally.

That's the way I was. Twenty-five years of marriage. Today, I'm forty-nine years old, a beautiful and successful woman, and I didn't know all this while I was married. And I'm starting a new life. It's hard. Almost impossible. And with the pain that came as a result of the failed relationship, a substantial and insufferable part of it was comprehending that it wasn't enough. Until this day, and perhaps forever, I'll carry this feeling of pain.

Iris

23

*For who knoweth what is good for man
in this life...*

(Ecclesiastes 6:12)

I came back to my empty house, and took a shower, and cleaned
my face in front of the mirror, and looked at the tightly wrapped
towel enveloping me. The sight of my unimpressive breasts, shoved
into the material, reminded me of a conversation that we had had
several months ago, after one of our friends had a boob job, and
we suddenly discovered that all of us wanted one too. That all of
us wouldn't mind lifting or filling, inflating or reducing. Because
none of us loved her own breasts. Each one of us would have been
happy to get her friend's, because they always looked better to us.
And I thought about the princess, and how I had always thought
things were better for her than for me. And how we all think the
same about someone else's body, and her work, and the amount
of money she has, and the lovely family she has. And her troubles,
which aren't as bad as our own. And then on the other hand each
of us had her own things that were much better than what other
women had. Compared to some women, we had a better body,
and a better job, and we knew how to manage our lives much
more efficiently, and we had more money, and a family that was
so much more wonderful than theirs. And our troubles were a lot
less awful than theirs.

And this was how we lived. As if in a swimming pool. Living in a swamp of comparison, with each party trying to justify itself at the expense of the other party. Comparing and feeling weaker. Comparing and feeling stronger. The size of our ass compared with Jennifer Lopez's ass; the size of our house compared to that of the neighbors, or the houses of other friends. Our success compared to male success; the success of our man compared to that of other men. We constantly see handbags more beautiful than our own, coffee tables more beautiful than ours, houses much more charming than ours, backsides and boobs more toned than ours, women who are better mothers than ourselves, women who are better mothers than our own mothers, husbands who are nicer and help more than ours, children who are better raised and better behaved than our own, families who go on trips far more successful than our trips, and it seems to us that everyone else has it easier, better, and if only we had what they have, then we'd be happy. If only we'd lose ten pounds, we'd be just as happy as that good-looking woman over there, and as adored as she is, and if we'd renovate the kitchen, then we'd entertain with so much more enjoyment; if only we had what we don't have, then we'd be happy. Because we want things to be perfect. Because we were taught not to compromise. We've internalized that compromising is surrendering; it's a concession, and we aren't willing to give up, because we deserve the best. Without the scratches.

> Several months ago, I wrote to you about me and my daughter. I asked you for help concerning writing, and in the meantime, I decided that there are other things I want to do, and who knows, maybe one day I'll write about what happened to

me. In the meantime, I finished chemotherapy and
radiation, and my hair started growing in, slowly
but surely, and everyone is even complimenting me
endlessly on my short hairdo. I'm also completing
a course that I took on personal coaching, which
I started five days after I finished chemotherapy.
But as far as I'm concerned, the most important
thing I did was sign my daughter up for preschool.
I decided to muster my courage and do it, and I
consider it a dream come true. I have no idea
what I'll do with her next year, but at the moment
she's happy and so are we. And that's about it.

Sometimes I still have fears and anxieties,
but I try to repress them. Right now, I really
want to study interior decorating and change
directions in life. So thanks for everything, and
I'm also enclosing a photograph, so you can see
the face behind the words. All the best.

Yael

The prince and the princess agreed that there was no point in
unnecessary wars that would make them even more miserable,
because as it was, both of them were going through an extremely
difficult period. It was clear to them that the only important
thing was to minimize the children's pain as much as possible.
So they ended it nicely. In the agreement drawn up between
them, they agreed that the prince would take the heirs twice a
week, and every other weekend. They divided the money that
they had between them fairly, and the prince spent most of his
share on a rented apartment. "It's fine," he told her when she
asked. "I just need to paint it." And he didn't invite her to come
over and see it.

When they told the children that they were separating, the heir lowered his gaze and didn't say anything. Then he went to his room and refused to speak with them. They sat in the living room, which once belonged to both of them, and would soon belong only to her, and their hearts broke. The heir's reaction frightened both of them. The princess said that they'd have to give him some time; it was still all new to him, and it was a shock. The heiress, who was still too young to understand the significance of the entire matter, was excited by the idea of having two houses and getting a lot of new toys – because that's how they presented it to her – and she had many questions about what toys she'd get and if she'd finally get that Bratz rock singer that she'd been wanting for so long. When she heard that she would, she was satisfied and asked Daddy to tell her a bedtime story.

The princess waited in the living room while the prince tucked the heiress in, and when he left the room, he didn't sit down, but started talking to her about what he intended to take from the apartment. This itemization choked the princess, as well as his cold way of speaking, and she told him to take whatever he wanted. She knew that he wouldn't take what he didn't need because she knew him, her decent prince. And she thought that if they behaved themselves, they could remain friends. "Tomorrow morning, when you're at work, I'll come pick up my stuff," he said, and left.

The next day, she came home after he had dropped by to take some things. He took some books, and left the bookshelves with more than half of the books. He took the armchair that he loved sitting on while watching television; several CDs – more than half; two pictures that left white squares on the wall; several pots; and his side of the closet. And his side of the bathroom counter. And a few towels. She looked around and saw that everything was the same. Except there was more space. Spaces that yawned without any logical order. Several empty shelves and several full; some corners that remained as though nothing had touched them, and some corners with nothing left in them. And the princess noticed that he didn't take any bedding and didn't take clothes for the children. She thought it would be a shame for him to buy new clothes because there was enough, and she'd put together a bag of stuff and give it to him when he dropped by. She wanted to call him and tell him not to buy anything, and ask him how he was managing, and just tell him that if he thought of anything, he could always drop by and pick it up, and to remember to send the heiress to preschool with a white shirt. And then she saw that he had left his house key on the table.

And she didn't call him.

> I'm 41 years old. I was married to an army man for 20 years. From the start, I gave up on a career with the excuse that one careerist is enough at home. We always lived on air force bases – a new base every two years. In order not to lose myself, I invented a method: after organizing the house, placing the children in their respective schools, and providing my husband with extensive support in his new position, I was more than ready to find a job. Despite the extreme difficulty of convincing the employers to hire me, I always found work in large companies, filling responsible positions that weren't taught in any university, like administrative management or being a CEO's personal assistant.

I didn't forget my job as a mother for one minute, which included volunteering to lead the class committee, quietly, modestly, without making a big deal out of it. And I waited for a promotion, for a raise, for an award of excellence and appreciation. And I also hoped that when the time came, my dear man, who received endless support from me, would repay me when discharged from the army, and we'd exchange roles. But no such luck. Thing is, when you accustom the people surrounding you to thinking that you're in a position of giving and that you're happy with it, and suddenly you come out with a certain small demand, entirely insignificant, you're stared at with an amazed expression that seems to ask, "What's going on?"

So my husband retired from the army and from me (I got divorced a year ago), and two weeks ago, my boss quit and left me jobless. After some crazy job interviews (I've done everything apart from bungee jumping), I decided that I'm the only one who can help myself and I'm channeling all my energy, my soul, my talent, and the work of my two hands toward myself. In the last few days, I've been calling all sorts of tax consultants and personal coaches, have been surfing in the Career Women's Forum and am trying to do something independent.

Debby

The princess, who so many times had told him, *don't forget, and bring this, and come home early, and remember what we need for tomorrow, and it's about time, give the kids a bath, you didn't pay the parking ticket and today was the last day,* wandered about the house, picked up the books that lay on the shelf and moved the remaining armchair, and didn't call to tell him. For so long, these details, and the proceedings surrounding them, were the sole source of communication between them. Between him and her. The CEO and assistant CEO of the family business. A business that they had to run efficiently. A business in which something happened every day, and that they constantly had to take care of, and act in response to, and do, and bring, and pick up, and there was work, and they needed money. An operation that slowly crushed her energies. His energies. And crushed their love. Crushed and ground their love until it became dust and all it took was a light breeze for it to blow away to kingdom come, without leaving anything behind. Just some dust. Some dust that had to be cleaned. And a towel that needed to be picked up. And a bill to be paid. And he forgot again, and she just reminded, and just mentioned, and another towel was misplaced, and another word said at the wrong minute, the wrong word, a word that couldn't be taken back. A word that left a scratch. Another scratch in their perfect family picture. If only he had tried harder. If only he had done what she asked him to, how she wanted, and how she imagined, then everything could've been so amazing. And so perfect.

She just wanted him to try harder, and she wanted him to help more, appreciate more. To love her and show her that he loved her. And to just bring her a flower to make her happy. To just make an extra effort. And he didn't. So she was angry and disappointed. Because he promised her. He promised happiness and love straight from the fairy tales, in front of all those witnesses. And he broke that promise. He – who once upon a time only wanted for her to be happy; who was willing to cross oceans and continents and slay dragons just to please her; who was willing to suffer injury and scratches just to bring her a flower; who promised her happily ever after and love forever, and together through thick and thin – promised but couldn't keep his promise. And he didn't even remember to bring the milk when she asked him to. And years had passed since he last brought her a flower, for no special reason.

> I wanted to share with you a lovely farewell letter that I wrote to my sleeping beauty. "My beauty, I fell in love with you the moment I saw you that Saturday, wearing your blue dress, with a smile and eyes that told me, 'Haven't we met before?' I saw your amazing beauty and heart, so thirsty for love. I believed that through the force of my kiss, the force of me being a prince who managed to overcome all those monsters and evil witches with good intentions (or the opposite), I could sweep you up in my strong arms and carry you off on my white horse (if I'm not mistaken, a Fiat Punto) toward the horizon. My love and belief were so profound that I forgot to check whether you were a willing participant, whether you wanted to take the risk and come down from your tower – come out from behind your high, secure walls and find love with me. I thought that it was possible, but I guess that the wicked witch, or perhaps your (not-quite step-) mother did a good job, and my sword couldn't slay all the dragons surrounding you.
>
> "The chill that blows from your lovely lips continues to send waves of frost that threaten

to freeze my heart, and from a handsome prince on his white horse, I am slowly shrinking and turning into a frog. And from floor level, the swamp doesn't look so nice, and the smell isn't so good either. And suddenly there are three dwarves (not to mention a house, a mortgage, and a poodle). And you're glamorous and brilliant, successful, and prettier than ever. But I'm dead and you're dead and this is how, nowadays, the fairy tale ends. So you live in a castle with a housekeeper and a gardener, the children are brilliant, charming, and happy, but the house is dead; it's cold, and not only from outside. That's the end of the fairy tale these days, when people chase things that are insignificant in life, and lose the map that leads to the true treasure, which is the only thing that will save us (nobody ever told us that fairy tales don't end with 'happily ever after')."

Jonathan

24

Thou hast put gladness in my heart...

(Psalms 4:8)

The prince came to take the children from the princess's house. He exchanged very few words with her, and was cold, and she didn't say much either. She found it strange to part from the heirs. It was strange to spend two days with them and then one day without. And a week passed by, and then two more, and he once again picked them up and brought them back. And it hurt her to see the children moved constantly like packages, from here to there, from there to here, involving all the *bring them, take them, and I forgot and you forgot*. And the heiress couldn't get used to his house and her new bed and cried and it broke her heart and the prince's heart. And they were both worried by the heir's silence.

The prince tried to reduce the damage inflicted on the heirs, taking care to do everything that had to be done. He made sure never to run late, always to arrive on time, to come to every school party and every parents' meeting. The princess saw how all of a sudden he could leave work in the middle of the day, knew which classes the heirs had on which day, had the time to sit with the heir on his homework and with the heiress on her drawings. She saw that he could suddenly do all the things that she had yearned for him to do, all the things that she had fought for, and she couldn't understand why he didn't do it before. Why was it that when she desperately wanted his help, this partnership, this togetherness, he couldn't do it, couldn't make the effort; and now, when she no longer found it important, when it no longer mattered or helped, and she even hoped, in all honesty, that he would screw up, or forget, or run late, he could suddenly do all these things. And do them perfectly. And it angered her to discover that he could do everything, and probably could have done so all along; if he had only wanted to, he could have done these things for her when they were together, all these things he was doing now, to spite her. Now he wanted to show her what a wonderful dad he could be. What a wonderful partner he could be, although he was no longer her partner. And he wasn't willing to do it for her.

And time passed, and the heir still wasn't really talking to them, and gradually immersed himself in a hostile silence that he presented to them, and they went to consult with a psychologist. They were very worried, and extremely frightened. They sat with her and had a shared goal: to stop the heir's suffering. And they were both worried about him. No one in the world would worry about him, the princess knew, like they would. Only they, his parents. Living together or separately, it didn't matter. He's his father, and she's his mother, forever. And the psychologist asked questions about the heir, and the prince started talking about him. He told the psychologist things that she didn't even know that he knew, that she never assumed that he saw, and it surprised her. She was surprised by how many things he knew about the heir. When the psychologist asked them some more questions, they answered almost uniformly, and with the same words.

When the princess sat there, and saw how they could talk when they had one huge, common goal, a goal that they would always share, and saw how much the prince loved the heirs, how he cared, she asked herself if they really had done everything they could have to end this differently. Had they really tried everything? Maybe they had given up too quickly. Maybe *she* had given up too quickly. And she knew that perhaps she had. And that thought made her profoundly sad.

Because she knew that it was too late. She saw how he looked at her, how cold he was toward her, and she knew that he was in a different place. And the heiress had already told her, a while ago, that Daddy has a girlfriend, and that she's very nice, and that she even helped her comb her hair yesterday into two pigtails.

> My sister married a man who left his wife for her.
> Four years have gone by and they have a son, but
> his half-brothers don't want to see him, and they
> won't acknowledge him or my sister. Her husband
> is frustrated because his ex-wife prevents any
> contact between him and his children. Perhaps
> someone can explain to women that even if a man
> is a crappy father, it's still wonderful for a
> child to have a father, and a woman who loves
> her husband will love his children if she gets a
> chance. All attempts to make contact have been
> blocked by his ex-wife. I truly understand the
> slighted woman, but sometimes, life is tough. Why
> doesn't she let her children enjoy a father who
> wants to be with them and loves them? How can you
> make women understand these consequences?
> Mona

One week after that evening at the bar, I arrived at noon to pick up my son from school, and met the prince at the school gate when he was coming to pick up the heir. I asked him how he was getting by. He said that he was fine. And I told him that that was great. He looked at me crossly, and I knew that I should have said something else. So I told him that I was sorry.

And he said that he didn't understand her. He didn't understand what she wanted.

And I told him what she said about the picture and the scratch, and how she sees only the scratch, and then the children came and we said goodbye, and that we'd talk, and I knew that we wouldn't really talk again, and that the most that would happen was that we'd meet at the heirs' birthday parties, or at a parents' meeting. And each of us walked toward our cars.

And suddenly he called out to me, and we walked back toward each other.

And he said that it was only a scratch.

I didn't understand.

So he said that maybe there really was a scratch, because old things are always scratched, and he's so sorry that the princess chose to see only the scratch. She could've chosen differently. It was such a shame. Because now, he said, their picture was completely torn.

Millions of women depress themselves, most of the time without the help of a man. It stems from our desire to succeed in everything, and to content ourselves with nothing but the best. This is how we cause ourselves, with our own two hands and through our own actions, to change from beautiful, energetic, and vivacious women into blurry, unkempt women (at least not internally, in our souls, where it counts the most). We're tired and

frustrated from once again failing to satisfy the
entire world, and we're left drained and lacking
in energy. One month ago, I made a decision: to
read books and not only to my children, to resume
exercising, to smile more, and to take a cleaning
person once a week, regardless of my pathetic
income. Since then, the house isn't cleaner (I
have two small children and my husband's teenage
girls from his first marriage), but I am free of
the burden of thinking about "When will I clean?
When will I have time to clean?" which enables me
to smile more often, and I've even finished *The
Master and Margarita* by Mikhail Bulgakov.

Naava

That evening I tucked the children in bed, and as usual, it took
ridiculously long and I started losing patience. He didn't want
to wear his pajamas and insisted on sleeping only in his ninja
costume, and she didn't want the night light, and preferred to sleep
with the overhead light on. And I counted to ten. And counted
again. And in the end, I gave up. And I passed through the house
that night to check that the windows were closed and that the
door was locked, and after I tidied up a bit, and before I went to
bed, I went into their rooms and looked at them. I looked at how
she had fallen asleep with that bright light and he with the ninja
costume, and I didn't understand what had upset me so much,
and why did I care anyway, and who said that kids have to sleep
in pajamas and in the dark, and it's just plain stupid. It's stupid
to waste this life – my only round in this crazy amusement park
of life –worrying about things running like they should. Because
there's no such thing.

I listened to the silence. And I thought about how, all this time, I had just been giving, and everyone needed something from me, and needed me, and I tried so hard to be okay, to be good, to be a good wife, a woman who takes care of everyone, who first and foremost takes care of everyone else, like I was taught. Not to think about myself. Not to take care of myself, but to take care of everyone else. To take care of my children, my husband, my parents, my friends, and my job. To make sure everything was in place, and there was food on the table. And like every good wife, I ate the leftovers. Because a good woman always sacrifices herself so that everyone else will be happy. Because a good woman doesn't say, *now it's me, now it's my turn.* She doesn't say, *today I don't feel like driving you to your after-school activities, and I don't feel like preparing food, and I don't feel like cleaning. So the house will be filthy. So my son won't go to judo this one time. So today I'll work until late and my children won't see me, and it's just one day out of 365 days a year and I'll finish my work obligations instead of complaining that I don't have enough time for anything.*

I didn't say those things. No. I was a wonderful woman, a fantastic mother, and an excellent daughter, and I gave and sacrificed. I sacrificed without asking if anyone even needed all this sacrifice. And I gave without checking if anyone even cared about all this giving. Because it was obvious that I knew what everyone needed. Because I decided that I knew what I had to give, and what my children needed, and what my husband needed, and I didn't even ask if anyone was interested whether I bought food or cooked, or whether my husband cared if the house was clean, or would rather have me rest and smile at him when he got home instead of cleaning. Whether my children even wanted all this running around and all these crazy activities, or whether they wanted a mother who would occasionally close the door, disconnect her phone, and watch a movie in bed with them. And hug them. And I didn't do that.

Instead, I struggled to make time and do and give all of myself, without anyone even asking me to, without daring to ask for help, without any pampering, without putting myself on top of my list of priorities, and I hoped and believed that one day it would happen: the day would come and everyone would understand, and bow their heads in admiration. I expected, like we all expect. Someone – the other mothers, teachers, or preferably our husbands or mothers – will notice how much we gave, and how wonderful we are, and how much we sacrificed for everyone else, and they'll call us up to the victor's stand in a celebratory ceremony, and everyone will cheer as we receive a medal. Because we really deserve it.

But no one hands out a medal, and no one invites anyone to the stand, and even if someone occasionally remembers to say thank you at some family event or celebration, even then the bitterness within remains. Because these little expressions of thanks aren't really worth the sacrifice. Yet, we continue to sacrifice and continue to expect admiration and a huge thanks. And we sacrifice and seethe, seethe and sacrifice, and become victims. Victims of our own sacrifices.

> Sometimes I think that you underrate what you have. Don't get me wrong, I don't envy you personally, but I do envy the family unit that you've created and that you don't appreciate. With all the running around, the errands, the children's chaos, and the dreams, perhaps you forgot that this is all a gift. Family and daily

problems are your biggest asset as a woman. You
have a family. I don't. The pictures smiling
at you from the living room wall when you're
eighty-five will be the familiar faces of your
grandchildren and great-grandchildren. A gift
that you can't buy with all the money in the
world. You built an empire that I will never
have. During the holidays, I watched television
and heard the neighbors singing. I desperately
yearned for a similar burden, the little fights,
the who'll-bring-what and who'll-do-the-dishes.
What you take for granted, I consider a lifetime
ambition. It isn't a lot to ask for, is it?

Maya

And I thought about what the prince had told me. And I knew
that he was right and that nothing was ever perfect, and that there
will always be scratches. He was right, because life isn't something
that can be organized according to personal will. Neither are
families, husbands, and children. Life isn't something that we
can design according to our dreams. Or according to what we
think we should have. Or deserve. And we point at them with
our unmanicured fingers and blame them. Blame them, our men,
for an unfulfilled promise, and for everything that went wrong in
our lives.

And I thought about how preoccupied I was with what I
wanted to change, and how wonderful my life could have been
had my child not been a special child. And how preoccupied I
was with how I wanted my husband to be and to behave, and
how my friends and colleagues and employers and mother
should treat me, and how I'd like everything to run. And I was

shrouded by a screen, this blinding screen of disappointment at life's imperfection, and I hadn't been happy with what I did have for so long. For so long, I had failed to see how many good things I had in my life.

> I can only recommend warmly, as a mother who ran through hospital corridors with an infant and left there shattered, don't forget those promises that you promised yourself, at least the important ones. You got a free lesson. I, who paid an unbearably high price, know how much this lesson is worth.
>
> Naomi

For example, that I love my man with all my heart.

25

*There came out two women,
and the wind was in their wings…*

(Zechariah 5:9)

That night, I knew there was no point in trying to sleep. I went to the living room and sat in the armchair in front of the silent television. The armchair that was full of stains, with its armrest in which a little thread had become unraveled a long time ago, and every person who sat in it played with it a bit, and pulled the thread this way and that, and by now there was a big hole that I repeatedly said that I'd repair, and then I said that it's simpler to buy a new armchair because it will cost more to reupholster it anyway.

I sat in my armchair, and I hated the silence. And I understood that I hadn't even seen. I understood that I had been so preoccupied with sorrow and anger, and with the small details, that I hadn't looked at the big picture. And I hadn't appreciated the fact that my man had done what he had promised to do. He had kept the most important part of the promise. In order to protect me, he had fought dragons. And I hadn't granted him even a smile. And I certainly hadn't expressed joy. In this moment of clarity I suddenly understood a number of things.

I have to stop wasting my life. I have to start separating between what is important and what isn't. To let go. Because you can't control everything anyway. I won't be able to save my daughter, even if I do devote all my time to her – my entire life, all my energies, all of myself. Because sometimes you just can't save someone. I have to stop being angry about what was, agonizing over the past and worrying about the future, because whatever will be, will be. I have to remember that the here and now is also important, and I have to enjoy it. Because *now* will never come again.

This moment can be good. And this one good moment plus another one is what happiness is made of. Because happiness is something that suddenly emerges, illuminating the sky for one second, for one moment, and then it passes. It's so easy to miss them, those tiny moments of happiness. For too many years, I let them pass without even noticing them. Without even stopping to rejoice in them.

And for the first time in years, I thought about what I wanted. Not what I wanted from other people – not what I wanted others to do, to be, to give me – but what I wanted from myself. And I wanted so many things. To find a job that I loved and give it the time and place that it deserves, instead of counting the minutes that it steals from me, because it's my time. To exercise twice a week as though exercising is one of the Ten Commandments, and to understand that it's easier and less frustrating than hating my body. To go out at least two evenings a week, and if necessary, to grab a quick nap in the afternoon. So the kids will watch more television. Big deal. To entertain casually. To understand that I don't have to prepare lavish dinners for friends who drop by during the evening, because the entire world is on a diet anyway. To throw away all the rags in my closet and leave only clothes that flatter my figure, because it won't hurt me to look good even while I'm doing stuff at home. To clean my face thoroughly every day, morning and evening, because the years are starting to show. And a good facial cream won't hurt either. To stop deliberating so much. To know that sometimes I can make mistakes and that there's nothing wrong with that. To ensure that my little girl gets the best treatment possible, and that she's happy, but to know that there will also be days when I won't be sure that I'm doing the right thing, and to understand that there's always tomorrow. To make certain that my son is happy, and that he receives all the support he needs, and to understand that I won't always be able to help him. To make sure that I remain friends with my stepson, and spend time with him, alone. To dedicate time to my wonderful parents, yet not to overly involve them in all that I'm going through because it's not healthy, for either side. To learn how to manage my time correctly. To read more and see better movies. To occasionally go away on a vacation, and enjoy it without agonizing over the fact that I committed a terrible crime against my country and abandoned my children. To drink more water. To dance at least once a month with a head jammed with alcohol. To remember that I'm allowed to say no. Nothing will happen. The worst that will happen is that someone won't like me. There will always be people who won't like me. To set boundaries on the amount of advice and criticism that I'm willing to listen to. To stop thinking that I'm the only one who can do things like they should be done. To stop saying to myself that it's simpler to do things myself than to ask someone else; it's all bullshit. To learn how to accept help gracefully. To let anyone who wants to help me, help me. To learn how to ask for help. To spend money happily on a babysitter or on a nanny, and if necessary, to buy fewer pairs of shoes. And buy only comfortable shoes. To seize opportunities. To try things and to realize that it's okay to fail. And it's okay to fall. And to stop complaining, already.

I knew it wouldn't be easy, that I would have to change myself. But considering the fact that I hadn't smiled for so long, that years had passed since I had last laughed, and that I had pretty much ruined my life, I didn't really have anything to lose.

> We women constantly need a soft, gentle, appreciative word for our insane efforts, before we're hit with scathing criticism that crushes everything we do and paints everything in a tiresome black of helplessness. So take a few minutes of kindness and tell yourself that you're wonderful, spectacular, and you're allowed to make a mistake. Are you sitting down? Hold on tight: you're human. And part of human nature is making human mistakes.
>
> Nina

After a short while, the princess started adjusting. She got used to being alone with the children; she got used to the house being empty twice a week; she got used to being without the children on the weekends that they spent with him, even though it was hard, especially on Friday evening, when she didn't make plans, and she was all alone at home, and she got used to calling the prince's house to say goodnight. It hurt, but gradually it hurt less. She even got used to that cold manner in which he spoke with her and how he never asked how she was.

And suddenly she had time. Those two days a week when the prince spent time with the children enabled her to go to her course without looking at her watch even once, to stay with her classmates and have a coffee, to set a leisurely appointment with the hairdresser, to get a manicure, pedicure, exercise, and then work in the evenings, advance, and earn money. And even though she didn't earn a lot, and even though she was slightly stressed out by the weight of the financial responsibility, she could do whatever she wanted with that money and she didn't have to answer to anyone if she occasionally splurged on a jacket. And on weekends that the heirs spent with him, she could go out until the wee hours and sleep until noon on Saturday, and one Friday, she went out with the gang from the course to celebrate that they had passed the exam and received their licenses, and she remembered how much she loves to dance, and how she loves when people look at her, and compliment her, and flirt with her. And she started surfing the net, and logged into several dating sites and registered, and looked at a few guys' pictures, but still didn't have the courage to write to anyone, let alone upload her photograph.

She stayed in touch with the young people from her course, and befriended some of her colleagues, and after a while, she started going out more, and having fun, and one morning, after a wild night of dancing and drinking, she woke up in a strange bed with someone she'd met the night before. And she felt odd. And even though she was supposed to be happy that someone wanted her after all, that someone thought she was charming in spite of everything, she felt like she'd done something wrong. Something forbidden. She was mortified and collected her things quickly and even though he offered her coffee, she didn't stay. And then she realized that she was waiting. Waiting for him to call, even though she knew that it was a relationship without a future, without a

chance. And she felt uncomfortable with herself for waiting. And
he didn't call.

> With the beginning of this new year, my wish for
> myself and for my unmarried friends is that this
> will be the year it happens. This year we'll
> find our man, the one who will ask us over dinner
> about our day. But this year, unlike other years,
> I'm deathly afraid. What if it doesn't happen?!
> What if he doesn't come this year either? And I'm
> wondering, why are so many girls searching? Some
> say we've become too career-oriented, yet the
> truth is that this is the only way to hold on to
> the apartment *and* the car. Others say we're too
> picky, but show me a girl who genuinely dreams
> of becoming a single mother and hearing someone
> hollering, "Mommy!" 24/7 without having the
> option to hiss between clenched teeth, "Go to
> Daddy." And then it hits me: maybe it's because
> we've become so strong, and we can use a computer
> all by ourselves, and manipulate data and people
> - maybe that's why men think they're no longer
> necessary. So listen up, you, I want you to know
> that I still crave your kind word and embrace.
> And I need you to kill a cockroach or two.
>
> Gabriella

And the princess realized that she didn't really want to be alone.
She wanted someone she could be with. Someone who'd stand by
her. A friend. And that she wasn't so good at being alone. That
she felt empty, and lonely. And she put her picture on one of
those sites. Some men wrote to her. Some of them were too old,

others too young. Some were disgusting and wanted to talk about what she likes in bed, and one of them made her laugh. And she realized that she was waiting for his messages. Waiting eagerly.

And they decided to meet.

■ ■ ■

The sun was rising, chasing away the darkness, and I cried. And I decided. I decided that I was saying goodbye to that sad, angry, embittered woman I had become. And morning arrived and I knew that I wouldn't always succeed, and that it was a long journey, but at least I'd know that I tried. That I made an effort to be happy about the good things. That I made an effort to enjoy my only life. To really be content. Because that was the only thing that no one could do for me. Because no one is responsible for my happiness.

> It's Oren. Yael went on a vacation with her sister, to Italy. When the whole story started, her sister said that when the treatments end, she'll take her to Italy (an old dream of Yael's), and it's happening right this minute. And I'm here with my girls. Anyway, thanks for your interest. I'll tell her to be in touch when she returns.

And I called my man and I asked him out on a date that evening.

I invited him out not as an old-time couple carrying sacks of information on their backs, who know all there is to know about each other, but as a man and woman who want to get to know each other. Fifteen years had passed since I made the first move on him, and I did it again. Fortunately, he agreed to go on a date with me.

And we sat at a small table, two people in mid-life. That evening, I met a man who charmed me and made me laugh, and whom I found interesting. By chance, he was also the father of my children. And he also met a lovely woman (at least, that's what he said, and I was happy to take his word for it). A woman who was, incidentally, the mother of his children. We had a lovely evening, and I laughed a lot. And I was happy.

Made in United States
North Haven, CT
14 March 2023

34074441R00114